# PRISON
# OF
# WOMEN

# PRISON OF WOMEN

## Testimonies of War and Resistance in Spain, 1939–1975

TOMASA CUEVAS

Translated and Edited by
MARY E. GILES

State University
of New York
Press

Published by
State University of New York Press, Albany

© 1998  State University of New York

Production by Susan Geraghty
Marketing by Anne Valentine

Printed in the United States of America

For information, address State University of New York
Press, State University Plaza, Albany, N.Y., 12246

Cover art by Antoni Tàpies

**Library of Congress Cataloging-in-Publication Data**

Cuevas, Tomasa, 1917–
    [Cárcel de mujeres, 1939–1945. English]
    Prison of women : testimonies of war and resistance in Spain,
1939–1975 / by Tomasa Cuevas ; translated and edited by Mary E.
Giles.
        p.    cm.
    Translation of Cárcel de mujeres and Mujeres de la resistencia.
    ISBN 0-7914-3857-0 (hc : alk. paper). — ISBN 0-7914-3858-9 (pb :
alk. paper)
    1. Cuevas, Tomasa, 1917–     . 2. Women political prisoners—Spain-
-Biography. 3. Francoism. 4. Reformatories for women—Spain.
5. Women communists—Spain—Biography. 6. Guerrillas—Spain-
-History—20th century. 7. Government, Resistance to—Spain-
-History—20th century. 8. Spain—Politics and
government—1939–1975. I. Giles, Mary E. II. Cuevas, Tomasa,
1917–     Mujeres de la resistencia. English. III. Title.
HV9742.5.C84A313  1998
365′.45′0820946—dc21                                          97-33352
                                                                                          CIP

10  9  8  7  6  5  4  3  2  1

# CONTENTS

# INTRODUCTION

## Mary E. Giles

Something about the book on the top shelf caught my eye. Standing on tip-toe, I turned my head awkwardly to read the title sideways: *Cárcel de mujeres. 1939–1945 (Prison of Women, 1939–1945)*. I managed to pry the volume loose from the books squeezed tightly on each side. Leaning against the shelves, I read on the back cover how a certain Tomasa Cuevas had gathered oral testimonies from women who had been incarcerated in the months and years following the end of the Civil War in Spain in 1939. Leafing through the pages, I paused to read a paragraph here and there.

I left the Madrid bookstore with the volume tucked in my purse and walked back to my pension a block off the Castellana avenue. Later that afternoon I settled near a window in the parlor of the pension and began to read. An hour or two passed. I let the book rest open on my lap and looked pensively out the window on the busy street below, reflecting this hot July evening in 1989 on a strange coincidence of events.

I'd come to Madrid three weeks before to read documents of the Inquisition in the National Historical Archives. Each morning I would leave the pension with notebooks under my arm and walk the three miles or so to the archives, savoring the artful displays of elegant clothing in the boutiques that lined the avenue. From nine-thirty to two-thirty each day I undid cardboard boxes tied with strings and searched through the documents for evidence on how women had fared in the courts of the Holy Office.

Here was a letter from the daughter of an old woman exiled to a neighboring village as punishment for suspected judaizing; now, the daughter pleaded, with the old woman paralyzed by strokes, could she please bring her mother home? There was a request from a younger woman to wear red skirts, which the Inquisition had forbidden as part of her punishment; without colorful clothing, she argued, how could she keep her husband from straying? Letters, petitions, records of proceedings, on and on the documents gave up their grim secrets, the ways large and small that women had suffered the heavy arm of the church.

From the courts and prisons of the Inquisition, I now returned each day to Franco's prisons. Reading from *Cárcel de mujeres* I lost all sense of time and place. How was one prison different from the other? Had one system of terror simply replaced another?

That was the summer of 1989. Five years would elapse before I met Tomasa Cuevas. During that time I thought about the testimonies and how they deserved an audience outside the Spanish-speaking world. I even tried my hand at translating two or three of them and wrote to the publisher in Barcelona about bringing them out in English. But when no reply came and other projects intruded on my attention, I let slide the idea of translating the testimonies.

Then, at an academic conference in 1993 in conversation with a friend, I happened to mention my intriguing encounter with two different sets of prison texts that summer in Madrid. Coincidence again carried the day: my colleague had met Tomasa at a conference organized by a colloquium of universities to observe the fiftieth anniversary of the outbreak of the Spanish Civil War. Tomasa had been brought in as a distinguished speaker along with other women and men. Through our mutual friend, Tomasa and I began to correspond and agreed to collaborate on an English translation of the testimonies. The first step was to select an appropriate number of representative testimonies for one book. By this time I had discovered that Tomasa had published two more volumes: *Cárcel de mujeres: Ventas, Segovia, Les Corts* (*Prison of Women: Ventas, Segovia, Les Corts*) and *Mujeres de la resistencia* (*Women of the Resistance*).

In the summer of 1994 I traveled to Spain, this time with Joanne Allen, whom I'd known since 1966 when both of us were beginning our academic careers as Spanish teachers. Joanne and I had made our first trip to Spain together in 1967, traveling by car for a month throughout the Iberian peninsula. Fresh from graduate studies at the University of California, Berkeley, we were wide-eyed romantics, more ready to quote Machado's poetry at the sight of poplar trees in the lands of Castile than question the legitimacy of a state authority wrested by terror.

Even though professors of ours at Berkeley had been political refugees from Spain, we were blithely unaware of the implications of their status in terms of the current political situation within Spain. We might wince at the sight of the dreaded Civil Guard patrolling by foot or motorcyle in pairs, but our fears stemmed more from allusions in García Lorca's poetry than from the reality of ordinary men and women being imprisoned and tortured right then. Much later, working with Tomasa's books, I would be jolted time and again on realizing what this woman whose story I was translating had been enduring while I was skimming about the Spanish countryside agog at castles and cathedrals.

The woman who opened the door to greet us was small, barely five feet tall, probably in her late seventies, and despite the added flesh that comes with age, still petite. Her nickname, Peque, which means "little one," suited her. Tomasa's expression was open and lively. Even with the reserve normal in first meetings, I knew that here was a woman I would like and trust.

As we worked together for three days selecting and ordering the testimonies, I came to appreciate Tomasa's natural intelligence. Shy on formal education, she nonetheless quickly learned techniques of editing. Soon she was rereading her material with a critical eye, alert to repetition and obscurity. At one point, when she'd finished working on a long section of her own story, she looked at me proudly: "See, Mary, I'm doing what you did."

If Tomasa learned from me, far more did I learn from her, not merely the outline of her story, but the character of this woman born to poverty and refined in adversity: damaged spinal column, diabetes, heart problems, deteriorating vision, arthritis—effects of age, yes, but also the marks of imprisonment and torture. But if she mentioned her infirmities at all, her tone was matter-of-fact. In large part suffering defines her life. But so, too, does joy: the calls from her husband in Madrid; visits from friends; her daughter, Estrella, and the four grandchildren; the glass of wine and stories we shared at dinners in the nearby restaurant; the champagne and dessert she served our first evening together in traditional celebration of the Eve of the Feast of St. John the Baptist. In spite of age and infirmities, what an alive woman this Tomasa Cuevas!

Tomasa already had seen the need to reduce the number of testimonies when I conferred with her at her home in Vilanova i la Geltrú, a seaport some forty-five miles south of Barcelona. But the length of the original material wasn't the only problem. I soon realized that a straightforward translation of the material would not suffice for non-Spanish readers. The material itself had to be reshaped: first, to reduce its length and number of different narrators and then to find coherence in those stories. I'd already spoken with Tomasa about bringing her own story sharply into the foreground in order to make her a kind of guide for the reader unfamiliar with the Spanish Civil War and the Franco era.

The need to sharpen the focus on Tomasa grew in the following months when I was translating the stories. Tomasa's voice was emerging from the aggregate of testimonies as an especially strong and insightful one. Through her I was seeing the forces that shaped political and personal decisions during and after the war more clearly than from the other testimonies, individually or collectively. I credit this understanding to Tomasa's ability to recapture scenes, conversations, and feelings. But

other women's stories were important, too; they imparted further cred-
ibility to Tomasa's story, widening and texturing the canvas of her narrative. Together the stories attest to the magnitude of oppression and,
paradoxically, sharpen the brutality inflicted on the individual woman.

The first draft of the translation revealed another vexing problem—
repetition. With two or more women narrating their experiences in the
same prison, some redundancy was inevitable. But the volume of repetition was making it very difficult to distinguish one voice from another.
Convinced that each woman did have her unique voice, I realized with
increasing earnestness that my responsibility was to sort out and
enhance the individual voices.

At times the task was relatively easy, as with Rosario Sánchez Mora
whose job as a dynamiter before imprisonment was a key to her strong
personality, or María del Carmen Cuesta, whose innate sense of the dramatic immediately sets her story apart. Other voices are less identifiable
but nonetheless powerful: the very inability to articulate eloquently
demonstrates in its own way how disfiguring cruelty is to the human
spirit. If some testimonies are writ in small letters, they remind us that
everyday existence in prison has, like ours, its own kind of humdrum
rhythm. Perhaps that humdrum rhythm is as true a representation, if not
a truer one, than the sensibility-shattering din of torture and killing.

Editing the testimonies by trimming away repetition and reordering
events for the sake of chronological clarity and narrative interest still left
unsolved a problem that was inherent in Tomasa's original methodol-
ogy. In the late 1970s Tomasa had set out on her quest to collect from
women she had known in prisons their testimonies about prison life. In
the prologues to their stories we hear Tomasa speak about how she met
the women, some of whom she'd not seen since their prison days
together. In her purse she carried a tape recorder. We can picture the
two women seated at a table with tape recorder between them, recalling
old times. Now Tomasa interjects a question; now the questions and
answers become a dialogue; now the story is an uninterrupted mono-
logue.

But the image of two women in conversation persists—women rem-
iniscing about a common past. For them no explanations are needed.
They know where they are in the past; they can see and hear and smell
the prison. If one woman refers to the uprising at the Montaña barracks
or the Casado coup, the allusion strikes immediate recognition in the
other woman. So on the women go, talking about a world to them familiar and firm. They don't require explanations and footnotes to set the
context for the life they recount. That context is in their shared memory.

But the reader who stands outside that memory, a stranger to the
setting for the events to which the women allude, that reader is like a

person listening to a conversation in a foreign language; she strains to catch a word here or there to get her bearings. Such is our response to much of oral literature, which by nature is informed with assumptions about the listener/reader's familiarity with the subject matter either by dint of shared experience or through research. Tomasa is not oblivious to the possibility that readers are unlettered in her school of experience; she begins her introduction to the first volume of testimonies by referring to the young people of her day who express interest in the early years of the Communist Party and especially want to know about brutality and torture in the prisons of Franco.

Tomasa's awareness of a potential audience beyond a circle of readers from within the context of the Civil War and the Franco years may account in part for her eye to details of time, place, and emotions in the telling of her own story. I think it is clear, too, that the "young people" include Tomasa's own grandchildren, a generation far removed in time and concern from her experiences. She may even have had in mind her daughter, Estrella, who emerges as a vital part of Tomasa's story in Part 2.

So as we listen to the women talking about "old times," we're aware over and over that we are outsiders. We're brought up sharply by a reference to the uprising at the Montaña barracks, unable to get the drift of the conversation just right and fearful to interfere with its flow. But what is the uprising of the Montaña barracks and how are we to appreciate the urgency in voice if we lack information about the event? Certainly, it would not do to interrupt the story with a paragraph of information. Nor would it be realistic to put this information in the mouth of one woman as if she were telling the other one what she didn't know. I decided to provide a context in two ways: notes within the text and a glossary of names, abbreviations, and events. Some events, however, appear so frequently in the testimonies and are of such pivotal importance to the unfolding of the Civil War and resistance to the Franco regime that I have elected to treat them briefly here in the introduction.[1]

The October Revolution of 1934 was a prelude to the outbreak of hostilities in 1936 and, for Tomasa, a coming-of-age event in her career as political dissident. For about two weeks during the so-called Red Days of October workers' committees of the Socialist Republic and workers' militia controlled the mining districts of Asturias. Socialists, Anarchists, and Communists forged solidarity among the miners, resulting in a kind of civil war. The uprising was part of an unsuccessful general strike to protest the claiming of the offices of agriculture, labor, and justice by the conservative party, CEDA, Confederación Española de Derechas Autónomas (Spanish Confederation of Autonomous Rights). The government brought in foreign legionnaires from Morocco to help put down the uprising. An estimated one thousand died and some 30,000 were imprisoned. A major result of the failed uprising was to unify the political left around the program of amnesty for the prisoners. Many women were imprisoned and many others mobilized their voices in a call for amnesty for jailed husbands and sons. Although Tomasa did not live in Asturias, she, too, rallied around the call for amnesty for political prisoners.

The unification of leftist groups during the October Revolution of 1934 later acquired identity as the Popular Front and emerged in the elections of February 16, 1936, as a major force in the political scene. Composed of Socialists, Republican Left, Republican Union, Esquerra (Left Republican Catalan nationalist party), and Communists, the Popular Front won 4,176,156 votes as opposed to 130,000 for the Basque Nationalists, 681,047 for the Center, and 3,783,601 for the National Front, that is, the parties of the right. The Popular Front thus won more votes and more seats than did the other alliances. The Communists, however, gained only a total of seventeen seats, a number that indicates the relatively minor position of the party at that time. This is the period, from 1934 to 1936, when Tomasa worked as a political activist in the areas of propaganda and what she calls "agitation." The elections are the ones that she and her friends faithfully commemorated from within prison.

A little more than two years after the election, civil war broke out in the peninsula, triggered by uprisings from within the army. The successful uprising by officers in the Army of Africa on July 17, 1936, spawned military responses in garrisons throughout Spain whereby the army intended to take control of the nation. The focal point for the uprising in Madrid was the Montaña barracks, located in the western part of the city on a site overlooking the Manzanares river. By early afternoon on July 19, 1936, General Fanjul and officers from other barracks in Madrid met at the Montaña barracks where the general gave a speech on the political aims and loyal intent of rebelling against the duly-elected government. The military attempted to go out into the streets with their rebellion, but they were prevented by large crowds that by then had gathered. The barracks fired with machine guns and the crowds responded with gunfire of their own.

The night was frenzied as more than fifty churches were burned and the workers and their parties extended their control of the city. By the following morning an even larger crowd marched on the barracks and bombarded it for five hours, supplemented by aircraft and artillery. General Fanjul requested help from General García de la Herrán, but it proved impossible to get through to the barracks. At ten-thirty in the morning the general, along with the previous head of the barracks, were wounded and one-half hour later, the white flag of surrender appeared. But when the crowd went forward to accept surrender, they were met with machine-gun fire until, shortly after noon, they broke down the massive door of the barracks. Historians agree that what followed was a massacre, with most of the officers killed. The survivors from within the barracks were put in the Model prison and General Fanjul was taken away for trial.

The uprising failed in part because the soldiers themselves were divided in their loyalties and in part because the forces of the Republican Assault Guards were overwhelming in number and force. A similar situation obtained in other barracks throughout the city with the result that the city remained loyal to the Republic.

The uprisings of July 19–20, 1936, against the Republican government took place not only in Madrid but also to the south in Toledo and east in Guadalajara where Tomasa and her family lived. As news of the other uprisings reached Madrid, the militia, or fighting units made up of workers rather than regular soldiers, left the capital in taxis, trucks, and private cars to combat the rebels, capturing Alcalá de Henares and then, in spite of resistance by the Civil Guard, Guadalajara. The militias held Guadalajara and by the end of July had captured Sigüenza to the north. Tomasa's account of these days and months of turmoil reveals the terror and suffering for the ordinary person.

By 1937, when Guadalajara was headquarters for the Russian air squadron, the leaders of the rebel Nationalist forces decided to attack Madrid from the northeast, advancing against Guadalajara and once again jeopardizing Tomasa and her family. The attacking force included 30,000 Italians divided into four divisions, 250 tanks, 180 pieces of mobile artillery, a chemical warfare company, a flame-thrower company, about fifty fighter planes, and twelve reconnaissance planes. The advance began on March 8, 1937, hindered by foul weather. On the morning of March 10 Tomasa's birthplace of Brihuega fell to the Italian Black Flame and Black Arrow soldiers. About noon Italian forces who supported the Republic defeated the Black Flame patrol; fighting between the two Italian forces continued throughout the day. At this time Republican aircraft dropped pamphlets promising safe conduct to all Italian deserters from the Nationalists, and rewards of up to 100 pesetas if they surrendered with their arms. The Thaelmann Brigade sustained heavy casualties.[2] On March 12 Republican bombers pounded the Italian mechanized columns and the Republican forces retook Brihuega. On March 18 Republican aircraft bombed the surroundings of Brihuega, followed by heavy Republican artillery. By early afternoon two divisions with tanks attacked, one on the west, the other in the east, thus encircling the town. They had almost completed this maneuver when the Italians got the order to retreat. The retreat turned into a rout.

In the final days of the war Guadalajara fell to the Nationalists. On March 27, 1939, the Nationalist army broke through the Guadalajara front and joined up with rebel forces advancing from Toledo. The bombings in the final days of the war Tomasa describes in haunting detail.

From Tomasa's story we see how she lived out the war from her corner of the world in Brihuega and Guadalajara: she worked in hospitals, organized sewing shops to make overalls for the militias, planned diversions for the troops, set up laundries for washing soldiers' clothing, recruited men for the front, and persuaded women to take over men's jobs. In short, Tomasa was like countless women in Republican Spain who were mobilized for the war effort.[3]

For Communists the war ended ignominiously with the coup led by Colonel Segismundo Casado, the Republican commander of the Army of the Center who opposed Prime Minister Juan Negrín's policy to continue resisting the Nationalists at a time, in the early months of 1939, when the Republican cause seemed lost. Casado and like-minded opponents of the policy of resistance were especially disillusioned when on February 27, 1939, France and Britain recognized the Nationalist government that had headquarters in the city of Burgos.

Even though Prime Minister Negrín apparently came to agree with Casado's policy of ending resistance and showed his favor by promoting the colonel to the rank of general, Casado proceeded to form an opposition government. At midnight of March 4, Casado broadcast the revolt to the people of anti-Fascist Spain. In the meantime the Communist Party, which had not given up resistance to the Nationalists, defied Casado's action by moving troops against him. Even when Negrín and Communist supporters flew to France on March 5, party resistance continued in Madrid until most of the city was under its control. But by March 12 strife within Republican ranks was appeased and by the terms of an agreement reached with Casado, Communist forces returned to the positions they had held on March 2. The bitterness with which Tomasa and her friends refer to the Casado coup is explainable in part by the next action of the council that Casado had formed; by its order the Communists Colonel Barceló and his commissar were arrested and shot. By March 19 Casado had sent a negotiating delegation to Nationalist headquarters in Burgos. A week of negotiations brought only one outcome—unconditional surrender. On March 27 Casado ordered the surrender of Madrid to the Nationalist commander in University City; two days later he flew to Valencia and from there to Gandia, boarding a British ship for Marseilles. Meanwhile, on the preceding day high-ranking Communist leaders had flown to Orán from Cartagena, leaving behind a party in disarray and its members, among them young Tomasa, to fend for themselves.

If readers are short on contextual information so also are the narrators themselves. Over and over I am reminded both from the text and conversations with Tomasa that she and the other women interpreted the larger context of the Civil War and the dictatorship according to their own necessarily limited experience. Their moral judgments about who is right and who is wrong are based on their experiences. Tomasa states repeatedly that she is no theorist, that her role in the Communist Party always has been that of a doer. Policy making is for the theorists, among whom her husband, Miguel Núñez, is a notable example. She has been one of the many rank-and-file members who have put policy into action.

At times Tomasa does hint at the larger picture, as in allusions to the party's change of policy about the *guerrilla* when she and Miguel worked and lived at a dam near Seville. The word *guerrilla* means a little war, and it refers to the subversive actions carried on by opponents of the regime both inside and outside of Spain. The fact that the people carrying out the "little war," that is, the guerrillas, were operating in both Spain and France gave rise to a clash in leadership between the two resistance groups. In October of 1944 guerrillas from southern France attempted to join effort with guerrillas in place within Spain to spark a general uprising against the Franco regime. When that effort failed, the Communist Party changed its policy; the new policy was to infiltrate Spain with small groups of guerrillas from France so that by collaborating with groups inside Spain they could wear down the regime through terrorism—blowing up trains, attacking Civil Guard barracks, destroying power lines.

From 1945 to 1948 these tactics demanded the regime's attention, but they did not mobilize wide-spread revolution. The policy was effectively laid aside in October, 1948 when the Soviet Union Communist Party called for the evacuation of guerrillas, a decision carried out in 1950 and 1951. Tomasa refers to this decision by the party to end guerrilla action; she states that it was 1948 when she and Miguel were carrying out that decision in southern Spain.

Meanwhile the *guerrilla* continued in cities with bank robberies and attacks on Falangist offices, terrorist activities that did not go uncontested from within Communist ranks. Tomasa's friend, Victoria Pujolar, mentions Cristino García and Gabriel León Trilla, both of whom favored terrorist tactics. Their fate demonstrates party strife with respect to urban *guerrilla*: on September 6, 1945, Trilla was stabbed to death in an abandoned cemetery for his disagreement with the view of party leadership that terrorism was counterproductive, while Cristino García was arrested on September 22, 1946, in Alcalá de Henares and shot on February 21, 1947, along with nine other guerrillas.[4]

The testimonies reveal that Tomasa and the friends she mentions in Part 2, Victoria Pujolar, Adelaida Abarca, and Angelita Ramis, were involved in urban resistance, though it is not clear if or to what extent they participated in terrorist activities. From their accounts the women set up contacts between the party and prisons, provided support for prisoners, and made connections between party leadership in Spain and in France. Only in Esperanza Martínez's testimony do we see first hand the life of rural guerrillas. Captured in 1952, Esperanza had been with the guerrillas during years when groups lived a hand-to-mouth existence and their activities were primarily defensive.

For Esperanza, Tomasa, and the other women who tell their stories, their understanding of the politics that informed the life-and-death struggle in which they found themselves is limited. For the most part, these women began their work in the Communist Party by joining the youth movement. Although the Communist Youth could claim only 14,000 members before the elections of February, 1936, after joining with its Socialist counterpart in April, 1936 to form the JSU, Juventudes Socialistas Unificadas (Unified Socialist Youth), membership dramatically increased.

Tomasa's initial attraction to the party is understandable in light of the grueling hardships of her youth. Not only does the opportunity for a better life that the party promised appeal to the young teenager but also the trust that older members place in her. Subsequent events—war and imprisonment—confirmed her commitment to the party.

Although Tomasa was in no position to assess the role of the party in the political life of the Republic, historians tend to view the effects of the Communist Party as problematic. The PCE, Partido Comunista de España (Communist Party of Spain), had been founded in 1921 when a younger radical youth group joined with members who had left the PSOE, the Partido Socialista Obrero Español (Spanish Socialist Workers Party), a Marxist-Leninist party founded in 1879 by Pablo Iglesias that advocated a workers' state and government. The role of the PCE in Spanish political life was minimal until the war because the party was unable to have an impact on either the PSOE or the CNT. The CNT, the Confederación Nacional del Trabajo (National Confederation of Work), was an anarchist labor union founded in 1910–1911 that believed in no government at all outside of unions or libertarian communes.

At the outbreak of the war the Communists had only sixteen deputies out of 473 in parliament, and the total number of Communists in Spain probably did not exceed 50,000. At the end of the first year of the war, the numbers had increased to about 300,000, thanks in large part to the growing popularity of the Soviet Union for sending military aid to the Republic while western democracies stood by in silence.

But the PCE was not without internal strife, another fact that receives scant attention from Tomasa and her companions for whom the party was the model of discipline and loyalty. In its internal wrangling, the party reflected the state of the Republic in general in that supporters were far from agreement in their political aspirations and methods in spite of the threat of a common enemy. Granted a coalition of left-wing Republicans, Socialists, and Communists had been formed under the rubric of Popular Front prior to the February, 1936 elections, but the name was no guarantee against the danger posed by competing ideologies from within Republican ranks.

In early May of 1937 wrangling turned to out-and-out warfare in Barcelona, the city to which Tomasa repeatedly turns and returns as the center of her political life. At the heart of what has been called a mini-civil war within the Civil War was long-standing acrimony between POUM and PSUC. POUM, Partido Obrero de Unificación Marxista (Workers' Party of Marxist Unification), was a revolutionary Marxist party founded in September, 1935 from a Trotskyist Left Communist Party composed of workers and peasants. Holding to the belief that workers must seize political power, POUM and the CNT united in opposition to PSUC, the Partido Socialista Unificado de Cataluña (Unified Socialist Party of Catalonia). PSUC had been established in July, 1936 with the uniting of the Catalan Communist Party, the Catalan branch of PSOE, and two other organizations. In effect, PSUC was the Communist Party in Catalonia.

Ideological differences among these factions were acute, and they inform the thinking and activities of Tomasa and her husband, Miguel Núñez. The PSUC was derided for its conservative bent with respect to the Catalan middle class and the defense of private property and the free market. Its main target was Largo Caballero, Prime Minister from September 4, 1936 to May 17, 1937. The PSUC wanted Largo Caballero out of office because he opposed the party's proposals to create a united Socialist and Communist Party and to bring the army under the control of the party and Soviet advisers.

By the spring of 1937 PSUC had succeeded in regularizing the militia and the militia patrols, thus depriving the workers of their own army and police force. This action, among other measures, triggered fighting in the streets of Barcelona. On May 3 the PSUC police commissioner seized the ground floor of the central telephone exchange, a building long held by the CNT. Fighting spread to the streets, with members of

PSUC on one side and the CNT and POUM on the other firing at each other from behind street barricades. The hostilities were heated but short-lived; on May 7 the CNT broadcast an appeal for the cessation of fighting. Casualities from the riots totalled 400 dead and 1,000 wounded. Subsequently, the Communists forced the resignation of Largo Caballero, who was replaced by Dr. Juan Negrín, a man whom Socialists, Communists, and Republicans could support.

Historians tend to draw a line between the policy and the methods of the Communist Party. The party's policy of strong central government made sense in the teeth of the larger war being waged against the Nationalists, but its terrorist methods against opposition from within the Republican side drew harsh criticism. The Stalinist secret police in Spain, headed by Alexander Orlov, was especially vicious in the months following the May uprising, virtually eliminating POUM and murdering its leader, Andrés Nin. One of its most outspoken critics was George Orwell, who in articles and in his book, *Homage to Catalonia*, exposed as trumped-up the charge of siding with fascism brought against POUM leaders at their trial in October of 1937. In spite of such criticism, POUM leaders were convicted of rebellion against the Republic and of conspiring with Franco.

One aspect of Spanish Communism that is fresh in the women's testimonies is the role of women in the party. Esperanza Martínez concludes her story with biting criticism of the party for its general disparagement of women: on the one hand, women were not sufficiently educated in party philosophy to assume leadership responsibility, and on the other, the same men who criticized women for lack of education were reluctant to facilitate the education that would qualify them for positions of leadership. Ironically, this double bind is precisely the same one by which the church had dominated women for centuries.

After the war the PCE emerged as the principal clandestine opposition to the Franco regime from within Spain. But internal strife continued to weaken the party, and discontent with what members perceived as a failure in the party's own democracy led to its near demise. During the process of transition to democracy after Franco's death in 1975, the PCE lost out to PSOE, which came to power in the elections of October, 1982 and dominated Spanish politics until its loss in the March, 1996 elections. Meanwhile elections of 1986 had seen the PCE forming the nucleus of a leftist coalition known as Izquierda Unida (United Left), and most recently, in the 1996 elections, the political fortunes of Spanish Communism declined even further.

Although some women allude to the failure of democracy within the party, they do not remotely suggest that Spanish Communists were guilty of political crimes or even consider the possibility that brutality marked the Republican as well as the Nationalist side. Here again, we must remember that these women's vision was that of participant rather than observer or historian. Prisoner to filth, hunger, torture, and uncertainty of execution, the Communist woman could not be expected to rationalize her suffering on the basis that her enemies might be enduring like conditions. Historians may cite the figure of over 89,000 executions and murders in Republican Spain during the war and describe in brutal detail the torture and murder of nearly 8,000 priests and nuns as evidence that suffering was not exclusive to Republican sympathizers, but even today those reports are no source of comfort to women like Tomasa whose understanding of events was forged in torture and refined in the sounds of executions carried out at dawn.

Nor do the women hint at the dark workings of SIM, the Servicio de Investigación Militar (Bureau of Military Investigation), which was a secret police under the direction of the Communists, supposedly for the purpose of ferreting out spies. Its methods of torture were the same as those used by the Soviet secret police in Spain and many men were said to have been murdered by its agents.

We who stand apart from the events that Tomasa and her companions relate must appreciate the necessary limitations on their vision and grant to them the truth of their experience. At the same time, we ought not dismiss the possibility—and in this case the fact—that war generates a cruelty that may infect the best of political intentions. If there is a larger lesson to be learned from the map of human suffering that is the Spanish Civil War, that lesson is the immeasurable value of peace. Or, as Tomasa says at the end of her story in the original Spanish text: "*Peace* and democracy for all oppressed peoples. *Peace* for all the world."

Conversation over dinner in the summer of 1994 at the home of Joanne Allen's friends in Vilanova was powerful testimony to the truth that we measure the world from the window of our own experience. The friends who had invited the three of us for dinner were a couple in their late seventies, the same age as Tomasa. No sooner had we sat down to the table than Mr. García leaned toward Tomasa, seated at the other end of the large table, and said, "Tell me, Señora Tomasa, what did you do during the war?"

I gasped inwardly at the sudden and only too-real prospect of a "nice" dinner turning ugly. For two hours, Tomasa and Mr. García talked; after feeble attempts to change the subject, Joanne and I resigned ourselves to silence and perhaps an early leave-taking. All three people had supported the Republic, but there the similarity stopped. Mrs. García had inherited the family home and land; Mr. García owned a small business; Tomasa was a proletarian by birth and experience. The Garcías had no sympathy for Communist theories or practices. Mr. García told Tomasa outright that her party was dead. She, in turn, did not deny the truth of his observations, but neither did she second his opinion. For a woman who had validated her belief in the party through imprisonment and years of separation from husband and child, silence was a telling response. What words could substitute for the reality of self-sacrifice?

All the while Mrs. García was busy serving her guests from the abundance of delicious food she had prepared. But suddenly she erupted. In a rapid-fire barrage of Spanish and Catalan she told her story: how her family home had been run over by the dregs of a popular army, by men who were little better than beasts—dirty, boorish, cruel. She didn't care if they fought for or against the Republic: they had violated her family home and she would never forgive them. If the Tomasa-Mr. García confrontation made us squirm uncomfortably— though by this time Joanne and I had given up responsibility for what we were sure was a disaster in-the-making—Mrs. García's outburst confirmed our worst fears. The sweet, motherly Mrs. García bearing plates of food from kitchen to dining room had metamorphosed before our very eyes into a kind of maenad, crazed by memories of brutish soldiers blaspheming the God of hearth and family. Not one of us uttered a word: Tomasa, Mr. García, Joanne, and I, a silenced Greek chorus, as it were.

As suddenly as Mrs. García had launched the denunciation, she ceased. She turned to pouring coffee and heaped our dessert plates with sponge cake and Spanish meringue. Soon Mr. García and I were deep in discussion about business in Spain and the United States. Mrs. García, Tomasa, and Joanne went outside to sit on the verandah and look at family pictures. And Tomasa was the first person to answer Mrs. García's invitation to see the upstairs apartment they had made for their married son and family. When the five of us said good-bye, it was as if we were all the best of friends. Tomasa might mutter "fascists" under her breath on the drive home, but she had known the Garcías' political leanings beforehand and it was clear that nothing would have stopped her from going with us to their house for dinner.

Of course, Mr. and Mrs. García were not fascists. But their politics were realized in different circumstances than were Tomasa's. And just as Tomasa's views cannot be changed neither can theirs.

That scene has replayed itself many times in my head. I've come to see it as a microcosm of Spanish society today. Old hostilities and old pains are not dead; they rise up in the particular event of a conversation and form a disposition to the meaning of life and death that ultimately defines individual identity.

There is one other aspect of Tomasa that remains for the telling—her relationship with her husband, Miguel Núñez. I've not met Miguel personally, but his presence I feel everywhere in their Vilanova flat: a photo of him taken in Cuba, handsome still in his middle years, with every bit the look of the intellectual; shelf upon shelf of books on politics, philosophy, history, sociology, literature; paintings and photographs revolutionary in mood. And I wonder at this union of the intellectual and the proletarian, as if Miguel and Tomasa were a metaphor for the ideals they advocate as Communists.

But there is something between them rooted more deeply in the heart than political commitment. There is a love I hear in Tomasa's voice when Miguel calls from Madrid, three or four times a day to see how she's feeling, as happened on our visit in January, 1996, when she was suffering from a cold and flu. The Catalan writer, Teresa Pamiès, honored their relationship in her preface to the first volume of testimonies where she wrote with deep admiration of Tomasa's strength to claim her identity apart from her well-known husband, who has served as a member of the PSUC executive committee and the Central Committee of the PCE:

> If Tomasa Cuevas had not been the companion of a leader, surely today she would occupy a position of responsibility commensurate with her proven organizational talents and a natural intelligence enhanced by an unblemished record. But the heart has its reasons and no one should inquire into the life of a couple. In this society made by men, a woman who has the "misfortune" to fall in love with a leader must resign herself to life as his lover, secretary or nurse or else renounce union with him.

Noting that neither option was right for Tomasa, Pamiès admires her for being her own person rather than simply "the tail of the comet." "Tomasa radiates her own light," continues the writer, "and only she knows how difficult it has been to share the militant life with her husband. Her light may not dazzle, it is true," writes Pamiès, "but it is no less authentic."

In this prologue Teresa Pamiès honors as well Tomasa's determination to gather these women's stories and bring them into print. Others would have thrown in the sponge in face of the mountain of work required by the project, asserts Pamiès:

> Kilometers and kilometers of tapes; hundreds of notebooks filled with transcripts of the tapes done by young friends, leaving to her—because she was the only one who could do it—the horrendous job of putting in order, coordinating, and verifying material that was important but often repetitive. Trips to various cities and villages, the search for old

friends dispersed throughout Spain or exiled, prodding the recalcitrant and the weary—and all that in spite of a health broken by a life of painful physical work since childhood, abuse in police stations, precarious living conditions and taking care of sick and aged family members.

When I began to translate these testimonies about women and prison, I could not foresee the effects that knowing Tomasa in person and in her story would have on me and on my attitude toward the work of translation and editing. What began as an intellectual enterprise with moral overtones has become a spiritual odyssey, brought to fruition in part by intellectual skills. But the full fruit of this odyssey is the realization that more than anything I would like to honor my friend, Tomasa, by helping to bring *her* story to the appreciation of a new audience.

## ACKNOWLEDGMENTS

I would like to acknowledge the following people for their generous help in the preparation of this book: Joanne Allen, for accompanying me on two visits to Tomasa's home and with her sense of humor and linguistic skills forming in large part the bridge of trust and understanding that is necessary in this kind of collaborative work; Amanda Powell, for putting Tomasa and me in contact with each other and reading thoroughly the completed manuscript; Robert Richardson, my colleague at California State University, Sacramento, and cartographer par excellence, who generated the maps for the book; and Terence Manns, Director of Graduate Research and Studies at the university, who made possible partial funding for the first trip to meet with Tomasa.

# PART 1

# *War and Prison*

Map by Robert Richardson, California State University, Sacramento

# CHAPTER 1

# *Growing Up in Prewar Spain*

I was born on March 7, 1917, in Brihuega, a little village not far from the provincial capital of Guadalajara. I was a girl when I left the village but in my imagination I still see it as it was. Not long after beginning this account in 1975, I visited my village and wandered through it as if I had lived there all my life. My family was of the working class. My maternal grandfather was a mason and my other grandfather was a baker. My father was only a boy when he began working in a flour mill in the village and delivering sacks of flour by horseback to homes. There were five children in our family: Antonia, Alejandro, who was two years younger, Angel and Concha, who both died of childhood diseases, and me.

I must have been three or four years old when my father had a bad accident. His horse slipped and fell; my father's leg was pinned under the horse and badly cut and broken in three places. When my father was taken to the hospital, the horse tried so hard to follow that it took several people to hold it back. The story went around that whenever the man hired to replace my father left the horse alone so he could deliver flour, the animal would run off to the hospital. That little horse was my father's best friend. Another of his friends was the dog, Canela, who always walked next to father and right between the horses' feet. This dog was the one who told my mother of father's accident. When Canela ran barking into the house as if she was crying, my mother realized something was wrong.

My mother suffered terribly during the two years my father was in the hospital. Even after he came home, life didn't improve. The mill wouldn't hire him because they considered him useless. It's true he limped a little, but he was as strong as ever. He might have been able to get field work but he didn't know anything about working in the field. The only solution was to leave the village. We decided to move to Guadalajara where my sister was working doing housework and cooking. There my father went from white to black. Before he'd delivered flour; now it was coal. My sister was able to help us a little; she'd salvage what she could from the leftovers in the kitchen where she worked. My brother only got day work, now here, now there, never in one place; he hadn't learned a trade or gone to school.

I must have been six or seven years old when I began to attend school, not on a regular basis, though, because that was when my mother got so sick. The doctors said she had a stomach ulcer or something that caused internal bleeding. She hemorrhaged so severely she almost died; for several years we were on the verge of losing her. The doctors said she couldn't stand an operation, so her only hope was to follow a strict diet, which in our economic situation was almost impossible. I was the only one in the family to set foot in school, but I missed a lot because I had to stay home with mother when she wasn't feeling well. We couldn't leave her alone. The school I attended was run by nuns. When I had to miss several days to be with my mother, they didn't just ask me politely why I had been absent but they accused me of being a vagrant who didn't want to study. So I gradually gave up school. But I had learned to read and write a little bit.

Working and taking care of my mother left no time for play. I didn't even know what a toy was. Once, on the Feast of the Three Wise Men, my father brought me a little candy bar of caramel and roasted almond. Unused to such a delicacy, I covered my father with kisses. Tears in his eyes, he said: "Look, child, you're going to see the girls outside and they'll say that the Kings brought them this and the Kings brought them that, and they'll even show you the gifts the Kings brought. But, my child, the Kings don't exist, and the gifts they show you are ones their parents bought. Now we don't have the means to buy gifts." I told him not to worry; it wouldn't bother me to see the girls with their toys.

I saw my father go off to work. All that day I thought a lot about our situation and my father, a day laborer with a seriously ill wife. I went outside and just as my father had warned, there were the girls with their toys and dolls, embroidery hoops, sewing kits, and countless other gifts. When the girls asked me what the Kings had brought me, a small lie took shape in my imagination: "A darling doll, so pretty."

"Why don't you have it?"

"Oh, my mother won't let me bring the doll outside. Do you know what? You take her by the hand and she walks and says, 'Papa' and 'Mama.'"

I had heard about such dolls. The girls crowded around me begging to see the doll. I kept on saying that my mother wouldn't let me, wouldn't let me. I finally got away from them and went back in the house. I cried in a corner. My mother asked me why I was crying.

"It's nothing," I said. "I just feel like crying, that's all."

"Did you see the other girls' gifts?"

"Well, yes, but I don't care."

That's where the matter stayed until afternoon when several neighbors came to visit my mother for the holiday. But those damned girls!

They thought that if they came with their mothers they'd see the doll.

"Come on," they begged, hugging their mothers' skirts, "show us the doll."

Finally my mother realized the girls' scheme, but I kept on saying that I had put the doll away for safekeeping.

"But you can show us the doll in the house. Come on, tell your mother to let you show it."

I don't know how but I finally managed to drag them outside without showing them the doll. But they said: "Hey, you lied. You don't really have a doll!"

When I went in the house, my mother was crying bitterly.

"Mommy, are you feeling worse?"

"No, my daughter, I'm better. I'm crying because I truly wanted to buy you that doll."

At that the two of us started crying. My mother explained that I wasn't the only little girl not to receive toys that day; she said there were many, many children whose fathers earned just enough to put a little food on the table. And she repeated what my father had said that morning: "You're old enough to know the truth, my daughter. The parents are really the Kings."

I was only nine years old when I started working in a knitwear factory. In those days it was considered a factory, but today we'd call it a small workshop. I remember it perfectly. It was a tiny little store where they sold stockings and other machine-made things. There was a small show case and a shop in back with four knitting machines, one for socks, another for stockings, and two for pants and skirts. My job was mending stockings. I began by earning two *reales* a week, and I stayed at that level for some time. Later I asked for a raise and received one more little *real* a week.

I was a rebel by nature and I was becoming more and more rebellious. I didn't let an opportunity slip by without asking for a raise. The answer was always the same: "Who do you think you are, you brat? Don't you know how many people would like to earn what you do?" But I wasn't convinced. Those three *reales* were very little pay. I knew what they earned from my work because in each little parcel of repair work they would put the price that had to be paid. Always grumbling and always arguing, they would raise my wages one more *real*, then another and another, until by the time I was eleven years old I was earning seventy-five. Mending wasn't my only job. On Sundays I worked as a nanny in a house where my brother's fiancée was employed. The regular nanny had Sundays off. I learned a lesson in life from my two jobs: you have to stand up for yourself. We needed more money at home so I asked for another raise. My employer said: "I've told you many times that you earn more than your work deserves. Be quiet and don't ask me again."

I didn't argue with her that day. But I began to jot down in a little notebook everything I earned for the shop during the week. When it was time to be paid the following week, I said to my employer: "Well, I'm going to insist again on a raise."

When she repeated that I wasn't earning my pay as it was, I took out the little notebook with the record of my work. "And this," I asked, "what is this? Look at how much I made for you this week and how miserably you pay me."

I thought the woman would go crazy. I was afraid she might even hit me. But no, the only thing she did was to say good-bye to me, call my father and tell him he had a very rebellious daughter and he ought to be careful with me and remember that Guadalajara was a small place and that she was well known in the community and could make it impossible for me to get work. And she put me out in the street. So at the age of eleven I began to look for work. I found a job in a factory that made pasta for soup. At the same time I asked a relative of my mother if he would put an advertisement in the liberal paper he published. I placed an ad for mending at home. My first customers came from the shop where I had mended stockings previously. When they called from the shop to complain that I was taking their customers away, I answered very calmly: "Well, you're wrong, Señora Isidra, because I didn't knock on the doors of these women who come to my house. The only thing I did was to advertise in a liberal newspaper, just as you advertise in the other paper. They knock at my door. But me? I never knock at theirs. So whenever you want to denounce me, go right ahead."

I worked days in the factory and at night mended stockings at home. The mending was difficult because we had only one light in the house and it was high up in the ceiling. I would put a chair on the table, climb up on the table, and sit there to do the mending. Usually I worked until midnight or one o'clock, and the next day when I left for work I would leave the little parcels with my mother to give the ladies who came for them.

The economic situation at home was increasingly bad. My mother needed a glass of milk every two hours. Such an expense was impossible for us. But I found out that a dairy farm was looking for a girl to deliver milk from six to eight o'clock in the morning. I got the job. They only paid me fifteen pesetas a month but they gave me three liters of milk free. Winter was the hardest time. I put on wool gloves to pick up those containers of milk, but my hands got so cold that when I knocked at customers' doors they would have to serve themselves the milk because my hands were too numb to move.

Matters went from bad to worse. We owed a month's rent on the house. I learned that the owner needed someone to bring water from one-half kilometer away; the owners still didn't have running water in the house. So in the afternoon when I left the factory, I went to fill jugs of water. I carried one jug on my hip and a pail in my hand. In the morning milk, then the factory, carrying water in the afternoon, and mending stockings at night. Sometimes I wondered how I possibly could do so many things. It must have been the necessity I felt to do it and love for my mother and seeing that my efforts did help my family and home. But all that made me rebellious. I rebelled against everything that exploited me.

My job delivering milk ended when they began using a little cart. Then I found a house that needed someone to wash clothes. Very early every morning I would go to the public washing place where I'd seen women washing clothes from morning to night. How angry I felt to be there. I put in the soap and went off to the factory. I returned from the factory and washed. When I left the factory I did the rinsing. There I was, running in circles from one job to the other. The baskets of clothes were so heavy I couldn't lift them; my brother would carry them from the washing place to our home or the customer's house.

At the factory I was the person who protested the most. I protested everything, but not just for me, for all the others, too. From carrying heavy trays of wet pasta while I was still growing my arms started to become deformed. But that is where I learned to fight. And that is where I met one of our companions, Santos Puertos. I'll always remember him as the person who guided my steps to the struggle that I carry on today. It happened like this.

One day he said: "Peque, come here, please."

And he took me over to a window and showed me some men in front of the factory. "Do you see those men?" he asked. "They're police. They're waiting to arrest me. Do you understand? I'm a Communist and they don't like Communists. But you could help me. You're a good girl and you can make something of yourself."

"What do I have to do?"

"Look, I have a little package I can't take out. If you keep the package for me, the police won't get it if they arrest me. You carry it to your house and hide it. But don't tell a soul, do you understand?"

"Yes, I promise. Not a word to anyone."

"Good. I'll give it to you before you leave."

There was no way I could say no to him because he was the only person who helped me take up the trays of pasta when the supervisor wasn't looking.

So we had an agreement. The next afternoon on the way to work I met a peasant, Raimundo Serrano, known as Peregrino. Everybody knew he was a Communist. The police arrested him frequently and made life impossible for him; he couldn't get work or even feed his family.

"What's new, Peque, are you off to work?"

"Yes."

"What do you know about Santos?"

"They arrested him yesterday."

"Oh! Listen, before they arrested him, did he give you anything?"

"Me? No! Why would he give me anything?"

"Well, look, there's something very important that I have to collect."

"It must have been some other girl from the factory. Santos didn't give me anything."

"Look, don't treat me like this, girl. This is an important matter."

"It can be as important as you like but I don't have anything."

"Okay, okay, so you don't have anything."

The next day he approached me again with the same questions. I insisted again it was a mistake, that I wasn't the one, that I didn't know anything, that I didn't have a thing to do with Santos. On the third day he brought me a note from Santos and said: "Look, I managed to get this letter from Santos out of jail. Now you'll see that he wants you to give me the package." I was convinced. That night I gave him the package.

That was my first clandestine work for the Communist Party in Spain. After this little job members of the party trusted me to set up connections or arrange meetings. One day I asked one of the men why the Communist Party had to work secretly when their demands for the people were just. He explained very clearly that capitalism and the middle class didn't want to recognize the workers' claims. He explained in more or less these words:

"Is it true that you don't want to continue being exploited? Is it true that you want to live better than you do now and work fewer hours? Is it true that you would have liked to go to school like our bosses' children, like middle-class children, and not had to go to work when you were nine years old? Well, that's what we want and that's what we ask for. And that's what we work for. Now, don't think it's easy. The struggle will cost us a lot: imprisonment, even blood, who knows? But we have to fight. We have to live better. We have to make Spain democratic."

His words affected me deeply. "You can count on me," I said. "I'll always be with you even if it costs me my life."

I worked with them in the party until 1931. When the Communist Youth[1] was founded in our region, I became a member and began work in propaganda and what we called "agitation," things that I could do in spite of my lack of education. Using an old, ugly machine, we published the *Joven Guardia* (*Young Guard*) and handed it out on the streets. These were the years of the big campaigns for freedom conducted by the internationally known Communist leaders, Carlos Prestes and Ernst Thaelmann.[2] We campaigned by painting slogans and signs on walls and roads and organizing gatherings in the country to meet with other young people. We had to be very careful because by then the Assault Guards had been organized as a special security force to defend the Republic. These shock troops were made up of officers and men thought to be especially loyal to the Republic.

My life at home and at work improved. Through friends I made in and out of the party I was able to get construction jobs for my brother. His income made it possible for me to quit my extra jobs. Meanwhile my sister had married a farmer and they provided us with fresh vegetables from their garden. My mother was improving thanks to her milk treatment. At least at home we were beginning to see our way clear.

My brother bought his first suit, on installment of course. And I bought something for myself—shoes with heels. How grand they made me feel, I who had worn nothing but sandals all my life. Sometimes at home I had tried on my sister's shoes when she wasn't there. Of course, she got angry with me and said I was going to break the heels or make them misshapen. But I loved to wear shoes with heels. As far as how I dressed, I looked nice. I was lucky enough to have a sister who could make a dress out of any piece of cloth they gave her in the houses where she worked. From any little thing at all she made me skirts and blouses so that I was always well turned out and very pretty. She loved to see me like that. She also made herself some beautiful dresses. She was very good looking, the cute type, with blue eyes like my mother's and long blond hair that she wore in a big top knot. People would call her "the blond with the top knot." I remember that after the elections of April 14, 1931, which was the first year we celebrated May Day, she made me a darling pleated red dress in just twenty-four hours because I was going to carry the banner for the *casa del pueblo* that day. The *casas del pueblo* were a kind of Socialist club house that the local trade unions used for meetings, and they had a cafe and lending library. I saw my sister near the sidewalk watching the demonstrators march by, her baby boy in her arms, and I could see the happiness in her face and eyes as she watched me in the dress she'd made for the occasion.

That May Day was and is unforgettable for me. The demonstration developed in a way that none of us expected as people from surrounding villages came to Guadalajara. All kinds of revolutionary songs were in the air.

My brother got married around the year 1934, leaving only my parents and me at home. I, too, had a sweetheart, a fellow from a working-class family who had a job as an electrical mechanic. If I had a job to do for the youth group and he came to take me out, I'd tell him I had mend-

ing to do. We'd chat a while at the door and then he'd be off. As soon
as he left, I'd go out. He didn't know I was active in the Communist
Youth. Sometimes he was the one who'd come to tell me he was going
with a friend to do some extra job. These boys were the kind who
handed over their entire salary to help out at home; for their own spending they depended on odd jobs.

One day it happened that we both had odd jobs. That day—and it
was now 1934—a bigger meeting was scheduled. If I remember correctly, the purpose of the meeting was to discuss preparations for a
national strike. To reach the house where the meeting was to take place,
I had to go a roundabout way to avoid walking across the central
square. Still I had to cross it at one point. Just as I was crossing, I met
some groups of young people. In one group I spotted my sweetheart. He
left the group, very angry. "Are you following me?" he asked. "Don't
you take my word for it that I have a job to do? I'm just here for a little while with some friends and then we have to get to work. I'm not
very happy if you've followed me."

I looked at him calmly, almost figuring out what was going on.
"Follow you? Follow you? It never crossed my mind. I met you by pure
chance. Go to your job and I'll go to mine. I'm off to deliver some stockings. See you later."

I reached my destination and went in the house. People were coming in, some now, some later. In one of the groups coming in I saw my
boyfriend. Both of us were happy to find the other in the same place;
from then on we worked more together than individually. One of the
jobs the two of us did was acquire paper for printing. We got some of
the paper from a boy whose father had a print shop. When the boy's
father finished his work, he locked the print shop, put the keys in his
jacket pocket and went home. The routine never varied: arrive home,
take off the jacket, hang it on the hook. The boy would wait a moment,
then say to his parents, "See you later." Going through the hall, he
would put his hand in the jacket, take the keys, go to the shop and get
what paper he could. This was pretty dangerous for him because he
might be seen at any time. Then we made a deal: the boy would continue the business with the key while my sweetheart courted me at the
window, right by the door. Without lifting the latch, the boy handed us
the paper through the window and off we went. That way the boy left
with clean hands. When the war broke out in Guadalajara in 1936 and
the fascists took the city within twenty-four hours, there were few casualties. But this fine young man was one of them.

# CHAPTER 2

# *Coming of Age in Politics and War*

My first arrest was in 1934. In late November or early December, I don't remember which, some children from Asturias whose parents had been killed or incarcerated or who had fled their homes were passing through Guadalajara on their way to live with other families. I went to the municipal square where the two cars carrying the children were due to stop. I don't know what had happened, but when I got there I saw an assault guard threatening a small child. I flew like a streak toward the guard and looking up at him—he was very tall and I was just a cute little snotty-nosed gal—I said: "You touch that kid and I'll blast you and curse your mother." I think I would have had to stand on a chair to hit him. He grabbed me by the arm, "Yes? What's that? You're under arrest."

He took me to city hall and they threw me in jail. The jail was full of rats that scurried over my feet. I was desperately afraid. When my father heard about my arrest, he went to the jail to find out why I was being held. "Come now," they told him, "she's in politics up to her eyeballs." My father answered that I was much too busy with three jobs and a sweetheart to have time for politics. In short, the police had to be mistaken. I must have been with those little children by accident. Besides I wouldn't behave like that toward a policeman. When they brought me out to make a statement and asked me what I had done, I answered, "Nothing."

Then they brought in the policeman who had arrested me. "Why did you arrest this girl?"

"Because she threatened me and cursed my mother."

"No, sir," I replied. "I didn't 'curse your mother.' I said that if you touched the child, I was going to curse your mother and hit you. But you didn't touch the child, so I did not curse your mother and I didn't hit you."

The policemen laughed because my statement was so simple and straightforward. But they still wanted to pull some information out of us. What had I been doing there? Who had given the orders? Who was I with? If I gave them just one name, they said, nothing would happen to me.

"Me? I just happened to be there. I was passing by, saw the children and stopped. Then I saw this man mistreating one of the kids and it just popped into my head to say what I did. But, since I didn't hit him or shit on his mother, I don't think you should hold me as if I'd committed some crime."

But they did hold me, for three days, even though they weren't much interested in the business with the policeman. What they wanted to know was who had sent us to welcome the children. "Nothing will happen to you," they said, over and over, "if you give us a name." All they got for their trouble were empty wishes. Finally they let me go.

My father was my best friend, the person who appreciated everything I did around the house. I knew how much he loved me. But that time he was waiting for me in the hall with a slipper in hand to shake the truth out of me. As I walked toward the open front door, he slowly backed away. And as he backed up, I reached the door leading to the attic where I kept my Communist Youth membership card. I seized the card and held it under his nose.

"Look, father, you and mother are what I love most. But I've put my dreams in this. See, it's my membership card in the Communist Youth. I've been fighting for it for some time. If you touch me, it's all over. I assure you I'll leave home, and you know that I've been able to support myself for many years. Do what you want. I'll stay on at home and continue to help you as always, but I'll do it as a member of the Communist Youth."

The slipper fell from my father's hand. "Don't worry, Pequeña, don't worry. I'm not going to hit you. Stand up for your rights because I've never known how to stand up for mine." The two of us embraced weeping. My mother, who was in the dining room awaiting the outcome, said: "And that's what you were going to tell her and what you were going to do to her? Well, it's all over now. That's the last straw. You've given her wings."

The campaigns for the elections of February 16, 1936, were hard fought. More than once people came to Guadalajara from Madrid to hold meetings and go around the villages promising people the moon. If there wasn't running water in the villages, they'd install a central fountain. They'd provide help with the harvests. They'd even bring in the railroad. Even before the Republic we'd always been promised a railroad. The promise never materialized. We also campaigned, but we didn't promise anything we couldn't deliver. We only reminded people that nothing could be accomplished in our country without a united front. Only by uniting our efforts could we free ourselves from slavery, distribute to the peasants the uncultivated land belonging to the large landowners, and form collectives of small farmers so they could earn more money working together than from small parcels of land held individually.

I was one of the members who went out to the villages for two or three days at a time. I don't know why I was chosen to speak, but the fact is that people in those little towns liked me and when I left they would promise to vote for the Republic. One time some people in government were planning a big meeting in the bullring at Guadalajara. Our job was to make sure the meeting didn't take place. In the morning a bunch of cars arrived and they began passing out leaflets and calling people to the bullring. We didn't interrupt their propagandizing, but the story changed when the cars of the representatives tried to get near the bullring. Stones rained down everywhere. The police appeared, and the Civil Guard and the Assault Guard were on horseback. In spite of efforts by the police to clear the area, we were able to prevent the meeting from taking place. The cars backed off with fresh dents and broken windows.

The elections were a success. Right away we asked for a general amnesty for the loads of political prisoners all over Spain and especially in the north. Guadalajara had two prisons, one civil, the other military; both were full of political prisoners. At three o'clock one afternoon I left the factory and joined workers from all over for a rally to support amnesty. Out in the street we met groups of friends who'd also left their work. At the rally the officials agreed to the amnesty but said they had to communicate with Madrid first. We didn't accept that plan and shouted for amnesty. We divided into two groups, one going to the civil prison, the other to the military one, shouting "Amnesty, amnesty, amnesty!" Our actions were communicated to Madrid and the order was given to release the prisoners. I remember that I was in the group that went to the military prison. Among the men released was a certain Lieutenant Castillo. We carried him to the *casa del pueblo* where we celebrated his release the best we could. The men embraced one another, those that were freed and those who had rallied. Lieutenant Castillo's voice was heard: "Well, now, it's good for men to embrace one another, but bring on the girls. They're the ones I want to hug." Little could we imagine that that man, with his courage and valor, that handsome, strong man, would be assassinated from behind just a few months later.

In April of 1936 our youth group was strengthened with the unification of the Socialist and Communist groups. The new organization was called the Unified Socialist Youth, commonly referred to as the JSU. On May 1, 1936, we Communist members of the JSU went out to celebrate wearing our uniforms; the only change in the uniforms was that now we wore a blue and red handkerchief with our blue shirts instead of the plain red one of before. The rally was very exciting. The Falange came into the street and tried to break us up. They didn't succeed but there were skirmishes and punching and kicking.

The following months were full of worry and fear from threats hanging over our heads. We had to endure constant provocations from the Falangists. Assassinations and betrayal spread throughout Spain. The assassination of Calvo Sotelo on July 13, 1936, was the final blow; Sotelo had pushed for the restoration of the monarchy and authoritarian rule. War broke out. We already had heard about uprisings in the south. The day we learned about the uprising in Madrid I went to warn my sister who lived in the country; she had a five-year-old child, a little girl two and a half years old, and a third child was due any day. I told her to keep the children away from the garden and not leave the house. My sister and her family stayed in their house for a few days, but when bombs started falling all around, they took refuge in the train station.

On the way home from my sister's house, I met several friends crossing the fields and some workers on the way to the afternoon shift at the Hispano-Suiza plane factory. When the workers left at two o'clock in the afternoon, they didn't use the main doors because the forces of the Civil Guard and the Army already were out front with machine guns. They all fled, running through the fields toward the villages of Cabanillas and Marchemalo. They wanted to know where I was going.

That's when I realized there wasn't anything else for me to do but return to Guadalajara. My parents were there and they would have been extremely worried if I didn't return from my sister's house. I couldn't go by the main highway because of the shooting there, so I went up along the side of the cemetery. I finally made it home to my parents, but I didn't know what to do. I could see resistance was useless; we were far outnumbered by the fascist troops.

That night we turned off the lights inside the house and peered out the window. A group of people appeared; among them we recognized Falangists. They approached the door. The three of us looked at each other, waiting to hear the knock. It didn't come. Then we saw them going along the street. Why hadn't they knocked? When my father opened the door to investigate, he saw the sign of a cross scrawled on the door, a sure sign they'd intended to make an arrest. My father warned me to get out of Guadalajara. He told me to stay off main streets, go by way of a gully leading to a small poplar grove, and from there cross the main highway to reach the road leading to the village of Iriepal. My father was sure I could find refuge with friends there. By now it was late at night and very dark. I was scared. As I reached the knoll between Guadalajara and Iriepal, I looked at the bundles of wheat in the fields, set in rows like little huts, and asked myself: "What if the fascists are arresting people in Iriepal. Am I putting myself in the wolf's mouth?"

I waited for dawn to come in that field of wheat bundles. When the skies began to turn light, I heard the sound of planes flying very low. Looking in the direction of Guadalajara, I saw planes circling the capital and dropping leaflets. I made out the flag of the Republic painted on the wings. The planes were ours. I soon was to find out that the leaflets were warning citizens to evacuate Guadalajara, especially old people, women, and children. The workers' militias from Madrid, who had fought heroically against the fascist uprising and had won the battle of the Montaña Barracks on July 19–20, were en route to Guadalajara to free us from the fascist hordes. Then I saw whole families fleeing across the fields with their children. But a little later I saw the fascists and armed forces running, looking back and firing from time to time.

Then I began to see the situation more clearly. I was running a greater risk out there in the wheat fields than in town. However great the danger of returning to Guadalajara to see if the city was being liberated, chances were there wouldn't be enough enemy forces left to do anything against us. But first I went on to Iriepal to the home of my friend, María Andrés. She told me my parents were with neighbors in a nearby house. My old father was overjoyed to see me. I told them I was going to Guadalajara since we were beginning to get news that the liberation was complete and the city was once again in the hands of the people. In Guadalajara I would be able to make contact with the party and the youth organization.

So much has been written about the Spanish Civil War that I'll only say I served wherever needed. I worked for a while in a hospital in the region of Alcarria and in hospitals of the International Brigades; helped organize sewing shops in Guadalajara making coveralls for the militias; organized diversions for the troops that came to the villages for a few days of rest; set up laundries for washing the soldiers' clothes; established sewing shops; recruited men from villages for the front; and convinced women to take over men's jobs.

During one of the many severe bombings of Guadalajara our house was ruined. Fortunately we didn't suffer personal injury because my father was working, I was at party headquarters, and my mother as usual had run outside as soon as she heard the planes. My mother was so afraid of the bombings that she wouldn't even stay in the house at night with my father and me; she'd take her little mattress and sleep in the shelter.

The worst bombing took place one day around three o'clock in the afternoon. I remember how brightly the sun was shining and then, when a mass of bomb-laden Junkers came overhead, how an eerie darkness settled over the city. Not one ray of sun could penetrate the darkness formed by those planes overhead. The bombing was horrible. They dropped incendiary bombs in the city center, and the fires destroyed many, many buildings, including the National Museum. I was among the people who went by car and ambulance to help the wounded and dead. The sight that met my eye paralyzed me. I saw a friend who was probably sixteen or seventeen years old, hopping along on one foot. She was carrying one of her feet in her hand and she'd wrapped the stump of her leg in her blouse. I began searching in the rubble for my family. Where could they be? Children, women, all kinds of people were there. You could recognize them only by their clothes; their bodies and faces were blown away. As I searched through the rubble, I felt someone catch me by the shoulders and almost lift me off the ground.

"What are you looking for here?"

"For my sister and her children."

"They're not here; I saw them on the way to El Molino."

I took off for El Molino, shouting, "Antonia, Antonia!"

"We're here, we're here," came the answer.

I warned her to stay put and I would let her husband know where to find her. No sooner had I left El Molino than I met him crossing the highway. As we embraced, I began to cry from nervous tension. He got frightened, but I said: "No, don't be afraid, nothing's happened. Antonia and the children are in El Molino. Go get them and take them to your parents' house, but don't go home now. There's nothing but death and destruction."

That same day the fascist prisoners attempted an uprising in the hope that they were going to be liberated soon. Some of them even had pistols and fired through the prison windows. The townspeople were so incensed over the horrendous air raid that they marched to the prison demanding the prisoners be killed. A huge rally formed in the central streets of Guadalajara, with the people shouting for justice. They wanted the prisoners to pay with their lives for the bombings that had caused so many deaths. When I arrived from the station, the rally was already underway; I joined in. The consequences of this rally later on were something to remember. When some of my companions were arrested after the war, they declared that I was the one who had organized the rally. At the time they thought I was safely out of the country. My impression is that the rally was an entirely spontaneous event. No one person or group organized it.

In March, 1939 the party informed the JSU that some soldiers from the Republican army were coming to rest for a few days in Guadalajara and we were asked to arrange a party for them and let them use the game room in the *casa del pueblo*. The room was in disrepair, and the billiard tables were in such bad shape they couldn't be used. Nonetheless, we immediately began to put the room in order and make life more agreeable for the soldiers during their rest in Guadalajara. We couldn't find any felt to cover the billiard tables, so I went to Madrid with a boy named Ramón to look for felt. It must have been the fourth of March when we left for Madrid in the middle of the morning.[1] No sooner had we arrived in Madrid than we did our shopping and by noon were loaded with packages of things the leadership had asked us to buy. It was Ramón's idea to stay in Madrid until the next day; he wanted to spend some time with other kids in the JSU. So we went to the Hotel Atocha near the Atocha railroad station to reserve rooms and leave the packages. This done, we went our separate ways, agreeing to meet at the hotel at nine o'clock that night to see if we might want to catch the night train or wait for the morning one. I went to my cousin's house in Ventas. She was surprised to see me.

"Girl," she said, "what are you doing here?"

"I came with a friend to do some shopping."

"Don't you know the war is ending?"

"Ending? Don't tell me that! Who told you so?"

"Get with it. The news is everywhere in Madrid. The war will end any day now."

I was completely unsuspecting that the war was nearly over. Neither the leadership of the party nor the JSU had informed us of this. I didn't know what to believe. I took it for a passing rumor and we changed the subject. I ate supper with them; we chatted about the family and ourselves and after a while I walked with my cousin to Manuel Becerra street where she was going to do some shopping and I could get a streetcar for Cibeles. I planned to walk to the hotel from Cibeles, but before we reached the Puerta de Alcalá the streetcar stopped and I heard shouts I couldn't understand. People began to get off the streetcar so I did too. I walked to the Puerta de Alcalá where I heard more shouts. This time I could make out the words: "Long live the Republic! Long live the Republic!" And, "Long live the junta of Casado!" And, "At last, the war is ending!"

The worst part is that there were shots along with the shouts. People were already lying dead in the street. Several times I had to duck into doorways to dodge bullets. I was scared and didn't know what to think. I finally made it back to the hotel. Things were confusing there but at least there wasn't the shooting that was going on in the Puerta de Alcalá. I went up to the room, not knowing what to do or if something had happened to Ramón. The best course was to do what we had agreed on and just wait. When Ramón got there, he was scared, too, and indignant: "It's horrible, do you understand? Colonel Casado—he's the Republican commander of the Central Army—well, he's formed a junta. He's selling us out, selling us out to Franco."

"Who told you that?"

"The JSU. They're preparing to defend themselves. And we've got to fight, too. We've got to defend ourselves. We can't let Casado's junta sell us out."

"Sell out" became the watchword of the JSU and the Communist Party in Madrid. We both were silent for a moment. Perhaps we were thinking the same thing. We were young and didn't know politically what to think of everything we'd seen in the last couple of hours. Ramón was probably eighteen or nineteen years old and I, I was twenty-one. I had been active in the JSU for some time but I didn't understand anything about politics. Finally the boy broke the silence: "Come on, let's collect our packages and get to the station. We'll take the first train out. Maybe we'll be able to do something in Guadalajara."

We went down to the vestibule and stopped to pay for the rooms. The concierge charged us for only one room since we hadn't slept in them. He urged us to hurry to the station because the night train always filled up quickly. We took off running for the station. We asked the man there what time the train for Guadalajara left and he said at half past ten. It was about a quarter past nine. Just then a freight train was leaving. We asked where the train was going and the man said: "To Guadalajara. It's carrying a special load, but if you catch it, you'll get there sooner." The door to the last car was open and the conductor was standing there. We threw him our packages and thanks to him got on the moving train. When we climbed into the car and sat down, we were very sad and subdued. The conductor asked: "What is it, kids? Where are you going?"

"To Guadalajara."

"Well, what's happened to you?"

"What do you think? The war's ending."

"I saw shootings in the Puerta de Alcalá," I added.

"So? Were you afraid?"

"Yes, a little. Is it true what they're saying about Casado's junta?"

"Yes, child, it is. The people who truly fought for freedom and for the Republic don't want it, but it seems to me they won't get anywhere simply by not wanting it. Me, I think it's all over. Still, we should fight as long as we can. We shouldn't let ourselves get caught because we're not going to have an easy time of it. Do you belong to some organization?" We answered that yes, we belonged to the JSU. "Well, kids, if it's true and if you've been activists, then you better find yourselves some corner where they can't find you because you're not going to have it easy."

The conductor talked with us the entire trip. He explained that we couldn't win the war because Hitler and Mussolini had helped Franco and the arms from the Soviet Union were stacked at the border because of the nonintervention policy.

"Oh, if we had those arms sitting at the border, the story would be different. In '36 we didn't have any arms and they didn't take Madrid. But that old goat Casado rushed ahead of events. He's betrayed the people of Spain. He'll pay for it dearly because we'll keep on fighting. They won't defeat us."

We finally reached Guadalajara. The man embraced us: "My children," he said, "I wish you lots of luck, lots of luck." I think tears came to his eyes. I felt a lump in my throat. We left the station and had walked for a while when we heard someone call out to us, a neighborhood boy: "Hey, are you going home?"

"Of course, where else would we be going?"

"Well, be careful. Some of your friends have been arrested already."

"Arrested? Who arrested them?"

"How would I know! But around here people are saying that the war is over and Franco has won."

We entered the city very cautiously, avoiding the center of town. Going up Market Street, we came out in front of a building where the local chapter of the JSU had offices. We were astonished to see the black and red flag of Franco's forces flying from the balcony. Now we really did cry. When I got home, my mother was very upset: "Why did you come back, my daughter?"

"What's happening, mother?"

"They've been here looking for you. They came to arrest you. A whole bunch of girls have been arrested. There's a Mercedes and a Trini. And a lot of men have been detained. I guess the war's over. So, look, you better leave. I'm afraid they'll catch you."

I went to a friend's house. She asked me what I was doing there. "Don't you know they're arresting people?" she asked.

"So, if they're arresting people, why haven't they taken you?"

"Because they're arresting the leaders."

"I'm no leader."

"Maybe not, but they've already gone to arrest you."

"And you, why don't you go away?"

"Because they're saying nothing will happen to us if we don't have blood on our hands."

"Ah, I don't have bloody hands!"

"No, but you really stood out."

"Okay, I stood out, but I never did anything they could arrest me for."

I realized that my mother was afraid for me to stay on in the house. Mother had been housing a young woman from La Solana in the province of Ciudad Real. This girl, Agustina was her name, invited me to go home with her. The first night in the village we had a scare. It must have been midnight when we were awakened by shouting. They were arresting people at that hour and shooting them in the village square or beating them nearly dead before putting them in jail. It was horrible to hear the men moaning as they were hit. Horrible to hear the women shouting for help for their husbands and fathers and brothers.

The next night the shootings and beatings resumed. I couldn't stand it. It was as if they were doing it to me. I thought they were punishing the people who had fought for the Republic, those simple country folk who fought for freedom and their country. The noise went on until two or three o'clock. I couldn't go to sleep. I was crying, my face buried in my pillow. I felt ashamed to be there, as if I were in hiding, as if it didn't matter to me what was happening in our Spain. I cried tears of rage and sorrow.

The next day I moved to Agustina's sister's house. But the arrests, the beatings, the shootings went on in that village, too. One day her sister came back from the store with the rumor that the authorities knew someone was around who wasn't from the village. She thought they'd come for me that very night. I told her not to worry. I'd leave for Madrid immediately.

I got on the train without buying a ticket. But the train was enough to make me sick. It was full of Franco's mercenary soldiers from North Africa, quarrelsome foreigners and soldiers covered with dirt, filth, and scabies. They were all the same, so I got out at the first station. I made my way to Madrid by following the railroad tracks, sometimes walking along them, sometimes near them. I don't know how many kilometers I walked. But my feet were a disaster. In Madrid I went to my aunt's house. She soaked my feet in salt water, gave me something hot to eat, and got me into bed. But my relatives were afraid to have me in their house.

The next day I went to my cousin Pura's house in Ventas, but no one was at home. Then I remembered the address of a friend from the JSU who had been in Guadalajara several times. I set off for her house in Cuatro Caminos. When I knocked at the door, her mother was taken aback. They'd come many times to arrest her daughter but hadn't taken her away because she had typhoid fever and was confined to bed. They were expecting the ambulance at any moment to take her to the hospital. Her mother was concerned that the police might have seen me. I hadn't been there five minutes when we heard the ambulance. "Get under the bed," the mother said. "I'll give the key to a neighbor and go with my daughter in the ambulance."

The men came in with a stretcher, along with the police. The mother asked the police if she could accompany her daughter in the ambulance; they agreed but said they didn't know if she would be going to the hospital or to the prison in Ventas. Possibly she would be taken to the hospital because her illness was contagious, but they weren't the ones to decide. All this I heard from under the bed. As my friend's mother was leaving, she said to a neighbor in a voice loud enough for me to hear: "Take the key. I left the door open because they're coming to disinfect the house. When they've finished, lock it up. I'll get the key from you later."

I left immediately. I wandered around Madrid from one place to another, not knowing where to go. In an effort to find housework, I went to several homes, but when they asked me for verification of "good conduct" I was at a loss. I couldn't just pull such a verification out of my hat. I realized that under such conditions it was useless to continue looking for employment. So round and round I wandered in Madrid. It was disgusting to go along those streets, filled with strangers and legionnaires harassing girls. Later some girls fell victim to those conquerors who had *carte blanche* to do whatever they liked. I looked at them with hate, with fury, with disgust. I thought about the men, women, and young people who had fought and suffered to defend Madrid, and to what avail? So that fascism could trample her because a traitor and coward sold us out? I didn't know what to do. I decided that I'd rather go home than fall victim to one of these good-for-nothings. I didn't care about prison. All I cared about was morale. I was tired. I was hungry. I had no money. I went to the station but the few coins left from what mother had given me weren't enough to pay the fare. Besides I was afraid of meeting someone I knew from Guadalajara. So I left the station. An African soldier who'd seen me counting my money apparently realized I didn't have enough and started following me. He began to talk and offer me things. I started to run. He ran after me. But my legs were quicker than his. I ran down the Avenida del Prado as if rushing to put out a fire.

I finally reached the Post Office building. I mixed among the crowd there, all the while keeping the fellow in view. He went from one place to another looking for me. When I saw he had his back to the door, I slipped out of the building. Once in the street I calmed down. Then I caught a streetcar for Ventas and went on to Canillejas at the end of the line. I still didn't know what to do. The only solution that occurred to me was to walk down the highway. During the walk I thought about all that had happened to us during the war, the lives we had lost, and how everything had turned out so cruelly for us. I realized that we would go on losing lives and suffer imprisonment and separation from our families. The war was terrible; it separated loved ones, destroyed homes, ruined marriages.

How well I knew about personal losses. I had had to separate from a young man I'd loved since I was fifteen years old. He was a good man, but the war and postwar times raised havoc with homes. Then I met a young French soldier of Spanish parentage. We'd only spoken twice but carried on a relationship by letter from different fronts. Was I in love with him? I don't know. I only know that through letters I developed strong feelings for him. He helped me to forget. But he died at the battle of Ebro, fighting for Spain, defending the Republic. I contacted his family. His older brothers were very good about writing to me. Later when I was in prison I felt the warmth of that wonderful family who treated me like a daughter and sister, even though the young man and I were united only by letters. How much I would like to have met his family, but through all the years of clandestine living I lost touch with them.

By nature I was happy and in good spirits. But during the time I walked those kilometers I felt physically and morally exhausted. Finally I reached Guadalajara. I avoided the city center and took the alley beside the patio wall by the house. I thought the owners of the house probably had come back and that I was just asking for trouble. Climbing up on the wall, I peered inside. Yes, the owners were back. Where could my parents be? I went to the house of some close friends and knocked on the window pane with my knuckles. Señora Adela came out: "Pequeña, what are you doing here? Come in, come in." These friends explained that the owners of the house had come back and managed to have my parents evicted. So my poor parents were put out on the street with just their belongings and my brother was put in a concentration camp. It was hard for my father to find a place to live in one day. Finally a man nicknamed "Rata" who ran a coal yard let my father and mother take refuge there.

After resting a bit with Señora Adela and soaking my feet, I left to hunt for my parents. The big gate at the coal yard was closed but the little door in the gate was only partly shut. "Who's there?" It was the owner himself coming toward me.

"Girl," he said, "what are you doing here? You've caused your mother such sorrow and now, just when she's calmed down and thinking you've made it safely across the border, here you are in Guadalajara. Look, you're going to end up in prison. Your friends are there already."

"Okay, but my parents, where are they?"

I found the address he gave me. My poor parents were so upset. What a scene! "Why did you come?" my father asked. "What's going to happen to us? And to you? They've already been here several times looking for you. We've been lucky so far; some parents are arrested simply because their children haven't been found. Those bastards said they weren't going to arrest anyone, but of course they do. The military jail is full to the brim; the provincial jail, too. You should see the trucks coming in from the villages loaded with men and women. Half of Guadalajara is under arrest. Entire families. The entire Picazo family is in jail, except for Paquito and Carmen. Julia, the coal dealer, with all her family. The Morales are all in prison except for the two little ones who get some food from Social Aid and whatever they can scrounge for. In short, the list goes on and on. And I haven't said anything about the concentration camp there in the Polygon at the entrance to the road to Cabanillas. That's where they detain soldiers caught here when the war ended and those returning from the front. It's painful to see the men there, barely enough water to drink, one little meal a day, no way to shave or bathe. Dirt and mange everywhere. And if you protest, they kick you. That's where your brother is."

We talked until three in the morning about what was happening in Guadalajara and the surrounding villages. Father was worried I would be arrested as soon as it was known I had returned. I expected it, too, but first I wanted to see my brother released from the concentration camp so my parents wouldn't be alone. Father had told me that he could be released if we got a certain affidavit with three signatures. But that night I didn't have any idea where I could get the signatures. I was utterly worn out and only wanted to go to bed. But I was too tired to sleep. Then I remembered a lawyer whose daughters I had cared for. And there was Mr. Lucio, an old neighbor of ours, said to be a Falangist.

The next day I went to see the lawyer. When I explained what I wanted, he drew up the document immediately and asked me if I had two other possible signatures. I told him I hoped Mr. Lucio would agree to sign, but I didn't know where to get the third signature. He suggested another man who would sign just because he, the lawyer, had signed. True, that man signed right away when he saw the lawyer's signature. From there I went to Mr. Lucio's house, who also signed. My father was surprised how quickly I had gotten the signatures. I went to the camp to deliver my brother's document. Four or five hours later my brother was home.

By now I was feeling better about my parents' situation so I began to talk with friends about the possibility of reorganizing the JSU. Everyone said it was a crazy idea with the situation in Guadalajara, all the arrests, the Falangists, the *requetes*, the Civil Guard, the police. The next day the Civil Guard knocked on the door. They said they just wanted to know where I had been since the war ended. I told them I had been in Madrid living with an aunt of mine who was sick and had asked me to stay with her. They warned me I was being watched.

That day I hardly left the house. My father spent the day peering out the window to see who was there in the street. The next day, May 16, was my sister's birthday. I decided to go to the station to see if I could catch the train going from Madrid to Barcelona. If I met someone on the way I would say I was going to my sister's in the country to wish her a happy birthday. I crossed the tracks and hid among some houses. When the train arrived, I ran out and scrambled up into one of the last cars. I didn't know whether to sit down or go to another car. I decided to move to another, but I hadn't gone more than four steps when a neighbor from Guadalajara showed up. He called the Civil Guard and I was arrested. They took me straight to jail.

# CHAPTER 3

# *Prison Life Begins:*
# *Guadalajara 1939*

They put me in a cell and the accusations began. I couldn't deny the truth of their questions: I hadn't hidden away during the war but had worked for the party, for the JSU, and with other women. They hit me several times and then took me to a room called "the room of scabies." It was a mass of human beings. The huge number of women was placed so that no one could move unless we all changed position at the same time. The size of the room was meant for ten, at the most twelve women with their sleeping mats. We must have numbered about sixty. During the day we collected our scant bedding so the older women and mothers with small children could sit on it and the rest of us spent the day standing up. There were so many women that some even rested their head on the edge of the drain in the floor that served as our toilet. Everyone had scabies. I caught it, too. They gave us sulfur for scouring our bodies and then every two or three days we got buckets of water for washing off our bodies. But they allotted only three or four buckets for all the women whose bodies were covered with sulfur. Every three days they gave us a little drinking water, no more than would fill a can for condensed milk.

For several days they summoned me morning and afternoon to make declarations. They began by asking questions I didn't understand. That's when I decided not to talk, even if they kicked and hit me. I remembered the comrade who had told me years ago that we wouldn't be liberated without a struggle and maybe even bloodshed. I wouldn't talk even if they killed me. In spite of the kicks and punches I refused to recognize any of the names they mentioned. Finally they left me alone but not before they kicked me in the kidneys. I was bent round like a hoop by the time I returned to the cell. The next days I could do nothing but lie on the mat. They didn't summon me again.

All the women who returned from questioning were beaten up, some even demoralized, but others remained courageous and staunchly determined. I remember one particularly awful situation. One day the door opened and two children were pushed in. One was probably five years old and the other not much older than two and a half or three. We asked where their mother was, and the older one said she had been left with some men. The little one was crying desperately, calling for his mother. At last we got the children calmed down by playing with them. After two or three hours the door opened again and a woman was thrown in like a sack of potatoes. We wouldn't have recognized her if we hadn't known who she was. The older boy cried that it was his mother. He clutched her and sobbed: "Mama, mama! What did those bad men do to you? I'll kill them. How are you mommy? What's wrong? What did they do to you?"

The little one didn't want to get near his mother. He said it couldn't be his mommy, no, it couldn't be. And he sobbed and sobbed. The older boy said: "Yes, it is, it's mommy. Come, it's mommy."

"No, it's not my mommy," said the little one, covering his eyes.

I don't think there was a person in that cell who didn't cry at the sight of those little boys and that poor girl. A few days later the three were taken away. We never knew what happened to her. Later someone told me the woman had been killed after she was arrested on a train bound for Alcalá de Henares where she was doing clandestine work for the party.

As we gradually got over the scabies, we would go down to the patio where some seventy women lived in a space that in the best of conditions couldn't hold more than thirty. The older women, including women as old as eighty-two, and mothers with small children, preferred to stay inside since there was no protection from the sun on that patio.

They brought in expeditions of women from jails in nearby villages. That's how some women arrived from my native village of Brihuega. One of them was a young girl of about sixteen named Soledad Villa; she arrived with her head shaved and the letters UHP smeared with tar on her skull. The letters stood for Unión de Hermanos Proletarios (Union of Proletarian Brothers). I lived with Soledad, María Andrés from the village of Iriepal, and Ceferina Cortijo, a girl from the hills who had been arrested when the war ended just because her brothers hadn't appeared yet in the village. She was only nineteen years old and the one time she left her village was to go to prison. Because I was older, all of twenty-two, my friends called me "mother." We enjoyed our companionship in spite of what we suffered on that patio. We suffered horrible humiliations that I'll never forget, but our morale never broke for a moment.

We were always hungry. There were only two menus for months on end. The first was onion cooked with water and salt, the second, dirty lentils so full of sticks, bugs, and stones that you got sick just looking at them.

But we suffered even worse from the water; the little bit we got was brought from the river in gasoline tanks. We had a special way of asking for water; we would sing a song but instead of saying "desire" at the end we shouted out "water." With so many of us young women shouting, even people outside the prison could hear us. The officials and the Falangists at the prison became so annoyed when townspeople appeared with bottles of water for us that they wouldn't let them in. The only bottle that made it in full was from a woman who ran a restaurant called "La Mascota." The few other bottles that got in were empty. Sometimes the officials put the bottles at the top of the stairs leading down to the patio and emptied them. Then they'd call the person who had brought the bottle and return it to him.

There was a well in the patio, but it was sealed up. One day the Falangists opened it. The doctors among the prisoners warned us not to drink even one drop of that well water. They said the Falangists had opened the well just so we would get sick drinking this water that came from all the drains in the prison and the living quarters of the prison officials. Typhoid fever would be terrible during the summer months in those conditions. But we didn't take the warning: we tied several belts together, fastened them to a pot, drew up water and drank it. The first potful was drinkable but then it came out so dirty and murky we had to strain it through a handkerchief. We drained the well dry. Fortunately we didn't suffer serious illness.

Another time the men prisoners warned us that we women were going to be tricked into doing something for which we would be punished severely. The plan was to turn on the fountain in the center of the patio at midnight; the fountain was dried up, without a drop of water. The officials expected that when the fountain was turned on a bunch of us would go for water. They even expected us to riot. Then their plan was to clear out some of the women with the machine guns they would have placed at the top of the stairs. Afterward they could say we had started a riot in the prison. We thanked the men for telling us about the plan and immediately began to caution other women not to move from their mats or rush over there in case the fountain really did give out water. Some women didn't believe us, saying that since we were young we were making up stories. But we finally succeeded in getting the women to promise that they wouldn't stir from their mats.

We were so anxious waiting for night to come that we couldn't go to sleep. We heard the door open. We heard them set the machine gun in place. After a bit we heard the water running. Our throats were dry, dry like our lips. It was truly amazing. Someone was crying, thinking that the water was running and we couldn't get even one little sip. The poor children were so thirsty and we couldn't give them even one drop.

But not one person moved. Amazing! To tell the truth, I didn't expect this. I thought someone would go running with her bowl. After the water had been on for a long time and the Falangists realized no one was going for it, they began to shout hysterically that we must not be thirsty after all and that our shouting "water, water, water" must be just a line because here was the water running in the fountain and not one person was coming for it. Any person near the prison that night would have heard their shouting. Still we didn't move. Then one of the men approached the door at the entrance to the school where the *mandata* was sleeping. The mandata was the woman with the job of clapping her hands to have us line up for a head count, get our meals or water, or intervene in some disagreement.

"What are you doing to prevent these women from getting the water?" she was asked.

She answered very calmly: "Oh, is there water? Well, then, yes, why don't we get some. We certainly do need water."

She got up, clapped her hands, and said to us: "Come now. Everyone on her feet, but please, what time is it?" She looked at the clock: "It's after midnight. I don't want to hear even a single word. Line up with your bowl and get your ration of water."

With incredible discipline we lined up, collected our ration of water and returned to our places. The Falangists were astonished, but fortunately they couldn't do anything with their machine guns.

The men lived in the same conditions as the women. Sometimes their heads would appear at the windows and they'd ask us for water. They even asked for our children's pee to drink. But that was risky business because the guards on duty at the corners of the walls would shoot at anyone who looked out through the bars of the windows. Once we heard a shot and saw one of the men fall. Later we found out that he had died from a gunshot to the chest. How many awful hours we spent listening to the men's horrible moaning from the beatings. We cried with rage at our helplessness. Similar things happened to us, but not as frequently as with the men. I remember, for instance, Consuelo Verguizas. She and her husband were detained just because the Falangists hadn't been able to arrest their son who was a leader in the Communist Party and, as we found out later, had gone to France. His parents were arrested when the authorities couldn't find their son. They beat the father mercilessly. One day they opened the door to our patio and tossed in some bloody boots and clothing and called Consuelo: "Here's what's left of your husband." They'd done their job; now they didn't have to put him on trial. Consuelo was dumb-struck. Shortly after that they passed sentence on her, condemning her to twelve years and one day.

They didn't allow packages from the outside into the prison until

September of 1939. Hunger began to take its toll on our bodies and women almost fainted from weakness. The doctors told the prison directors that the situation couldn't continue; unless they allowed packages from the outside, they'd have people dying on them. But the officials didn't care; they wanted people to die. At last the doctors managed to have packages allowed in for people in poor health. To get the packages we had to have a medical check.

The doctors who checked us in the presence of the officials and Falangists selected the people they knew would share their packages with friends, and above all they took into account mothers with children and old people. Not all the imprisoned women who went to the infirmary were granted the privilege of receiving packages. The Falangists made their own selections and only the women they chose could receive packages. From my group they chose two of us, Soledad Villa and me. Soledad had no one to send her food because her brothers and sisters were in Madrid; besides, we weren't allowed to write relatives asking them to send packages. My parents could send me very little because they barely had enough to feed themselves, but my sister, who was living with her in-laws, sent greens, tomatoes, and peppers from her garden. We were allowed only two packages a week, but with trickery we increased our number to four a week. The other girl in the group was from the nearby village of Iriepal, and we managed to send a message to her family, who were better off than mine. Maria's family sent two packages each week addressed to Soledad Villa. But it was a long time before we ate anything from those packages. We wanted to get food to the men who were in worse condition than we women; we managed to tie belts together and using a small bag got food to them through the windows.

Every day we selected a different cell. Around one or two in the morning when the guards were tired and went to the guard tower for a rest, we carried out our mission, knowing that if we were seen we would pay dearly. We were especially careful not to let the woman who owned the restaurant "La Mascota" see us; we thought she was a fascist. Her restaurant sent her a big package every day and from time to time she would give something extra to the children and old people. Even though she didn't seem to be a bad person, we tried not to confide very much in her. Her mat was installed in the patio by the school door. Whenever we sent the package to the men, we would walk toward the toilet that was in the middle of the school so that if anyone did see us it would look as if we were going to use the toilet. One night, just as I was going to the toilet, "La Mascota" grabbed me by the leg and motioned for me to squat down.

"I know what you women are doing every night when I see you get up and go to the bathroom."

"What are we doing?"

"Giving food to the men."

I told her that wasn't true and she must be dreaming, but she insisted: "I've watched you for several nights; you can't deceive me."

"Well, what's the difference," I retorted. "The food's ours and they're our friends. We don't want them to die of hunger. We have to help them. So now you know. If you want, go tell the officials. It doesn't make any difference to us."

She answered that we would talk about it in the morning, for me to go to the toilet and then we'd see. When I got back to my group, I told the girls what had happened. To tell the truth we were a little afraid that she'd call those characters in the morning and tell them what we were doing. We knew, though, that we wouldn't be the only ones punished; we feared for the men. But nothing like that happened. To our surprise the woman came to see me in the morning.

"You already know," she said, "that I receive a package every day. You get one twice a week. You're young but you're wasting away because you're not eating enough for your age. On the other hand, I'm older and the food they send me is more than enough. I don't want any-one else to know about this, but every day I'll leave you a bag with food next to the well. You take it and do with it what you want; use it for your friends or for yourself. I know you consider me a fascist, and even the fascists think I am, but I've never been one. If I'm here, it's because they know I've shown a great deal of favor to the soldiers who came through my restaurant and to the militias when the war began. If they arrested me, it's because no soldier, not even one in full retreat, went without a meal in my restaurant, whether he could pay or not. I've told you that I don't hold to any idea, but I am a human being and I will not deny bread or a bowl of soup to another human being. That's the crime for which I'm in prison. Now think of me what you will."

One day the men threw in a note warning that they had heard three women were to be taken out and shot that night. One of their compan-ions had heard the same when he was taken out to give a statement and was tortured. They even had the names of the women: Blasa Rojo, the wife of the party's secretary (her husband hadn't been arrested because he had gone into exile); Isabel, the wife of Relano who was also in the party's leadership and had been shot; the third name was mine. They cautioned us about the risk we were running and urged us to do every-thing possible to remain calm so we would be prepared and could pre-pare the many women on the patio. It wasn't clear how those women would react if the officials appeared at midnight or dawn to take us away; if the women protested, there would be more deaths than ours.

The three of us got in touch with each other hoping to find out if it was true that our last hour was approaching. It must have been two or three in the morning when we heard the patio door open. There was a discussion among the fascists who had come for us and the guard on duty. That man had been a prison official for at least forty years. We knew that he treated us correctly because he was a true prison official and nothing else. The Falangists wanted to take us away at all costs, but the official answered that so long as he was on guard, they wouldn't take us away; he said he was responsible for the prison at that hour and would not hand us over. If we had committed a crime that deserved death, then they would have to ask for the death penalty in a trial, but without a trial he would never hand over the women. The discussion between the Falangists and this official was very brief. The official had his way and the Falangists quit trying to take us out that night; we owe that man our lives. A tremendous silence filled the patio. The door closed. We heard the Falangists walking down the hall away from the patio. We all breathed a sigh of relief.

By now they had begun to hold trials and hand down long sentences. Many of the men in the Central Prison were transferred to other prisons throughout Spain. With all the cells in the left gallery now empty, we women from the patio were taken there. Eighteen or twenty of us ended up in cells meant to hold one person, at the most two. This transfer split up our little group. Only María and I remained from the original group while Ceferina and Soledad went to another cell. In our cell was a little old woman, eighty-two years old, named Manuela Letón. We called her Letona. Her favorite place and the one where she was most comfortable was in the little corner that served as a toilet. There she spent the days with a handkerchief over her face and a rosary in her hands, praying constantly. We would ask her: "Granny, why do you pray?"

"So that none of that trial business you talk about will happen to me. I don't know what it is."

During the battles of Guadalajara the fascists occupied old Letona's village and then evacuated it. She carried everything she could on a little donkey. I don't remember her husband very well, but I think he died during the retreat. Her sons had volunteered for the front. She was in Guadalajara all the time and when the war ended and she still had her little donkey, she returned to her village. But before she got there the Falangists stopped her on the highway and asked about her sons. She said she didn't know where they were and that she was on her way to the village to see if they had come back now that the war was over. They told her her sons weren't in the village because they'd gone to look for them. Right there on the highway they cut her hair close to her scalp and made her swallow a liter of castor oil. When she couldn't swallow any more and refused to open her mouth, they forced the castor oil down through a funnel. The poor little donkey was standing on the shoulder of the highway and those beasts asked if the donkey was a Red. When the donkey moved its head up and down the way those animals do when they're standing still, the Falangists said the donkey was saying yes, he was a Red. So they beat it to death. Right there on the shoulder of the road they left that poor little animal and took Letona away to prison. The poor woman suffered frequent bouts of diarrhea because the purge of castor oil had damaged her intestines. For her the seat on the toilet was not only comfortable but necessary.

In the cell we also learned more and suffered more because we could hear even more clearly when the men were taken out and brought back dead or nearly dead from beatings. I'll never forget one day when our cell door was open—we thought the official, sadist that he was, had left the door open intentionally—and the door to the men's cell in front was also open. We could only see two men. One of them had been a priest; during the Republic he had taken off his clerical garb, married, and had two children. They had tortured him so brutally he couldn't even move. The other man was a professor. They had stuck matches under his fingernails and lit them; he couldn't move his hands at all. Apparently they had to feed the priest and help him dress because his hands were completely destroyed. We could hear his torturers come for him and beat him even more cruelly in his terrible condition. Those brutes still weren't satisfied. At dawn we would hear them come to take out the men they intended to kill, and above all we could hear the prison priest saying to them: "I've come to put myself at your service at this, your last hour." They would answer: "Yours might come tomorrow. We don't need your services. We aren't thieves or assassins." Our men faced death courageously. Seldom did we hear a lament or complaint. Usually the men went out singing revolutionary songs, shouting in support of the Republic, and calling the officials assassins.

Being young, we women had some good times in prison. Once a keepsake belonging to one of our friends disappeared. We searched our belongings, but the keepsake didn't turn up. Then a handkerchief disappeared. We were sure someone had to have it because handkerchiefs don't just fly off by themselves. But no one had it either. Then two belts from robes disappeared. We didn't find them either. At the same time we noticed more cracks showing up in the walls of our cell. One day a little piece of one of the belts appeared in a crack, then the whole belt. We began to pull on it and out came the handkerchief, the keepsake, the other belt—the thieves had been mice! They carried their loot back to their nests. The mice episode was a distraction for the four or five of us younger women.

But the rest of the women ranged in age from forty to eighty-two, the age of old Letona. The older women who had lived through the war hadn't been involved in politics; they were imprisoned just because their sons or husbands had been at the front or they had looked up and cursed the German planes dropping bombs on them or some neighbor woman of rightist inclination heard her cursing the planes and denounced her. These women thought we younger ones didn't care about the suffering all around us when we laughed or joked. That wasn't the case at all. We had to forget our circumstances for a little while; otherwise we would have gone crazy. Besides, we wanted to help the older women not worry about their families every minute.

From my point of view living together with friends was bearable even with the ever-present hunger and thirst. Some days we would go down to the patio and spend a couple of enjoyable hours chatting with other companions. We shared news and found out what was going on in the prison. The patio was a safety valve for our nerves after being locked up in cells. Once when I was down in the patio I met a woman from near my home. She was a dressmaker named Monica. She explained that before her arrest she had been bothered several times, so she always had her things ready in case of arrest. When my mother found out about Monica's arrest, she brought some material so Monica could make me a dress. My mother knew I was due to be sentenced, and she wanted me to look nice. Through Monica I found out about my family's severe difficulties. My brother, who lost both his son and wife in the war, was living with my parents and provided some comfort. But, Monica told me, people often came to tell my parents to pray for me if they were Catholic because I was going to be taken out and shot at dawn. So for months my poor father went out at dawn to hide in the brush of a ravine near the cemetery and watch the shootings. He saw some of his old friends from Guadalajara fall, men with whom he had shared many a drink. The poor man's nerves must have been destroyed watching the executions day after day. His life revolved around the prison, his home, and the cemetery. He would walk by the prison just to feel near to me. The penitentiary had very high walls and watch towers on the sides so it was impossible to see or talk with someone inside. And visits weren't allowed yet. But Monica told me my father consoled himself sitting behind the penitentiary facing the fields; he would stay there until it got dark. With no work or anything else to do, my father thought it was his duty to be near me and know what was happening to me.

The trials for women had begun. Some women were condemned to death; others received long prison sentences. During the time we spent in the Central Prison rumor was that people condemned to death, including women, were sent to the Military Prison. Perhaps that explains why we never saw a single woman taken out to be shot while we were in the Central Prison. But the people in town said that there were women in the executions. I wouldn't doubt it. When women from the Central Prison were transferred to the convent of the nuns that had been equipped to serve as a prison, the ones who went to trial petitioned removal of the death penalty. But they would return with the death sentence upheld and then be mixed in with the rest of the prisoners. You can imagine the anguish those prisoners felt as they watched their companions await the dawn and said good-bye when they went to their execution.

I found out that I carried the death penalty and my trial was coming soon. More than a month passed. I remember that whenever I went down to the patio, I talked with "La Mascota." "Look, Peque," she said one day, "if they give you the death penalty and take you to the Military Prison, I'll see that you lack for nothing in your last moments. I'll tell my husband to send you every day the best of whatever they have in the restaurant." I laughed to myself because I was thinking: "I don't care about dying with a full stomach. I'd like to feel full right now!"

Monica made a pretty dress for me to wear for my sentencing. What hands that girl had for sewing! Not one stitch showed. She barely finished the dress when she was set free without a trial. Toward the end of September I was advised that my trial was set for the twenty-seventh. They asked if there was someone in Guadalajara who would testify in my defense. I replied that I had no one but that all Guadalajara knew me, so they could decide for themselves on the defense witnesses. I didn't know which people wished me good and which bad, so I left the matter in their hands. "You're very generous," they said. " What if we choose Trallero or Galloso for you!" Those were two mean characters who'd taken lots of cheap shots at me.

"It's all the same to me," I answered. "Anyway, you'll do whatever you want. If you want to beat me, that's what you'll do."

They had the gall to say: "Well, no, because some people already have volunteered testimony on your behalf."

That stopped me for a minute. Who could have volunteered to testify in my defense? I was surprised to hear that one witness was the lawyer, José Sanz Vacas, and the other, our neighbor, Mr. Lucio.

I found this strange. The truth is that we hadn't asked anyone for help, so they must have offered to be my defense witnesses. I didn't think the two men would speak ill of me. They'd never seen me do anything to bother them or anyone else; my work was strictly political. There were never noisy meetings at my home or anything going on to disturb people. These two men must have presented many arguments for me because the hearing was very different from what I had expected.

Old Letona also went for sentencing that same day. Poor little woman, no sooner had she found out that she was to be sentenced than her bowels became terribly upset. She couldn't leave that hole where she sat. For two days she was unable to control her bowels. We asked the doctor for help, but he had no medicine at all left. The day of the hearing we got Letona ready the best we could. Since she didn't wear under-skirts, slips, or underpants, we folded up a towel and some petticoats and fastened them between her legs with safety pins so she wouldn't have an accident on the floor at the hearing.

There was a group of some twenty prisoners from another cell that also left; their only crime was that they had established a laundry and store for soldiers who came through their village and then organized parties for them in the town square. I knew two of the prisoners because I had been in the village to organize the laundry and store and had come in direct contact with them. These girls never said for one moment that I had been the person who'd gone to the village to set up the laundry and shop. One of the twenty or so women was set free but they sentenced the two girls who were most responsible to twelve years and one day and sentenced six other women as well.

We fixed ourselves up so nicely it looked as if we were off to a wedding instead of a military tribunal. I wasn't even thinking about whether they were going to ask for the death penalty for me. I was proud of my new dress and wanted to impress the tribunal with my courage and serenity. Naturally they took us out in handcuffs. Since Granny Letona and I were the only women from my cell, the two of us left together. I was terribly upset to see this little old woman whose only "crime" was that her sons had volunteered for the front.

When we went out the door of the prison, I saw my father. He was alone. His eyes glistened with tears at the sight of his daughter in hand-cuffs. He walked behind us down to the square where the military tribunal was. I glanced in the direction of my house; there was my mother at the door leaning against the wall with her head bandaged. My heart jumped: what could be the matter? Inside the court room I saw my sister with her children. One of the guards who had accompanied us had been a friend of my sister and her husband when we were young and my sister had asked him if she could talk with me and give me a hug. But he said it was forbidden. Little Pedro, who was probably seven years old, came up and hugged me. "Auntie, auntie, why are you here? Why are those men so bad?"

"Hush, my son, hush, don't say a word. If you talk like that they'll punish your mommy just like your aunt."

The boy fell silent.

"Do you know what's wrong with your dear grandmother?" I asked him. "Yes, she has a bad eye and had an operation." A Civil Guard came up, grabbed him and took him a way. Then a guard who was an old friend came in and said: "Because I've known you since you were a little girl, I'm giving you a very special favor. You can embrace your sister and father. But don't say a word; it's forbidden." My father was able to say that my mother had had a tumor in her eye. They operated in the hospital, but she lost her eye.

The trial of Granny Letona was grotesque. She was completely deaf so you had to yell in her ears. When they called her by her first and last names, she was supposed to reply to the last name. But since she couldn't hear a thing, Granny didn't respond. They repeated it three times and still she didn't answer. Then they asked very angrily why she didn't answer. I answered that she was stone deaf so if they wanted to speak with her they had to approach the little bench where she was. They answered that I should do it for her; I was to tell her to stand up and answer to her last name, which she did. The only accusation they made was that she had fried some eggs for two Republican soldiers who had bought them in the village and asked her to fry them. She also gave them bread and a little wine to have with the eggs. They asked if she knew who those men were; she answered that they were soldiers for the Republic, and she knew that if her sons at the front knocked at some door they would like to be cared for as she had cared for those boys. They answered her that they must have been bandits who probably had stolen the eggs because they didn't fry them where they bought them but instead brought them to her to cook them.

"Well," she said, "I think they were Republican soldiers."

Thus her trial ended. When they decided on twelve years and one day they asked if she had anything to say. I didn't even ask her but answered: "She has nothing to say." They asked me how I knew. "Well, I know you've already imposed a sentence and they denounced her in the village."

They had to take her out of the room because the poor woman's bowels were running again and the stench was very bad.

Then it was my turn. There were several accusations against me: demonstrations, meetings, organizing shops, recruiting village men for the front. In short, I was a Communist in service of the people defending the Republic and had fought the three years of the war to obtain our freedoms. My greatest surprise was hearing the sentence: thirty years. In truth I thought they would ask for the death penalty, as I had been forewarned. The reason I was not charged with the death penalty is that the two defense witnesses spoke on my behalf, which I had not expected. They asked me if I had anything to say. "No," I answered, adding that if the occasion presented itself again, I would do a thousand and one times what I had done to defend the freedom of my people and the Republic.

Then they judged the men. There were eighteen or twenty of them, I don't remember exactly, it's been so many years. The accusations were really serious; they had volunteered for the front; lent a bus or car to the militias at the outbreak of the war; contributed part of their harvest to help feed the soldiers. On that day in court there wasn't a single man accused of killing a Falangist, a priest, a nun, or any person from our village or surrounding towns. Nevertheless, if I remember correctly, seven men were condemned to death. Clearly all the sentences were prepared ahead of time; how else could they have tried forty people in less than three hours? By noon we were back in prison.

On the evening of September 27 thirty of us from the Provincial Prison in Guadalajara were told that we would be leaving in an expedition the next day. The truth is we didn't believe it would happen because the twenty-eighth is the feast of the Holy Innocents. Our first thought was that those "children" just wanted to make fun of us by seeing us get our packs ready for the trip. On the other hand we had heard rumors that with so many women in prison who already had been sentenced, some of us would be transferred. So we stationed one woman at the door to cover the peephole while the rest of us began to prepare our packs. If the rumor turned out to be true, we'd be ready; if not, then those "children" wouldn't have the fun of laughing at us because they wouldn't have seen our preparations.

The rumor was true. Thirty of us were called the next morning. Only four from my cell went, including poor old Letona. We were handcuffed two by two; in our free hand we carried our little packs. In front of the prison I saw my father, mother, and sister, but we couldn't even greet one another because the Civil Guard wouldn't allow it. We walked to the station.

My sister, brother-in-law, and nieces and nephews were there, but I didn't see my father. Nor did I have a chance to ask about him because they wouldn't let us near our families. We said our good-byes from a distance. Later I learned that my father had gone home because he couldn't stand to see me handcuffed walking with the Civil Guard. What they didn't tell me is that he suffered a stroke; the poor man was at the end of his rope. He died a year later. All that year he was obsessed with me, his *pequeña*, his little girl. The nun who cared for him in the hospital thought that when he spoke of his *pequeña*, he meant his little granddaughter. One day when my sister-in-law went to the hospital with the little girl, the nun said: "Oh, look, Señor Jesús, they've brought the girl today. Do you see her? Now you have your *pequeña* here."

"No," he said, "she's not my *pequeña*."

The nun looked at him in surprise and walked away. After the visit the nun said to my sister-in-law: "I don't understand your grandfather; he spends the whole day talking about his *pequeña*, his *pequeña* and today when you bring her he doesn't pay any attention to her."

My sister-in-law didn't say anything because the nuns didn't know that the little girl he asked for and wanted so badly to see was his own daughter. And that little girl was in prison.

*From those nine months I spent in the prison at Guadalajara I remember clearly and with deep emotion many companions of mine. Some of them I've mentioned already. Others I have asked to tell their stories themselves. In the following chapters we hear the voices of Blasa Rojo and Nieves Waldemer.*

# CHAPTER 4

# *Sisters Condemned to Death:*
# *Blasa Rojo at Guadalajara*

*April, 1975. After many years I meet Blasa Rojo again. I didn't let her know that I was coming. She's completely surprised but she welcomes me warmly with a big hug. She lives in a housing project; on the outside it looks nice but the houses are very simple. This entire area was once fields; it's all new to me. We chat in a room that has a little balcony overlooking the street. We sip coffee and eat cookies. She doesn't object to giving me her story. But she regrets that her memory is failing after all these years.*

When war broke out in 1936 my husband, Raimundo, and I were living in Guadalajara. We had been active in the Communist Party for some time. With the outbreak of war Raimundo was in charge of the workers' militias. Toward the end of 1938 he returned from the front at Humanaes. Unfortunately, he'd only come to say good-bye; he was being transferred to Catalonia. Later I found out that our army was retreating. I never saw my husband again. He crossed the border into France where he spent a year in a concentration camp. He was one of the first refugees to leave for Mexico. A friend saw him there some years later. Raimundo told him that he'd received news I'd been killed. He remarried in Mexico and had three children.

When Franco's forces entered Guadalajara, I left with my sister and the military buses for Alicante. But when we reached Alicante we weren't able to embark. They simply left us on the dock. Then a real odyssey began. The dock was mobbed. We women and men who were carrying guns took cover under the sail cloth on a boat used for carrying coal. We looked like little Negroes when we came out the next day. You couldn't see anything except our teeth.

We waited and waited for the ships. They never came. We waited until we began to see guards and priests. We were told to hand over our arms. Some people threw their weapons into the sea rather than surrender them. From the dock at Alicante we were taken to a theater. I spent eight days sitting on a theater seat. Then we were put in the prison at

Alicante for about two months. From that prison we were transferred to our home provinces.

No sooner was I back in Guadalajara than I secretly hurried to see my children. The following day, at eight o'clock in the morning, I was arrested. They took me to the commander's office and held me there for two nights to make a statement. Since I refused to say a word, I was sent to a prison and held for a year without an indictment from the provincial government. When the provincial jail filled up, I was taken with other prisoners to a convent that had been turned into a prison. That's where I was condemned to death. And that's where they condemned my sister, two times. I lived under the death penalty for six months, my sister for a whole year.

Who could forget the prison at Guadalajara? Hunger, thirst, at night the cries of men being beaten. I remember one night when they were going to hang a man from Torija who had been a chauffeur. They were getting the scaffold ready, putting it up right there in the patio. What a night! The poor man went crazy. He was young, only twenty-seven years old. "I'm innocent," he would cry, "and they're going to kill me. I'm innocent!" Oh, what a night! Hearing that poor boy's voice right up to the moment they killed him made my hair stand on end.

And I remember how they killed poor Raposo. They fastened him to those iron doors and beat him to death—just like Jesus Christ. Then there was that man, Chinas, I think his name was. He was a good-looking fellow, with dark hair. Eight days after his arrest I happened to see him looking out the cell window facing the patio. I was stunned. They'd beaten him so badly his hair had turned completely white.

But the worst was living with the death penalty. Your life hung by a thread. You'd think: "Today they're coming for her. Tomorrow it may be me." There were sixteen of us condemned women in one tiny cell. My sister was more nervous than me; she couldn't sleep. All night long she'd sit by the little window facing the street, watching to see if they were coming. "I hope they kill me," she'd say. "They've condemned me twice! Yes, I hope they kill me."

My sister had been denounced for something she hadn't done. The reason for my death penalty was political. I'd been president of the Antifascist Women, a member of the Women's Union, the International Red Cross, which was the party's relief agency, and the Communist Party. I was detained for my part in the arrest of a woman named Campoamor. My husband had sent me instead of the soldiers to detain the woman so she wouldn't be scared. She wasn't arrested. We just took her to headquarters to make a statement and then released her. For detaining that women I was condemned to death.

Our friend Dolores, poor Dolores, she was killed for doing something similar. The men had sent her to search for some nuns in Brihuega. Dolores refused to confess anything at all. She embraced us the night they took her away to be executed. They killed her and her three brothers. Her poor mother was left with Dolores's little boy, such a little thing. To care for him she had to go begging all through Brihuega. A few days after Dolores's execution some girls entered the prison from the police station. It happened that one of them had been chatting with a guard who'd been selected for the firing squad, and he'd told her: "When I got home I was crazy and wanted to go to my room and cry. I was so upset by the sight of such a pretty young girl being killed with her brothers." The girl who told us this was imprisoned because she and some other friends had crowned a young friend of theirs with flowers when she died: the flowers were red carnations. For just this all the girls were imprisoned.

We lived in constant fear. Besides the hunger and other suffering there was always the thought: "Oh, God, what if they come for me!"

When I talk about that time in my life with my children, my daughter will say: "Mother, it couldn't have been so bad."

"Look, my daughter, you had to have lived through it."

It's exactly for that reason that we must speak about those times. The young people think we're making up stories. We're not. I remember going by the jail when I was married to my husband and saying: "How I agonize over the people stuck there. It's a cemetery of the living dead."

What horrors those walls hide. After the year I spent in that prison there's nothing in the world worth having any member of my family endure what I did. I would rather they die than go through what I did. That kind of suffering makes you crazy. They say I have heart disease. Of course my heart hurts. And my head. And my stomach. When you're condemned to death and you see them come for this woman or that woman and you don't know if you'll be next! Six o'clock in the evening comes and you don't know. Of course you can hardly stand talking with anyone, not even your friends trying to pep you up. All you can think is: "What if the best I have is a few more hours here." Mother of mine, it was madness. And the madness went on for six months from one day to the next and one night to the next. That's the worst torture and the worst suffering a human being can endure. To spend just twenty-four hours under the death penalty is enough to pay for all the bad you might have done in your life. Imagine what it was like for me with six months and my sister with a year. It's no surprise that my sister just about turned into a beast, to the point of growing fuzz on her face like a monkey.

At first I'd try to console myself saying, "They won't execute a woman." But listen, the last thing we did when we left that prison was to write down the names of the executed women on a tile behind the window. Señora Antonia, the mother of the Morales woman, is on that list. Poor Morales, how desperate she was when they took her away.

You can't anticipate what the final reaction of a prisoner will be. I saw how bravely Señora Paca, the woman from Aunon, went when they took her, her niece, her daughter-in-law, and her daughter out to be shot. They had petitioned the Council of War to commute the niece's death penalty to thirty years. The niece thought her sentence was that, thirty years, because she wasn't being kept in the little cell with the other condemned women. I was with the women in that cell when they started calling the names: Valentina, Gregoria, Francisca, oh, I don't know how many. Then they called the name of the niece who thought she was sentenced to thirty years.

Señora Paca was seventy years old when they shot her, and Señora Gregoria, well, she hadn't done anything. She was married to one of the most revolutionary men in Aunon; he was a real character, that husband of hers. He'd been a fighting man for years, but she, she hadn't done a thing. Her home and family were her whole life. The poor woman didn't know one thing about politics. But they killed her. And they killed her husband and her sister and her mother and her cousin. They killed them all that same night. She was just an old woman who ran a grocery store.

The same with Valentina. I remember her words: "They're going to shoot me and I don't know if the family can save my husband." I don't know if her husband was shot. I think so. Poor Gregoria had three little children, the oldest only eleven. The poor children would walk to town or catch a ride and then come by the prison, calling through the window: "Mama, Mama." Poor little ones, barefoot, with running noses. Gregoria was crying that she was being killed and wasn't there one human being around to take her children? Wasn't there someone to put them in an orphanage? They were going to kill her, and she didn't know what would happen to her children. After they executed her, the city government placed the children in an orphanage.

And me? They destroyed the best part of my life. When Raimundo left, I was twenty-seven years old. They put me in prison, along with my sister, both of us condemned to death with no trial. They commuted my sentence and hers. She ended up spending thirteen years in prison and I was shuttled from one prison to another for eight years. First they took us out with a group of twenty women whose sentences had been commuted; we were transferred to the Canary Islands, but we couldn't stay in the prison there because it was also full. So they took us to a convent, then to a prison in Zaragoza, then to Torrero where we were locked up for eight days with almost nothing to eat. Then we went to Barcelona to the prison of Les Corts, then to Cáceres, Bilbao, Amorebieta, Motrico, and back to Amorebieta, where I was freed.

When I got out of prison, I was a wreck, homeless, without clothing or money. When you have nothing, you're a nuisance everywhere. My mother was too old to care for me. I went to one brother's home but soon saw that I annoyed him. I went to another brother's home. My anxiety to find out about my husband became my whole life. I finally got news. He was living with a woman; she was his whole life now.

My children have suffered the consequences of their parents' actions. My son finally stood his ground; he told his professors he hadn't taken part in the war and they should remember that if the outcome had been reversed, they'd be the ones suffering reprisals. They allowed him to finish his studies and now he has a good job.

Ever since prison I've done nothing except help my children. I know I've been selfish. I've closed myself up in my own needs, not worried about other people's needs. Why? Fear. Fear of going back to prison. Fear of all that pain and suffering.

*After finishing her story Blasa tells me that when she got out of prison she didn't get mixed up in politics any more because she was afraid of being imprisoned again. She acts as if she has been a failure in the revolution. But I know better. Blasa, you loved your husband so much you would have followed him to the ends of the earth. When he left, you poured all your love into your children. War doesn't only kill the ones we love. Even without killing, it destroys families.*

# CHAPTER 5

# Childbirth in Prison:
# Nieves Waldemer Santisteban
# at Guadalajara

*Two years after my visit with Blasa I found out through a friend, Clotilde, that other people from our home region were living in my neighborhood in Barcelona. Aurelio and Antonia are a fine couple. Aurelio is the son of Nieves Waldemer and he was born when she was in the Central Prison of Guadalajara. From the time I was sent from there on an expedition to another prison, I have known very little about the Waldemer family. Her son told me about his parents, and shortly after our visit, on one of my trips from Barcelona to Madrid, I went to my region of Guadalajara and spent some hours with Nieves. She lives in an old neighborhood, in a little house, tiny but comfortable. She's surprised to see me. She's still a handsome woman and in good shape. She welcomes me happily. She tells me many things and some I keep and present here as one more testimony.*

I was born and lived in Guadalajara. I was arrested on May 8, 1939, because I belonged to the Antifascist Women and had worked for the front sewing for the soldiers and taking care of them. I was also a member of the Union of Miscellaneous Work (Sindicato de Oficios Varios) and of the Communist Party, but until the war I had never taken part in any activities, either directly or indirectly. But war came and I had to help the cause of the Republic. I was eight months pregnant when I was arrested, which is how my son happened to be born in the Central Prison of Guadalajara.

I gave birth upstairs in the infirmary. Within half an hour I had to go downstairs because the baby was fussing so badly. When they put us on the ground with the blanket I found out what the matter was: there was a bunch of bedbugs, at least forty, under him. Afterward they put me in a room with four women who had chest problems. One of them suffered hemoptysis; she tried to cough into the little pan on the table between us, but my nightshirt got soaked instead. I spent the whole time with my back turned to her so none of the blood would touch the baby. When the military doctor—a *requete* wearing his pink-colored cap— came, he said: "Don't keep the new mother here, not for her sake but for this little boy who'll be a man one day soon." That guy wasn't wrong. Today my son is indeed a fine boy and a soldier in the PSUC.

The day after my son was born, they hanged two men in the patio. And they didn't give us any food. I had to eat what a prisoner gave me— two little tomatoes, that's all I had to eat the day after my son's birth. The men they hanged were the mayor of Tendilla and a boy who I think was from Torija, maybe twenty-two years old. All night long he shouted: "If only the people knew, they'd save me!"

I was in the Central Prison until the end of 1939. I was transferred on December 29. It was fiercely cold and we had to wait all night for the Civil Guard to take us to the convent of some French nuns that had been turned into a prison. Naturally we lived the life of cloistered women there! We mothers with our children were kept apart from the other women. Several of us shared a room about fourteen meters square with just one toilet. We were a mass of women and children and what one had the other caught: boils, scabies, all those illnesses that spread in close quarters. The room was almost a pig sty.

The women were simple folk, mostly from the country. I don't know why all of them were there, but judging from my own situation I imagine their cases were similar. They'd drummed up reasons to deprive them and their children of their freedom. What mistake, what crime had those children committed? Yet there they were, locked away like common criminals. I became friends with many of those women. They suffered terrible hardships, perhaps more than I did because at least my family brought me basic necessities. But those women didn't receive help of any kind; as villagers, the women and their families had been penalized with no way of defending themselves.

While I was in that convent-prison my sister, Mercedes, heard the horrible news that our father had been executed. She said some things the prison officials didn't like. The next day a certain Ramón, one of the officials, told her: "You compromised yourself with your words. What a shame. You don't deserve to be punished. It's clear that you were upset at the news of your father's execution and reacted as any daughter would. It's not right that you're here." The next day she was transferred out of the prison and taken with an expedition away from Guadalajara.

There was one women in the group who wasn't there for political reasons; in fact, she had been on the side of the regime. She was the wife of a sergeant in the national forces and had been imprisoned for stealing 400 pesetas from one of her husband's companions. Now I've seen some acts that are truly inhuman, which is why I bring her up. She might not have shared my ideas but she shared my life in prison. I'm mentioning her case to demonstrate how bad things were. If they treated this woman who was one of them so badly, imagine what they did to us. Well, she was imprisoned because she had committed a robbery in the house where she and her husband were guests. She had a little baby girl and was expecting another baby. When time came to say the rosary, the nuns left her covered with just a sheet and locked and bolted the door. She was already going into labor, but the nuns weren't concerned about her. When the rosary was over, the nuns returned to the cell. They saw blood running. The woman had given birth to a baby girl. But the poor woman was dead, dead because no one stayed to help her. All of us women lamented what had happened to that woman, even though she didn't think as we did. She was a human being, after all, and she didn't deserve that treatment.

You may wonder how the nuns treated us. Well, the treatment varied. There was one nun who was very decent to us. Then there was Sor Gertrudis; she was the worst of the lot—an evil woman. One nun, Mother Visitation, was more or less human, but the other nuns—one day they'd take the women to chapel as if they were off to a party and the next day the same nuns would take women out to be shot. I myself saw fourteen women taken away. Those women went to their deaths bravely. Two sisters-in-law from Aunon went out with their clenched fists raised high. One of them said: "Friends, remember my children. I'm leaving my little children."

The person I remember most vividly was a young girl from Zamora. María was her name. I was separated from the other women and kept in a little room with the mothers. But they didn't lock us in so we could go to the patio for water and wash the children. Well, this girl, María something, I don't remember her last name, they took out to be shot. Cabecilla himself, the one who had denounced her, came to get her. They held her in the chapel with the nuns all night and tried to make her kiss the crucifix. She refused. "You're the ones who've committed crimes," she told the nuns, "you're worse than we are. You're the ones who should confess."

The other two girls they killed were Virginia Martín and Olivia Villén. Olivia was blond; she looked English and had a darling figure. She was the sweetheart of one of Virginia's brothers and one of Olivia's brothers was Virginia's sweetheart. They killed the four of them on the same day.

I remember one Christmas Eve when we pooled the food our families had sent and the decent meal we were given that night: fried potatoes and lamb and lots of it. They let Eloisa Caro, who was condemned to death, go down to the patio because she got along with all the nuns.

They let her take some little pieces of charred wood and put them in a small can. It was so cold that Christmas Eve. She asked for a little coal from the kitchen and by blowing on it she was able to start a fire in the can. It seems to me there were eight of us women having supper, including my sister and three other women condemned to death. We were seated around the can when we realized that the "good mother" was coming to pay a visit. To hide our light we took a blanket and put a wash board on top. When Eloisa saw that the nun wasn't leaving, she sat down on top of the board to hide the light. Well, it burned her bottom and finally she cried out: "I can't stand it any longer. I'm getting scorched." It was a bit of comedy in an otherwise grim situation. "Oh, mother of mine, I'm burning up," she said. "My behind can't take any more!" If we hadn't done some silly things, we couldn't have stood the situation. You had to do something when all around you came the howls of men being beaten.

They didn't kill any of my brothers and sisters. But if we managed to keep going it was because of my mother. Not one of us was at home and our father had been executed when he was seventy-one years old. But that mother of ours! She brought us what she could. She did washing for other people and all kinds of housework. With her help we survived. My son was taken out of prison because he had an eye disease. My mother-in-law and a sister-in-law cared for him. His father was also a prisoner, in Cuenca, the town where he was born. Because they didn't have a denunciation against him in Guadalajara, they took him to Cuenca even though he'd never lived there. Then they transferred him to Guadalajara. He was released because the military tribunal had no evidence against him. After that I was freed.

We got along as best we could. We worked. I did jobs that I'd never done before, like picking beans or vetch or any other field crop by the day. I cleaned offices. I made gloves. In short, I did anything and everything except something wrong. That wasn't in me. And what can I say, with all six of us in jail. One brother of mine who had never hurt a fly they condemned to death. Another brother spent five years in jail. My sister, who lived rather well economically, was also imprisoned; she spent four years in prison. Another sister they kept in jail for ten years; first she was in for five years, got out, and then was caught again and kept at headquarters in Madrid where they subjected her to three months of beatings, every morning and every evening. She was left a broken woman: she lost her mind and lived for ten years just sitting or lying down, cared for by only her husband.

A long time has gone by. You remember many things. Other things, like names, you forget. Many people say hello to me around here, but I don't know who they are because I don't remember them. They've changed physically, just as I have. I used to be petite, but look at me now. Who could recognize me? I've changed so much, in character, too. Youth can endure everything, but now, well now we're no longer young.

*We say good-bye with a little lunch, some good ham, an even better Manchegan cheese, and good wine.*

# CHAPTER 6

# My Prison Odyssey:
# Durango 1939–1940

After nine months in the prison at Guadalajara I was sent on an expedition to the prison at Durango in northern Spain. To get to Durango we had to travel by way of Madrid. We got off at the Atocha station where the Civil Guard had a bus to take us to the North station. At that time the North station was under repair and there were no doors in the waiting room. We just about froze to death while we were waiting for a group from the Ventas prison to join our expedition.

We waited in the freezing cold for four or five hours; finally the expedition of 350 women arrived from Ventas and the loading began. It was a freight train, and we had to clean out the manure left from transporting animals. We didn't have time to do a thorough job so we had to travel in filth. The Civil Guard took out a square piece of the floor in each car so we could do our business. There were thirty of us to each car. When they stopped at stations for a change of guards, the guards climbed a ladder up to the little windows in the freight cars and called us by our first name; we were to reply with our last. I suppose they were afraid one of us had escaped through that little hole in the floor.

After three days of traveling like this we reached the town of Zumárraga at night. It was very cold, and even before we got to Zumárraga we could see the ground all white with snow. They pulled us onto a side track, for what reason we didn't know at the time. Later we found out that it was a narrow gauge track from Zumárraga to Durango. The Civil Guard that took charge of us in Zumárraga was very friendly; I would say that they were even good people. They let us get off the train for a little while to stretch our legs, numb after three days in cramped quarters. When the town found out that there were political prisoners at the station, many people hurried to see us and even bring us things, which the Civil Guard allowed so long as they didn't get near the prisoners. The guards themselves collected the little packages and handed them over to us.

The mayor of Zumárraga—what a shame I don't remember his name!—also did a strange and wonderful thing. When this man heard we were at the station, he came to see us; talking with the Civil Guard and listening to us he realized that we had started the trip with food enough for only twenty-four hours and now after seventy-two hours on the train we had absolutely nothing left to eat. So the mayor asked the captain of the Civil Guard if he could offer us hot soup. The captain agreed. So big pots of good hot soup were brought; it tasted glorious to us. He also brought a light for every car and a huge loaf of bread, the kind they called a *hogaza* in the villages of that region; it must weigh four or five kilograms. He offered, too, to pay for a pile of empty fruit boxes stacked there so we could have a little fire in the front of each car for warmth. We spent the night there in Zumárraga. The next morning they transferred us to the narrow gauge train for Durango.

I think the entire population of Durango had turned out at the station. It seems they didn't want political prisoners and a prison in their town. They were so adamant that the guards cordoned us off for fear the people would hit us. But no, the people didn't want to harm us; they just didn't want political prisoners in their town. Finally, though, they got us to the prison, which was a convent for French nuns that had been turned into a prison.

Every day new groups arrived in Durango. From all over the Spanish land the prisoners came. There weren't enough prisons in all of Spain for so many prisoners. That's why convents like the one at Durango were converted into prisons. Finally more than two thousand women were housed in the converted convent in Durango along with scores and scores of children ranging in age from a few months—some had been born in jail—to three and four years. Yes, there were many children, that is, until the government issued a decree that children older than two years couldn't stay in prison with their mothers. But if by chance all the family was imprisoned, where would the children go? To the orphanage? That created problems. In some cases friends and relatives came for the children, but we were up north and all the women were from central Spain, some even from Andalusia. The government set a date by which time the children had to leave prison. The mothers became desperate. What was to become of their children? Where would they be taken? Would they ever see their children again?

When the people of Durango realized the situation, they responded very well. They told the prison director that the children should be taken to their homes in Durango until their families could come for them. All children over the age of two were removed; one baby under two was even taken out. Those people of Durango dressed and fed the children very well and brought them to see their mothers on visiting days. Little by little the children disappeared from Durango as families and friends came for them. I think that one or another of the children remained in the region because their families were in prison and no one was left to claim them.

The poor little children who stayed with their mothers had to eat the same food as the adults; there was no milk or any kind of supplement necessary for little ones. It wasn't long before two of the children died. When we protested, the officials fixed up a room down below for mothers with children. I don't think their motive was to improve life for the little ones but to avoid people seeing that the situation was continuing the same. Later on townspeople became very upset at the news two little children had died and others were gravely ill. They brought jugs of milk which were distributed among the mothers. No thanks go to the prison administration but to the beautiful and compassionate people of Durango!

The Durango prison housed not only political prisoners but also common criminals. Some women were well-known thieves; others were prostitutes; still others, murderers. Next to us was a little girl not more than eighteen years old who had killed her sweetheart's sister for having objected to the relationship with her brother. She told of killing the girl with a knife as matter-of-factly as if she were telling the story of Snow White. Other women had committed murder out of revenge or jealousy. But for us political prisoners the worst criminals were the women of the street. It was disgusting to live next to them; it wasn't just that these women no longer had the fun of walking the streets but they were so immoral they even turned to sexual relations among themselves. We were so offended by them we felt obliged to denounce some of the incidents to the officials, but in those years, in '39 and '40, it didn't do any good. The nuns and officials in charge were no better than the prostitutes. In an attempt to heed our protests and demands, the prison director set aside one room for the younger girls. Since I acted as a mother to the young girls in our group, they refused to go to the room without me; so even though I was older, the officials took me too. But this arrangement didn't work because there were minors among the common criminals who were set aside with us.

In spite of the horrible conditions—and naturally the food and hygiene were terrible—we young women didn't lose our good humor. We were always happy, always singing and planning some joke to distract the older women, and sometimes the younger ones too, from thinking about their homes, their children, their husbands. We would do all sorts of pranks to divert the women who spent so many days under the death penalty. I remember vividly one such prank. Almost every night we staged a mock trial where we judged Franco. We cast lots for the part of Franco because naturally no one wanted to play that role. The unlucky woman would sit on a sleeping mat that served as the defendant's chair and the popular tribunal was formed around her. The entire room had the right to speak and render opinions. It was like an army of devils rising up. No one can begin to imagine what tortures the prisoners dreamed up to make Franco die little by little, to make. . . . Well, what can I say? It was horrifying.

I don't know if someone looked through the peephole or if some official going up the stairs happened to hear us, but suddenly one night the door opened. However, we always had one woman on the lookout, and she heard the keys in the door in time to warn us. We quickly lay down on the mats that had served as our seats; when the officials came in, they found every woman lying in her place. But they weren't convinced that we were just lying there; they searched us thoroughly thinking we had a radio transmitter that someone had been using. Then came the punishment: a week without mail and going to the patio. But we spent the week in a big way; every night we held the trial.

The room fixed up for the young girls didn't have a toilet or water. The toilet and sinks were out in the hall. Being locked in at night, we would have to call a guard to have the door opened so we could use the toilet. We decided to take matters into our own hands. We collected buckets, bottles, and anything else to use when we couldn't stand it any longer. But the solution wasn't satisfactory and certainly not hygienic. At that time the director's living quarters were directly under our room. So we decided to stir up a tremendous racket and make all the noise we could; maybe he'd get tired of our noise and move us. We pulled up our skirts so far our panties almost showed and tied them up with our belts. Then with ribbons in our hair we ran around in a circle playing a game called "potato wheel," stomping our feet as hard as we could. All of a sudden the door opened and there stood the director. He had an expression on his face as if he didn't know whether to laugh or scold us. The door closed and he left. He didn't say a word or punish us even though, as we found out later, a lamp in his dining room had fallen over and broken. What we did accomplish with our game was that they never closed the door to our room again; we could go to the toilet whenever necessary. The director must have thought we were crazy to dress up like little girls, but we made our point. Where demands had failed, a joke worked.

On the fourteenth of April we celebrated the anniversary of the establishment of the Second Republic in 1931.[1] We spoke about what the Republic had meant for Spain and how it had been betrayed. This the women with political education did for the others, speaking with several groups of women. We wanted to do something special for the first of May, but we couldn't agree what it should be. So the youngest ones of us took charge. One girl composed a charming, happy song set to music as if it were a march. There must have been fifty or sixty of us. We went out to the patio with one girl marching in front carrying an old broom and wearing a red sweater. The rest of us followed behind singing the words to the march. There was a terrible uproar because we were singing at the top of our lungs:

> When they ring the bells
> early in the morning
> I stretch disdainfully
> for I go to bed dreaming
> and dreaming I get up,
> when I laugh and when I sing.
>
> I weep not knowing why;
> it's because there await me
> hearts that love me
> and weep for me.
>
> I'm a prisoner, a prisoner
> I do not have, I do not have another sorrow,
> for my liberty I lost.
>
> Riches I do not want
> nor do I long for comfort
> to ease my pain.
> Only madly do I desire
> another first of May
> to live at home in peace.

When the officials heard the words "first of May," they came out furious, the director, the nuns, the officials, all of them shouting. Pushing, kicking, hitting, they made us return to our rooms. Fortunately, no one touched me. One thing that made me laugh, yes laugh, was that one of the officials kicking us lost his shoe and a prisoner grabbed it and passed it to another who in turn threw it down to the patio. He got really mad. I laughed so hard I almost fell in his hands. But being such a little worm of a thing, I scurried among the rest of the women so he never found me or knew who had been the one laughing. He was too mad and irritated to pay attention to the face of the woman who was laughing almost, almost in his face. So we did celebrate our first of May and the town of Durango did hear about our celebration and talk about it. The women who were caring for the children from the prison told the mothers on visiting days what was being said in town, including the news that the prisoners had celebrated the first of May.

Meanwhile the nuns had petitioned the state for the return of their convent. At last they won their case. The more than two thousand of us were taken from that prison and dispersed among several others. I was chosen to go to Santander with Daniela and Consuelo Verguizas and also old Letona while other women went to Amorebieta and Saturrarán. Departure at the station was emotional for it seemed as if all the townspeople had agreed to be there. Everyone wanted to give us packages; everyone wanted to say good-bye to us. Of course, the townspeople couldn't get close to us because of the guards, but the packages were handed over to us. We sang a song at the station just as the train began to leave and we could see some of those women of Durango in tears. We had set words to some music that is well known throughout Spain: "Greetings Durango, Durango of my affection, my affection. Greetings Durango, when we meet again I will be free. I do not leave because of the people, for they are good. I leave because they transfer me from the prison."

*I also formed strong friendships with many women in the Durango prison. One of my friends. Rosario Sánchez Mora, offers her testimony about prison life in Durango.*

# CHAPTER 7

# The Dynamiter:
# Rosario Sánchez Mora at Durango

*At some events on the Civil War held in Barcelona in 1979, I happen to meet Rosario Sánchez Mora again, a companion from the Durango prison. I invite her home and rather than staying in a hotel she spends the three or four days with me. Rosario is already retired in 1977. She lives in Madrid, is married and has children and grandchildren. As a hobby, she paints pictures, using her one hand. Her health is good and we spend a nice time together remembering things from the past. I use this time to take her testimony about life in Durango.*

I'm from Villarejo de Salvanes in the province of Madrid. My father had a shop where he made carts, wagons, and all kinds of work tools. I lived in the village with my parents until I was sixteen years old when I went to Madrid to live with some friends who had taken care of me after my mother died. The year was 1935. My father gave his permission for me to leave home provided I learned how to be a seamstress. I lived with this family until war broke out in 1936.

In the afternoons Carmen and I would take the children for a walk in the Moncloa area. That's where we met some young people who belonged to the JSU. As they explained the purpose of the JSU, I decided I would like to join the organization.

The house where we lived was very close to the Montaña barracks. The night the barracks were attacked neither Carmen nor her husband would let me leave the house. I can't pretend that I understood what was happening. I was a new member of the JSU and still didn't know much about politics. The explosions we heard coming from the barracks were very strong, but as soon as I could I managed to meet my JSU colleagues. When I got there, everything was chaos; the boys were running around getting orders. That same day there was fighting in several sectors of Madrid, and insistent calls for help were coming in from Somosierra and Guadarrama. With no thought for my own safety, I asked if I could go with the boys to help.

Every truck load of volunteer militia made up a company. The boys in my truck told me to stick near them and they would look out for me. I certainly wasn't afraid of those fellows; they showed no hint of aggressiveness toward me. I only have wonderful memories of those boys who fell, one by one, until they were all gone. We were approximately the same age, between seventeen and nineteen years old.

Even though we organized ourselves as a company, we hardly knew what we were doing. I certainly didn't know how to use the rifle when they handed it to us and showed where we could practice. They also gave us rudimentary muskets that must have weighed at least seven kilos each; that musket was such a museum piece I couldn't even figure out how to fire it. We spent three or four days there in a trench, without rest or relief. They brought us food whenever they could and we dozed at odd hours; things weren't very well organized.

Our job was to defend the so-called German rock, which was a pile of boulders and rocks that became famous. Many young people died there. It was considered an honor to have shot from that pile of boulders. The area around the "German rock" was arid and open, unprotected, except for a small uneven wall that marked the boundary between fields; the only protection for the defenders was behind parts of wall that jutted up.

There was a group of three or four fellows who tried to humiliate me because they were against women going to war. They wanted to see if I had the physical stamina to stand guard on the parapet. So they stationed me for several nights, in the greatest of danger, on the parapet of the infamous front line called the "German rock." They could never have imagined how seriously I took this responsibility and what strength I gained from doing that. If my eyes closed, I would shake my head as hard as I could and open them again. I always spent five or ten minutes longer than the time assigned me before I would call the boy who was supposed to relieve me. The guys began to lose their mistrust of women. Like all girls, I was a flirt, but during the war I combed my hair just to comb it and not to flirt. The guys respected us as girls who were under the direction of an organization. We weren't just girls they'd met somewhere; we were their comrades.

The time came when they considered taking me from the trenches and putting me with a group of dynamiters. This work was also dangerous, but I wouldn't have to stand guard at night and also I wouldn't be on the front lines. Between Buitrago and Gascones there was an old run-down shack that we used for making a small fine powder; powder is just the name we gave it because with so few materials at hand it couldn't really be called powder. The group the dynamiters belonged to had the dynamite there and that's where they made the bombs, right next to the front lines, only about five kilometers away. My job was to work with the dynamiters making bombs by hand using empty condensed milk cans, screws, nails, bits of glass, and old pieces of shrapnel. We made the bombs by mixing dynamite with all this stuff.

We were under the orders of a man who was the captain, an Asturian named Emilio González González from Sama de Langreo in Oviedo. He was a miner who knew how to handle dynamite very well. He didn't let us touch the fulminates; that was the most dangerous part of all because fulminates made the bombs discharge. He would touch the fulminate to the fuse and then squeeze it between his teeth to close them. I don't know if he did it this way because he didn't have any tools or whether he was used to doing it that way. The fulminate is a piece of metal that has a hollow part where half of the explosive is set and in the other half that's hollow the little piece of fuse is set; then the two halves are closed to hold in the fuse and this combination of fuse and fulminate is very carefully put inside the can and slightly flattened. That's how the bomb is made.

Along with the large musket this was the only material we had for defending ourselves; we didn't even have a machine gun. Later on they brought one and a mortar for every company, but at that time we only had the musket and the hand bombs. We tested them right there, behind the house. One day we were testing some fuses to find out whether they were fast enough or damp; if the fuse is damp it burns from within and isn't noticeable from outside. When the fuse is normal, you squeeze it with the thumb nail and when you're burned you release two more fingers of the fuse, that is, about three centimeters; you do this to keep it burning until there are only three centimeters of fuse left and then you have to throw the bomb. We weren't making this test with a bomb but with a cartridge of dynamite in order to find out if we could work with the fuse. Mine exploded in my hand. That's how I lost my hand.

When I entered the hospital they cut away what was left of my wrist. My hand had exploded with the dynamite, flying off in one piece. I didn't see it or realize what had happened. I only know that I was left with a piece of bone and blood running out through the veins. I fainted, bleeding copiously, and my companions picked me up. One comrade who was older than I—his name was Toquero and he was from Fuentelsar and had been exiled in Mexico—tore off the straps of his sandals and used them to make a tourniquet on my arm. He took me in his arms and stood in the middle of the highway to stop a car. The first one that came by stopped and Toquero took me to Buitrago, a village a few kilometers from where we were. Until now I had never noticed this man who was older than I; he was calmer than the other fellows who had all fled in horror so they wouldn't have to see me bleed like that. In Buitrago they applied first aid by treating me against tetanus and gangrene and then took me to the hospital at Cabrera for an operation to trim away what was left. I spent three days there. Normally they sent the wounded home after the first treatment.

Being there was painful. You had to be strong to see how people died from bleeding in the hospital. When the shots were in the bowels or stomach, the ambulance took them away because they didn't have any facilities there for operating on them. This was a Red Cross hospital and it was run marvelously. The staff had no rest for twenty-four hours of every day; when a group arrived they had to attend to them and rest in shifts in the hospital.

After the operation, I had the honor—and I don't say this to flatter myself—of a visit from the famous writer, Ortega y Gasset,[1] who had been told of my conduct during the weeks that I had been fighting on the front line at the "German rock" and making bombs.

"Where are you from?" Ortega asked.

"Villarejo de Salvanes."

"Well, listen, I go by there every day. This afternoon I'm going to Valencia. Do you want me to say something to your family?"

"Oh, no, sir, please don't tell my father about this. How unhappy he's going to be."

"But, child," he said, "he's going to have to find out somehow, don't you understand? It's best that he come; he can care for you and be at your side. I myself will give him the news. I know how to tell him. You'll see he won't be very upset."

"All right," I finally said, "we'll see."

That very evening my father, mother, and two friends, one the man who made fritters and the other a gentleman from our village, came to the hospital. When they arrived, the doctors went out to greet him so as to cheer him up and downplay the seriousness of my situation. But they didn't know my father. He said to them: "Look, I am very, very sorry that my oldest daughter has lost a hand. I have five more children and if my six children would all lose a hand for the same cause, I would be proud." My father didn't scold me at all or utter any recriminations. All he said was: "Why didn't you tell me you were here?" My father knew I was in Buitrago; what he didn't know was that I'd lost my hand.

They transferred me to the Red Cross hospital in Madrid. The wound where the hand had been scarred over without any complications. I spent fifteen days recuperating; with plenty of good food to eat. I didn't need any transfusions. Then they discharged me. My father took me to the pavilion of Philosophy and Letters where they had set up a rest home for convalescents. I'm not sure if it belonged to the Republican Left. I spent eight or ten days recuperating there. I left because the front line by the University City was getting nearer and also I had recovered enough to return to the division.

I served as a telephone operator for the general headquarters of the 10th Brigade. It was there I met the poet Miguel Hernández.[2] By this time several months had gone by and I continued to work in spite of missing a hand. One day Antonio Aparicio, a comrade of mine who was a poet, came up and said: "Listen, a very good poet is bringing a poem for you." I didn't know how good a poet he was, and besides I thought that it would just be some little thing like the poem another comrade had written for me. I didn't realize the repercussion this poem would have later, for the poet was none other than Miguel Hernández. Many prestigious intellectuals came through our division, including the Nobel Laureate Vicente Aleixandre[3] as well as Miguel Hernández.

I didn't know this great poet at all. On introducing me, Aparicio said: "We're going to carry this poem on the radio; he'll introduce it and then you'll read some stanzas." I was a little frightened but they encouraged me. I did it to please them and also out of curiosity, for I'd never seen a transmitter before and I wanted to find out what a radio was. First he read the poem and then I read the stanzas. For several months I had the good fortune amd great honor to work with Miguel Hernández, each of us at our own job but in the same vicinity. That's when I realized he was a sentimental man, simple, affectionate, a man of few words, a little introverted; he saw, he observed, and he smiled. He always had a kind word for everyone, and the people adored him—workers, women, children—everyone adored him. He made no distinctions between the upper and lower classes. What he did make was poetry; he was a soldier with the pen, and with the pen he defended the working classes. Inside of him was the beauty of the born poet. As for me, he didn't really know me; he only knew that I had been left without a hand when the bomb exploded. Then he wrote the poem for me, "Rosario, Dinamitera."

> Rosario, dynamiter,
> on your lovely hand
> the dynamite covered
> its fierce attributes.
> Looking at it no one would believe
> there was in its heart
> a desperation
> of crystals, of fire-shot
> eager for a battle
> thirsting for explosion.
>
> It was your right hand,
> capable of fusing lions,
> the flower of munitions
> and the desire of the fuse.

Rosario, you good harvest,
tall like a bell tower,
you seeded the adversary
of the furious dynamite
and your hand was
a maddened rose, Rosario.

The vulture has been witness
to the condition of lightning
of the deeds I keep silent
and of the hand of which I speak.
How well the hand of this maiden
knew the enemy!
but now it is not a hand because
not a single finger of it moves,
the dynamite captured it
and turned it into a star!

Rosario, dynamiter,
you can be a man and you are
the cream of women,
the foam of the trenches.
Proud like a flag
of triumphs and splendors,
shepherd to dynamiters,
see her spirit moving
and send to the wind
the bombs of the traitors'souls.

When I returned to my division I was given the most dangerous
jobs. Every day was a gamble with death. I was responsible for delivering mail to the front lines. There were many, many troops at the battle
of Brunete,[4] which went on from July 6 to July 25, 1937, but the 46th
Division was there an especially long time, for months, risking lives for
the town that one day was in our hands and the next in Franco's. Well,
my job was especially dangerous because there were always low-flying
planes shooting at any object or person that moved. Three of us went in
the mail car: myself, whose job was to deliver and collect mail; the
driver, a fine man named Valentín from Morata in the province of
Madrid; Fita, who came only on pay days and collected money from the
soldiers eager to get money to their families before they died.

One day when I was going by myself through an unprotected area
with a small delivery of mail for some troops near a bridge, I spotted a
low-flying plane. I saw a blanket on the ground covering what I thought
was a man: "I'm going to get under the blanket," I said to myself, "so
the plane doesn't see me." I spent who knows how long waiting for the

shooting to end; when I finally got up, I said to the one beside me: "Let's go. It's over." No answer. That's when I discovered there were four cadavers under the blanket left there to be picked up.

The closest I came to being shot was the day I was returning from the general staff of the 10th Brigade that was set up near a little bridge on the road. The shooting came nearer and nearer. That was also the last day I carried mail because our division was relieved and each brigade returned to the barracks. Then I went with the general staff to Alcalá de Henares where I worked in the office and served on the political committee for propaganda for our division. This was my last assignment. When the militia left for the Ebro, I remained with my parents in Madrid.

I would like to emphasize that I could have retired from service after I lost my hand, but I continued in the army without pay in order to defend the Republic. Let's not talk about danger because in war danger is everywhere, but I do want to speak about morale. Let me say that the women militia suffered very much in this sense because some sectors of society put us down just because we were women. Some people couldn't understand that we were risking our lives to fight valiantly for a noble ideal. Of course we were afraid, but we felt it was necessary to defend ourselves so that Franco couldn't wipe us out. With this ideal in her heart a woman is just as effective as a man wherever she serves. I want to praise the efforts and idealism of the women militia, especially in answer to those critics who accused us of being prostitutes.

When the war ended I tore up everything that might compromise me; I left my party card until last. It broke my heart to tear up my card; I felt as if I were breaking off all connection with my past. Finally I just slipped it under the table cloth. I left home kissing my mother and daughter good-bye, not knowing where to go. I went to the division to see if someone might be there who could take me to an airport or a sea-port. That's where I met Dora, a friend I'd known for several months, but there wasn't anyone else around to help us. Dora had enough money for us to spend two days in a hotel; that way we wouldn't be caught in our homes. Then she managed to find some friends with a truck who were going to Valencia.

When we reached Valencia, the city was over-flowing with people on the way to the port of Alicante, desperate to get out of Spain. What happened in Alicante is well known: the arrests, the concentration camps, horror and misery everywhere. But there's one fact I don't want to pass over. I remember a gentleman who took his own saffron harvest, carried it in two five-kilo cans, took it out by the fistfuls, threw it on the ground, and set fire to it. When he saw the Italian soldiers in the Littorio Division[5] that entered Alicante, he cried: "Look, here's my saffron harvest." This man was a true example of valor.

Dora and I were among the thousands who were captured and returned to Madrid. The trip took seven long days. What terrible shape we were in: skinny, dirty, dying of hunger, we looked like strange creatures. The guards left us in the Atocha station with the recommendation that we go home. There we were at three in the morning, not knowing what to do or what road to take. I went to the home of some acquaintances who were professors, a family of marvelous intellectuals called the Palacios. There I spent the night. Then I wandered from house to house until the police detained me in one of them and took me to the village. They held me for more than twenty days; they intended to cut my hair but it just so happened that on the day they were going to cut it the Civil Guard came for me to take a statement.

The women prisoners told me terrible things about what happened to the men: how they were beaten to make them confess and then left half dead; how the skin from their backs stuck to their shirts; how the men were taken down to the wells with their hands behind their back and their wrists tied with cords so tightly their shoulder bones were dislocated; how they were pushed in the wells with their heads under water to make them believe they were going to be drowned; how the men were taken down there over and over if they didn't confess.

In Villarejo the people were sent to two places. Some went to Aranjuez and others to Getafe. The worst was the prison of Getafe, which is where they sent me. In that prison—and everyone who has been there knows this—there were no toilets; we had to do everything in cans that were put in three or four rooms without doors where women prisoners were held. We had to use those cans for defecating as well as urinating. Those cans stayed there twenty-four hours a day and they only took them out once a day, at seven in the morning. Worst of all was the lack of hygiene; there were no sinks or running water for washing. The water was given us in a can that had been used for condensed milk, which means that each person had only one fourth of a liter for twenty-four hours. You couldn't ask for more, not even for the old women or the children. The young girls—I was twenty years old and we were all approximately the same age—would take a little swallow of water from the can and put the rest in a bottle in case an old woman or child got thirsty in the night.

Later in 1939 I was tried and sentenced to death, which came as no surprise. My denouncers were from my home town and were fascists in the style of Hitler. I was sent to Ventas under sentence of death. Compared to Getafe, Ventas was a paradise. They stuck me in the gallery of condemned women. That's where Matilde Landa was; she saved my life. I was in Ventas for only three months before I was taken to Durango. After eleven months in Durango, I was transferred to a prison in Bilbao and from there to Saturrarán. That was the last prison I was in, and probably the worst.

When I look back on the dangerous work I did during the war, I am proud, not just for me but for the history of women and especially for the "feminists" of today. The word *feminist* didn't even exist during the war because we women weren't considered separate from the men. It's true that women haven't been treated as equal to men throughout history, but I wonder if the majority of women have done anything to defend their rights. There's a lot of talk these days about feminism, but I'm not sure if fighting with words is the best way to achieve equality with men. Fighting side by side with men, we felt equal. I hope that my story will be a testimony to women's equality. Obviously I am only one of many women who worked alongside men in those war years. Many, many women took over men's jobs in shops, factories, agriculture, and administration. And it wasn't the physical work that made us equal. It was our sense of responsibility, our concern for companions, our idealism, our self-sacrifice—those inner qualities determined equality.

*We say good-bye at home, happy to see each other again. I am grateful to her for the testimony she gives for the book.*

# CHAPTER 8

# *Into the Storm:*
# *Santander 1940–1942*

There's a very funny story about our departure from Durango. In those first years after the war all the railroad cars in Spain had written on them "Franco, Franco, Franco." We saw some cars sitting on a side track with those three words, and underneath them the words, "Sal de España." Those three words mean "Salt from Spain," and they indicated that the cars were loaded with salt. Now the words were placed in such a way that you could read the whole car as "Franco, Franco, Franco, sal de España." We started shouting like the devil: "Bravo, bravo, that's it, that's it—Franco, Franco, Franco, get out of Spain." At first the guards didn't understand what was going on, but when they saw all of us looking toward the cars and laughing, they got the joke. The railroad worker who wrote those words so they could be read two ways must have been some joker!

We left Durango between eight and nine o'clock in the morning and reached Santander very late at night. With one hand manacled and the other clutching our personal belongings, we were forced to climb the steep Alta hill that runs from the station to the prison. Once again our prison originally had been a religious house, this one a monastery run by Salesian friars. We were exhausted after traveling all day, climbing the hill, and then having the hassle of finding a place to sleep. The prison was overflowing with people; we could scarcely find room to put down our narrow sleeping mats. Worse even was being mixed in with thieves, common criminals, and women of the street. Since Santander was a capital city, the custom was to imprison the prostitutes for ten, fifteen, or twenty days if they didn't pay their fines at the time of arrest.

Our group was split up when we reached Santander; one part went to Saturrarán, the other to Amorebieta. I became close friends with some of the women from Santander. I remember one woman from Santona whose husband had been killed, leaving her with five children, the eldest no more than fifteen. She would go out fishing with her son in a little boat they owned and then sell the fish to support her family. Her arrest came about when she was suspected of having gone fishing one night and not selling her catch. She tried to explain that she hadn't fished that night because her child was sick, but her protests didn't sway the authorities. If she had gone fishing, they wanted to know, and hadn't sold any fish, then where had the fish ended up? The officials assumed she had given the fish to the band of Cariñoso, who was a famous guerrilla in the area.

We also had to endure the misfortunes caused by the hurricane and fire that hit Santander while we were imprisoned there. I don't recall the exact date, but it must have been toward the end of 1941. One day such a strong wind began blowing that we couldn't stand to have the window open even a tiny crack. We hurried to secure all the windows. As the wind blew harder and harder, panic set in. Suddenly a gust of wind shook the windows; they flew open so hard that all the panes broke. I remember being beside one of the windows; I threw myself to the ground and covered myself with the mattress, not knowing what else to do. Papers were blowing all about, clothes spilling every place, women all around me screaming. We were in terrible danger because the room was so large it had lots and lots of windows and all of them were broken. We not only had to escape that hurricane and save what we could, but we also had to calm down the hysterical women, especially those women from Santander whose fear for their families added to their panic. We tried to give comfort by assuring them that probably nothing was happening down in Santander and that the wind was much fiercer up here on the Alta hill than down below in the city. We didn't know what was going on in the other rooms, but we heard shouts and screams of terror. All the women were screaming, running from one place to another. The nun in charge of our room we called "Big Shoes" because she was big and strong like a Percheron horse and must have worn at least a size forty-three shoe; she sounded like a man when she walked. And she was a brute in her own right. She would hit you on the head with the food ladle at the drop of a hat. But that day, for what reason I don't know, maybe she was in shock or genuinely upset at our helplessness, she spoke to us kindly: "Calm down now, calm down, don't get excited; go down the stairs very calmly, don't hurry, don't hurt yourselves." In fact we did behave in a disciplined way; we went down the stairs and into a lower part of the building.

Women were coming out of all the rooms toward the stairs. Then we found out that some of the sick women in the infirmary had been injured. Originally the infirmary had been one large room, but they had installed dividers to make compartments. One of those dividers had crashed and slid when the windows flew open. We had no more than left the rooms and reached the lower area when we heard the cross on top of the building come crashing down; it crossed the length of the building from top to bottom and pierced the ceiling of our room. Thank goodness we weren't there. Downstairs we were out of danger. There were some porches with tremendously thick walls, the church and a few rooms; with three floors above, we felt safe. The entrance door also came off; they asked us to help by holding the door up while they got heavy poles to brace it. Later the saying ran throughout Santander: Question: "How can you tell a perfect prisoner?" Answer: "She holds up the door so it won't open." The truth is that the last thing on our minds was escape. But of course there were some suspicious people who alerted the Falangists to set up a guard in front of the prison door just in case we tried to take advantage of the situation.

The priest took us to the church to offer his so-called encouragement and consolation, especially for the poor women from Santander.

"My daughters," he said, "resign yourselves, many people have died in Santander, many, and there are so many wounded that the hospitals can't take all of them."

He actually seemed to enjoy saying this to women who didn't know if their families were dead or alive, their homes still standing or destroyed. Besides being the priest in our prison, he also was priest to the Tabacalera prison for men. One of his duties was to take the men out to be executed and give them the coup de grace.

The hurricane finally began to subside. But then we heard the news that the storm had caused the electrical wiring in a drug store in Santander to short circuit and that fires were spreading throughout the city. "Big Shoes" said that some of us should volunteer to go with her to the rooms to collect our things and have them ready in case we had to evacuate the prison. Her words upset us because if they had to take us away, then what on earth was happening? When we went up to our room with its view of the whole city, the sight of the raging fires paralyzed us. All Santander seemed to be in flames. And the wind hadn't stopped. We watched in horror as the wind picked up burning beams and dropped them on houses and as the houses immediately burst into flame.

So we gathered up our belongings and made up the sleeping mats; everything was ready in case we had to evacuate. We spent three days waiting for the fire to be completely extinguished. We ate only canned food because the stoves couldn't be lit and we couldn't lie down because the sleeping mats remained rolled up by order of the prison directors. For three days we sat on our sleeping mats. We did take the little old women down to the porches where the poor souls could stretch out on the ground.

Next to our building in Santander was the Alta barracks. The soldiers had taken precautions; no sooner had they spotted the first fires than they began to transfer the munitions to the countryside. The commanders had even come to the prison to assure the officials of our safety; if something happened to the barracks there wouldn't be an explosion because all the munitions had been removed. That calmed us down, there's no doubt, but who could calm down the poor women from Santander who still had no news of their families? And if that beast of a priest came, he only recounted tragedies. Some of us were always going around the room sniffing out news of Santander; sometimes we would hear a voice from the street across the walls shouting the name of a prisoner to let her know her family had survived.

After three days life returned to normal. There were still small fires burning in Santander, but the hurricane was over. Orders were given to light the stoves so we could have something hot to eat, which our stomachs welcomed.

I have other memories of the Santander prison, especially of women from Guadalajara. There was Consuelo Verguizas, whose husband had been beaten to death. She was sentenced to twelve years and one day simply because the authorities hadn't been able to catch her son. She knew nothing about his whereabouts. On one occasion, through someone who was corresponding with people in France—they had begun to receive letters from family members—we found out that the boy had left Spain with the troops when the war ended. While we were in Santander his mother received a letter and photo of him along with his address; they got in touch with each other and from then on she received news of her son. I don't know if it was the shock of knowing that she had lost her husband because her son hadn't been caught and then finding out he was out of the country, but the fact is that Consuelo began to lose her mind. Perhaps it was hunger, too, for the poor woman suffered so much.

Consuelo and I were in the same room, though not close to each other; she was near the door while I was in the center of the room. Nonetheless, she was always near me. She was a very humble woman with little spunk, used to giving in to others. A good seamstress, Consuelo was always ready to sew something for her companions or for the children; she had no one at all outside of prison. The one other son had been killed a few months after the war began. Some nights the woman who slept next to me and I would wake up with the feeling that something was hovering over us. Sitting up on our sleeping mats, we'd recognize Consuelo.

"Consuelo, what are you doing here?"

"I'm afraid they're coming for me."

She would cross the room by dragging herself over the floor so they couldn't shoot her from the windows.

When we went to get our food and the nun put the ladle on her plate, Consuelo would look at her and say: "Hah, do you think I didn't see you put poison in my food?" I would take hold of her, lead her away and assure her that the food wasn't poisoned.

"Yes it is, yes it is. I saw it."

"All right, come along, take my plate and give me yours."

Then we would exchange plates and she would say to my friend, Amparito, who was also at her side: "Hah, Amparito, you, too, huh? Do you think I didn't see? Yours is poisoned, too."

Then I would say to the poor woman so she could eat: "Look, mine isn't poisoned because they don't want to kill me."

"No, not you, but me, yes they do."

"Good, well then so you can see there isn't any poison, let's you and I eat from the two plates." A spoonful for her, a spoonful for me, so it went until we finished the meal.

She even followed me to the toilet. I was, shall I say, bashful about doing some things in front of her, so I'd say: "Please, Consuelo, leave me alone for just a minute."

"Yes, of course, but as soon as they see me alone. . . . If they haven't killed me it's because of you. Without you my life is over."

We consulted the doctor about Consuelo. I would have preferred a specialist to examine her so she could be taken to the appropriate hospital for observation. But no, the woman doctor, who was herself a prisoner, looked at Consuelo there in the room with us. The doctor warned me to be careful: if Consuelo was so obstinate with me, it was likely she'd turn on me some day.

"Why would she turn on me?"

"Because people who are crazy or disturbed sometimes turn on the people they like the most."

I didn't believe her then and I never did, but it's true that I was always a little on the alert after that.

One day Consuelo refused to leave me alone when I wanted to use the toilet.

"Please, Consuelo, I can't do anything with you here. Leave."

She grabbed me by the throat and squeezed hard. I kicked on the door. Some of my friends came, pushed on the door and got me out of there. But it could have been bad for me because she had hold of me with a frightening nervous strength. It wasn't that she was a naturally strong woman but her nerves gave a strength to her fingers that she didn't even realize. She didn't know what she was doing. Later I asked her: "Consuelo, do you see what you did to me?"

"Who? Me? I did that to you? It can't be, my daughter, it can't be. I did that?"

She kissed me and caressed me.

"It can't be, my friend, it can't be. Are you sure I did it?"

One day I noticed that she was very subdued and barely came over to my sleeping mat. One moment I saw her seated pensively on her own mat, the next moment she was gone.

"Have you seen Consuelo?" I asked the girls.

"No, we didn't see where she went."

No sooner were those words spoken than we heard "Plom!" coming from the toilet. We went running and there was Consuelo—she had tried to hang herself by her girdle ties but they were too worn out to hold. She hurt her throat a little but that was all. All this we had to put up with, knowing that the prison administrators could have remedied the situation had they wanted. That woman could have been put in a hospital. She was no murderer. We submitted petitions to have her transferred to a hospital but our petitions disappeared with the wind.

So the days passed. We did handwork to earn a little money for buying necessities from the commissary, not only for ourselves but for the old women and for others who had no one outside to help them. We made large bags with pretty embroidered flowers, clusters of violets from pieces of soft bread the country women gave us; we went without bread so we could color and fashion the crumbs into lovely bouquets. We had many orders from Santander to sew flowers on jacket and coat lapels. Something else I liked to make were paper boxes. I used untrimmed paper cut lengthwise in strips of one centimeter. Four of these strips I would weave into what are called carnations. Then I'd make stars and turn them into the pattern I wanted and form a box. Next the inside was lined with cloth and the outside painted with a shellac to give it a wood color, like mahogany.

While Consuelo was improving with the treatment the doctor had given her, I was getting worse, in part because I was working very hard to earn money. Also I no longer had extra food because by this time Amparito and some other women whose families had brought in food had left the prison. And the truth is that my nerves had been affected by Consuelo's sickness. One day when I was making a flower, I stuck my finger and it got infected. The doctor, who had taken a liking to me, said: "Look, I'm going to take advantage of the fact you're running a slight fever because of the infection in your finger to send you to the infirmary. You look terrible. My advice is that as soon as you know there is calcium in the infirmary, you go down for an injection: put your name in for calcium because you need it. You're young but you don't eat. I don't know what's going to happen to you and many other women."

Old Letona was released from prison at Santander because of her age; she was more than eighty years old, eighty-three, I think. Poor little woman—how was she going to get to her home town all alone?

There was no one to come for her. But there are good people every-where. One of the prisoners had a nephew, her sister's son, doing mili-tary service in Alcalá de Henares and at that time he was on leave in San-tander. During a visit she asked her sister if it would be convenient for the young man to accompany old Letona on the train as far as Alcalá and then we'd arrange for someone to meet her in Guadalajara. Not only did the boy agree to accompany Letona but he asked for the address in Guadalajara where he could leave her so that she wouldn't have to change trains by herself in Alcalá. Poor Letona. I know that she reached home safely thanks to that young man. That's the last news I had of her.

We can't only speak about the hardships we endured in prison. We must also remember the times when we forgot our suffering and enjoyed ourselves like crazy—that's what the little old women called us, crazy. But it was our craziness that helped those women set aside their sad memories for a few moments and have a good time.

We had a choir that sang the rich songs of our home region of Guadalajara. The people of Santander would climb up the little road that ran between the barracks and the prison to listen to the women pris-oners sing in three parts. We always set a watch at the door so that if a nun came we would stop singing. The nuns were eager to get us into the church choir, but we wouldn't go near it.

That year many women arrived at the prison. There were Asturian women who hadn't been near their native land for years; some had left behind very small children they hadn't seen again even in a photograph. On the Feast of the Virgin of Mercy these children were brought to be with their mothers. When they came in, they had their names printed on little cards hanging around their necks. We welcomed these little ones by singing words that one of our companions had set to the hymn of San-tander. At first the children were scared, but we had prepared games for them and even made some toys. We organized a big party with a music band and uniforms we'd made from wrappings on the packages that came for us and cardboard top hats. The only musical instrument we had was a drum which, if I remember correctly, the soldiers from the Alta barracks had given us. I still have a photo that shows Rosario, a very pretty redhead from Santander, carrying the drum; to her left is a lovely little brunette, Enriqueta; Andrea is above; the first on the left, a strong young girl from the mountains; the rest, I remember their dear faces but, regretfully, not their names.

Once more a prison closed. As in Durango, the religious had been negotiating with the state to have the facility returned to their Salesian order for use as a school. They won. So we were taken away; the women who hadn't been tried yet were taken to the provincial prison of Santander while the rest of us were dispersed to other prisons. They selected me for Amorebieta. What a prison I got by chance! But the women who went to Saturrarán said that the prison there was much worse, so I kept a song on my lips and hope in my heart.

*I've already mentioned several women I knew well in the Santander prison. The friend who gave me her testimony is María del Carmen Cuesta.*

# CHAPTER 9

# A Minor in Prison:
# María del Carmen Cuesta at Santander

*During the years from 1940 to 1942 that I spent imprisoned in Santander, a city on the coast of the Cantabrian sea in the north of Spain, I met a young woman—actually she was legally a minor—named María del Carmen Cuesta. She was one of the hundreds of women prisoners in the Salesian convent that had been converted into a prison. She had come to Santander from the prison in Ocaña. We didn't have much to do with each other since she was on one floor and I was on another, in a room that held more than 800 women. But thirty-six years later, in 1978, I saw her again, in Valencia. And this is how it came about: Adelaida Abarca, a friend of mine from the prison of Les Corts in Barcelona in 1945 and 1946 (and whose testimony appears here a little further on), had kept in touch with me through the party ever since the 1950s when she escaped from Spain. Adelaida was still living in France in 1978 when she told me that María del Carmen was in Valencia and very interested in talking with me and giving her testimony. The day I visit her she is ill with flu and a fever. But she's so anxious to give me her testimony that she makes an effort to speak even though she's not feeling well. I like to talk with her because she has such a sweet way of expressing herself. She puts so much love and energy into telling her story that she relives it. And sometimes she breaks down crying and says to me: "Please forgive me, Tomasita, but I can't help it." But here is her personal testimony about that time in Santander from 1940 to 1942.*

About six or seven years ago there was a movie on television called "Fahrenheit 451." That movie had a tremendous impact on me because the plot concerned cultural repression under a dictatorship. There was a special unit of firemen who destroyed all the books they could find. Denunciations were rampant. Whenever a denunciation was received, the unit would appear, take inventory, and burn all the books. The people fled to the forest, but each person—man, woman, and child—had etched in his mind everything pertaining to universal literature, all the works and every literary genre. Each person was converted into a human-book in the hope that one day the books could be published again.

The movie made a huge impression on me because I thought that there were hundreds, no, more than hundreds, there were thousands of us women who, like the people in the movie, retained in our minds profound testimonies, testimonies we hoped would come out at a given time to fill all the pages of history, the history of the longest, darkest, and most brutal period of our country, the history of fascism.

I'm telling you this because it's exactly four weeks since the film was shown again on Spanish television. When I saw the film for the first time, I thought we women were so tightly gagged that our stories would never see the light of day. Seeing the film again, shame, pain, and helplessness consumed me even more. Now the gag has been removed, but a profound weight bears down on us that seems impossible to cast off; for some women the weight is political, for others, a kind of collective shame, born perhaps from so many years of distorting history. These weights pressure us not to speak too much about the Civil War and the subsequent repression, but this smoothing over of history's harsh events and the effort to calm those dark forces make it very difficult for new generations to realize the Franco repression in all its intensity.

I'm saying this as a way of explaining why we haven't been able to bring out these testimonies. But now it appears that the stories will be published, and so, let me begin my story by recounting how I joined the JSU. In 1934, when I was nine years old, I went to Sama de Langreo in Asturias to spend the summer with family. On my mother's side all the family were miners. At that time there was a lot of unrest among the miners in Asturias, and I began to breathe in the repression of the miners. Because of my age I didn't realize many things, but I was moved by affection for those family members I saw imprisoned deep in the well of the mine. I saw how families were prevented from taking food down to the miners and how little by little they had to eat the mules in order to endure the long days of the strike.

Later, in Madrid, I met Virtudes González. We immediately formed a deep, caring friendship. It was the fourteen-year-old Virtudes who talked with me about politics. Through her influence I gradually started working in the JSU and was active in the attempt to join the anarchist youth groups into what would be called the Antifascist Youth Alliance, which came about in November of 1937. By the end of 1938 I was involved in the Drama School of the JSU. By now times were grave and serious. I was given the post of secretary of the so-called Comets when the previous secretary was called to the front lines. We were called Comets rather than Pioneers in order to avoid sectarian affiliation. As a Comet I worked with children, trying to distance them from the problems of war and train them in everything relating to cultural movements, sports, and film. Unfortunately, the war was being waged so close by and so bitterly that it was impossible to meet all the children's needs. I also met men and women in the Provincial Committee.

When Casado's junta seized power in March, 1939 and was negotiating a cowardly surrender without even minimal defense of Madrid, the entire Provincial Committee had to leave the city. Virtudes and I left together, joined by other young people from Aranjuez, Villaconejos, and Chinchón on the roads out of Madrid. We spoke with them about what surrender to the troops of Franco meant. For us it meant that Spain would be soaked in blood. We were convinced of this from evidence of the persecutions, imprisonments, torture, and shootings that went on in the zones controlled by Franco's troops. Any doubts people might have had during the war now vanished; we had evidence that these brutalities were more than a case of excessive propaganda.

Returning to Madrid, we found the front lines in total collapse and the city under occupation by Franco's troops. Horror was everywhere. I ran to my parents' home, fearful that my father already was under arrest. Virtudes went to see her parents and brothers and sisters. We ran around like crazy ants, not knowing where to go or what to do. We knew that many people, thousands of people, were in jail but we couldn't grasp the situation. We were disoriented. I remember asking my father why he hadn't left; his answer was that there was no reason to leave because he didn't have blood on his hands. But two days later they came for him; the man who denounced him had spent the war years in hiding on the third floor. Not finding my father, they took me to the Office of General Security. As I said good-bye to my grandfather, I whispered in his ear: "Warn papa to leave." The next day my father appeared at the Office of General Security and I was released.

I went to find Virtudes, and we decided to make contact with as many of our friends as possible. We wanted to scrape together a little money to buy tobacco and food for the people in prison who we knew had nothing to live on. We didn't contact our friends at their homes but in the street. Every evening at seven or eight we met on Alcalá street, with a little ribbon pinned to our clothes to identify us. I served as the link between my sector and the Provincial Committee.

At that time an edict had been issued for everyone in possession of firearms to leave them at designated sites. The order was a laugh for the people of Madrid. No one dared hand over arms of any kind, especially since most people owned at least one pistol. My aunt had a pistol in her house which, she often told me fearfully, had belonged to her husband before he crossed the border with the army of the Ebro. She was very much afraid. I told her: "Don't worry, aunt, I'll get it out of here."

A friend we called "Pioneer" offered to help; he went to my aunt's house and brought the pistol to mine. Being young, we didn't think anything could happen to us for what we did, but one day a girl appeared who had been closely connected to our JSU when she worked as a typist for the Provincial Committee. She couldn't have been even sixteen years old. I don't know why, perhaps it was the threats and fear of torture, but she led the police to the houses of all of us out on the streets who had belonged to the JSU and had taken part in the war in some way. Around three o'clock one morning a detachment of probably eight men showed up at my house to arrest me.

I was only fifteen years old but already I had a sense of courage. They say that moments of terror bring out courage. I have never understood why, but it happened like that with me. My sister, who was four years older, almost died of fright and sobbed terribly. But me, I was calm, as if something inside of me had been set free. Perhaps it was my hate for these men that gave me such a calm appearance. They made us get dressed in front of them and after talking with the doormen, who didn't share our thinking, they took us to the infamous Jorge Juan police station. It was very dark, but I was able to recognize Virtudes, Victoria, Anita, and a bunch of others. Virtudes I knew by her laugh, which was something special, like a tinkerbell. She was brunette, with very Spanish features, a girl of good humor, young, happy, always full of life. Seeing that we were together again, we all began to laugh like crazy, not suspecting what truly horrifying days lay ahead.

By chance one of the men in the detachment that had come for us, a certain Emilio Gaspar, had been a member of the JSU. He was one of those people who always land on their feet and always find themselves in favor; they're vulgar, funny, don't bother anyone, and are welcome everywhere. Well, he appeared with the police squad. When they took me out to make a statement, he said: "Peque"—that was my nickname; it means "little one"—"Peque, don't be afraid. So long as I'm here, nothing will happen to you."

They put me in a car with Emilio Gaspar; the inspector also came. They took me to the walls of the East cemetery where I was told to show them where I had hidden the firearm. They said they knew I had had a weapon and had buried it in this cemetery. I told them that was impossible, that I'd never had a weapon, and that besides I was terrified of cemeteries and dead people. I imagine it was my naive way of speaking and my frightened expression that were convincing; they took me to a hotel in Ventas where the doorman had told them my mother was staying. When we reached the hotel, the inspector told my mother to get dressed. They were about to take her away when Emilio Gaspar said: "No, not that lady. She's got a bad heart." But my aunt, who lived in Ventas, they did take away.

When we returned to the police station, they called my sister to make a statement. The questioning was a shock for my sister; she was completely removed from political parties, being a Republican by conviction, but nothing more. At one moment, when they called the two of us, I said: "The fact is that my sister never belonged to the JSU."

Then, in a flash of courage, I added: "But I did, and what's more, with honor." All that got me was a whistling of blows, the only ones I received.

So began the interrogations. I don't know if we were in the police station for ten or fifteen days. In the first days nothing out of the ordinary happened except that they questioned us at any hour of the day. Sleep was impossible. We would just start to fall asleep when they would summon us. Always being on guard and alert wore down our resistance. At first we didn't pay much attention to what was going on around us, but after three or four days we became aware of terrible cries, shuddering, horrifying cries. They had begun to put some of our women companions in cold water baths and apply electric shocks. But something very serious, very grave, happened at that time, something that would mean the end for many of those young lives.

On July 27, 1939, a certain Lieutenant Colonel Gabaldo[1] was returning with his daughter and chauffeur from Talavera de la Reina to Madrid. I don't know the exact moment or kilometer it happened, but his car was machine-gunned and his daughter died along with the chauffeur. Gabaldo was hated because he was responsible for the archives and documents that made it possible for the military police to accuse us of being Masons and Communists. I don't know in what manner, either directly or indirectly, that "Pioneer" was blamed for the incident. Nor do I know exactly how they tortured him. But I do know that from the moment we heard "Pioneer" had been thrown out a window one night and killed, we began to experience true fear. The rumor everywhere was that they hadn't been able to get one word out of that eighteen-year-old boy. Had he uttered even one word about carrying the pistol from one house to the other, many more of us would have been arrested. But he didn't open his mouth. Whatever he knew he carried with him to the grave.

We spent about fifteen days in the police station. They let my sister go, but the rest of us were sent to the prison at Ventas. Now begins the most hellish part of our journey. It was in Ventas where my strength began to wane. Reaching Ventas at dawn, we were still happy and laughing because even in the midst of tragedy we felt the joy of our youth. But when those enormous bolts that looked like giants clanked shut behind us, I felt as if we were passing through the gates of hell that we had heard so much about as children. It was then I broke down. For the first time since my arrest I began to sob, uncontrollably.

The following morning they assigned us our places. The oldest women went to galleries and halls while we younger ones enjoyed the privilege of staying in the School of St. Mary. The school was a room where the minors were to live with two or three inmates to act as teachers and a prison official who would be with us at all times. Here we would live out our confinement, forbidden access to the other prisoners, family members, or our companions. For companionship we had only ourselves, the minors. We couldn't imagine how huge this tragedy was because at first we came up with some fifty-thousand schemes for escaping. With every escape attempt the companions outside the school and the rest of the inmate population greeted us with affection and hugs. When we were returned from an escape attempt, we would sing to the women, dance, and tell stories. The women would weep and laugh. I think that as we walked through those galleries, halls, and cells, we gave something of our youth to those women, reminding them of their own daughters left behind in villages, in Madrid, and other places. These women were enormously concerned about us, more so than for themselves. Perhaps news had reached them through their families that our trial would take place soon.

August 3, 1939, arrived for the occupants of the ill-named School of St. Mary. The entire prison of Ventas was in an uproar as the news spread rapidly: the minors were going to trial. All of us were convinced that we would be in the same proceedings, but the older women knew better. They were truly frightened for us. Virtudes came running with the news that she and some others were leaving for their trial. I was confused. "But aren't I going?" I asked.

"I don't know. Be ready in case they call your name."

Among the minors Anita López, Martina Barroso, Victoria Muñoz, and Virtudes left. Argimira Hampanera, Julia Vellisca, Mari Carmen Vives Samaniego, and I remained: four of us. We were stunned. Our friends left on the third and returned on the fourth. All Ventas waited impatiently, but we all knew that they would return with what we called "la pepa"—the death sentence.

After Virtudes returned, she spent two hours talking with me out on a little patio. I'll never forget those two hours. She spoke to me of what fascism meant and the time it would take to stamp it out. For the first time in my fifteen years I began to understand what I had never grasped before—the meaning of the fight the workers were waging. Virtudes spoke of many things, as if she wanted to pass along to me all her own experience. The way she was speaking reminds me of the old man in "Fahrenheit 451" who taught an entire work from memory to a child so the book would live on in the little boy and he in turn would pass it on to posterity.

"But Virtudes," I said, "nothing is going to happen to you. They'll commute the death penalty."

"No," she replied, "they won't commute our sentences."

Then in my impulsive way I said: "Well, I want to go with you because I'm from the Provincial Committee."

"No, Peque, you stay here for you must bear witness to all you will endure."

As we embraced, she said: "Don't forget anything I told you this afternoon. Don't ever forget it."

That night, at what time I don't know, with Victoria asleep beside me and Anita and Martina sleeping elsewhere, we were awakened with a blow to the shoulder. Victoria and I sat up like two automatons; in front of us were the director's lieutenant, Carmen de Castro, María Teresa Igual, and some other officials. I don't know who was outside the room, but Anita and Martina were already standing up and Victoria, with her curls falling over her forehead, clutched my neck, crying: "María, they're going to kill me. María, they're killing me!"

She clung to my neck so hard I couldn't loosen her grip. At last Martina and Anita drew close and Martina said to me: "You'd better put your affairs in order soon because if you don't, they'll kill you just like us."

And Anita said: "Please, Victoria, be brave."

Then Victoria stopped crying and I saw her go through the door, her head drooping. We were all speechless from shock. I don't think we even cried. I don't know whose idea it was to kneel down, but again, like robots, we all fell to our knees. We remained kneeling until we heard the sounds of a machine gun in the morning. Those sounds you could hear clearly, especially if there was a breeze coming from the east. Some nights we could count perfectly the shots of the coup de grace. That night we kneeled until we had counted sixty-five of those shots.

One-half hour later María Teresa Igual, a haughty, cold woman, came in to tell us of the valor and integrity with which our friends had met death. She told us that some of the girls had gone to confession—I don't know if that was true—and they had gone out singing JSU hymns and died shouting "*vivas.*" What's more, she told us that the machine-gun fire hadn't killed Anita López, the tallest of the girls. Anita was still alive when she fell. She had sat up and asked, "Well, aren't they going to kill me?" At that very moment the coup de grace was administered. This same woman, María Teresa Igual, who was present at the executions and told us everything, also brought our companions' personal belongings. To me they gave Virtudes's dress and from Joaquinita López, a belt from Africa.

When the minors arrived from the Salesian prison, their families had intended to go to Burgos to ask for clemency, or at least to have the death penalty commuted. Not all the families could afford the trip, but Virtudes's brother had gone to Burgos. Her mother, who adored Virtudes, came very early to the prison and pressed herself against its walls as if to feel the throbbing of her daughter through their stone. She wouldn't leave. How Virtudes suffered because of her mother's grief! When they took Virtudes to the bus, there was her mother. Seeing her daughter get in the bus, the mother began to shout: "Murderers! Leave my daughter alone! Murderers!" And she ran after the bus, running, running, until at last she fell flat on her face. Then she was put in prison, and every day she would appear at the door to the School of St. Mary. The prison officials left her alone, perhaps believing, as I did, that she had lost her mind. She would watch me until I left our room. I was permitted to go out. Then she would grab me by the arm, squeeze it with alarming strength, and direct me to the infirmary. When we reached the infirmary, she stationed herself by the window from where she could see the walls of the cemetery. Her breathing would become very rapid and deep, but she never said a word or cried. Then, with her squeezing my arm and breathing deeply, I took her back again to her sleeping mat and returned to the school. She was there for maybe two months before she was freed. I never found out if she died or went crazy.

After a few months the four of us minors still left were told of our upcoming trial. The prison director, Carmen de Castro, called us into her office to say that there had been some cases of clemency and she didn't think anything bad could happen to us.

The girl who initially had denounced all of us also went to trial. She was very ugly, like a little monkey. I remember that with our legs bandaged because of scabies, she and I looked like Egyptian mummies. I realize now that we treated her harshly. We were proud of our courage and intolerant of any weakness. No one would say a word to her, not one word. She sat completely alone in a little corner, drooping like a rag.

When the Civil Guard came in, they asked: "That one over there, who's she?"

Some of the prisoners replied: "That one, she's the beast."

That girl, the beast, they put in Ventas because of what she did. Look, after they took the minors away, this girl who had turned us in had to be put in a special room in the infirmary because they feared the reaction of the women. In a prison with thirteen thousand women there are all kinds; in a moment of anger and helplessness a woman can turn on a person who betrayed her companions.

How different that creature was from the notorious Roberto Conesa.[2] Conesa had been a member of the JSU before he began to work for the Francoist police. With his help, the police stepped up their arrests of Communists in July and August of 1939. Conesa was fully aware of what he was trying to do when he pushed for the arrest of JSU members. He knew that he was taking the first step in his professional career. He quit being an ordinary shopkeeper and found an opportunity to advance himself at the end of the war and the beginning of the repression. This he did by accusing young people of taking part in the plot to kill Franco. Of course, it's inconceivable that young people without any means could commit such an act in the first month after Franco's forces took Madrid. But the deaths of the minors had to be justified, which this man did and in so doing began his professional career.

Thanks to whom, I don't know, my sister was given permission to give me a kiss before I left for my trial. There the two of us were, me being strong and telling my sister that she had to be strong too, and my sister, desperate and crying, "Mari, no, Mari, no!" And I: "Be strong. Tell papa that I was strong, very strong, and tell mama, too; tell her I didn't cry."

On December 15 four minors, sixteen years old, appeared before a military tribunal along with some guerrillas. The Agency of Military Intelligence and Espionage tried us for taking part in the plot to kill Franco. The room was over-flowing with people, so many they had to close the doors. The sentences began to rain down. We were sentenced to twelve years and one day and returned to prison.

We remained in Ventas from the fifteenth of December until the middle of 1940 when we left with a group destined for the penitentiary at Gerona. The trip was interminable. We were transported in freight cars used for shipping cattle. We absorbed our own smells and excrement because we had to do our business in little pots or sardine cans they set up in each car. The rattling of the train wore us out. At first we stood up, but little by little the jostling of the train pushed us together until we sat down. We reached Tarragona where we stayed for fifteen days. With our sleeping mats on our shoulders the line of prisoners walked across the entire city to reach the convent of the Oblate nuns. From Tarragona we were taken to Les Corts for two months and finally to Gerona.

If comparisons could be made, we might say that we had gotten out of hell and made it into heaven because here, in Gerona, we began to experience a little equilibrium in our lives. The nuns in Gerona had a magnificent garden that belonged entirely to them. But one day Carmen de Castro appeared with the order to turn the garden into basketball courts so we could exercise.

We also were authorized to present plays at the discretion of the prison director and administrator. We were rehearsing *Life Is a Dream*, the seventeenth-century play by Calderón de la Barca, and I was playing the part of Prince Segismundo. In a letter to my boyfriend in Madrid I mentioned how difficult the part was for me because as Segismundo I had to throw my enemy off the balcony in one scene. He jokingly replied that it was impossible for me with my delicate constitution to grab my enemy and throw him off the balcony or through the window. On account of that letter I was taken to the superintendent; she interpreted my words as "political signals." I don't remember how many arguments I put forth to convince her otherwise, but the price I paid was transfer to the prison at Ocaña.

Ocaña was hell. After all these years I am relieved to be able to talk about those grievous times. One face and one name I've tried to forget but can't is that of Conesa. Today I can hardly believe that this man continues to hold positions of responsibility in the General Office of Security when evidence proves that he held interrogations and tortures and that he was the principal accuser and assassin of the minors. I don't think of him with revenge in my heart but in the process of remembering these events we have no recourse other than to remember the perpetrators of so much torture and so many shootings. In remembering Conesa, my thoughts go again to our young girl from the JSU who betrayed us. With the passage of time I've said that perhaps we were a little inhuman and we shouldn't have treated her as we did. Who knows a person's limits under torture? Who knows how long you can resist? I don't know if they beat that girl or tortured her. All I know is that she was sixteen years old, like me, a mere girl, another of the minors.

# CHAPTER 10

# *The Cemetery of the Living: Amorebieta 1942–1943*

There must have been 450 women in our expedition. It took all day to get from Santander to Amorebieta. When we arrived late in the afternoon, they held us for hour after hour in a solitary patio to count and recount us. They would call us by our first name and we would answer with our last. Seated on our bedrolls we didn't know if we were going to spend the night out there or what. Later we found out what was going on; the prison was jammed to the rafters with inmates and couldn't hold even one more person. But leading us by the nose, the officials still worked to find room for us. They began to take us up to the rooms at night; the women up there already had been counted. We'd been counted, too, and also given a little food.

We were led to different halls, each woman on her own to find a place to settle down. But we couldn't find room in any hall because the sleeping mats already were stretched out and women were lying on them to keep their places. There we were left standing, pushing this woman and that one to find a place to lie down. During the train trip and while we were in the patio, I had struck up a friendship with two pretty sisters, Elena and Elvira. The three of us took charge of finding room for poor Consuelo Verguizas, the nearly eighty-year-old Daniela Picaza, and Gloria Nolasco, who was seriously ill when we arrived. Elvira was tall and strong, and she immediately made room where she could, putting down the three women's sleeping mats with mine next to Gloria's. Lying there next to one another, Gloria and I looked like two little creatures stuck together. The hall was hell, cries everywhere, on one side coming from us prisoners, on the other, from the prison officials.

"Be quiet, please be quiet."

There we were trying to find a place to sleep for just that night. But we couldn't go to sleep. Before we knew it, it was dawn and we heard a little bell ringing, ringing.

"What's that?" we asked.

Someone was dying in the infirmary, we were told.

With morning we could see the faces of the women in Amorebieta.

Their skin was so yellow they looked as if they belonged to another race. Obviously these women were wasting away. I remember one little girl who called me by name and came up to hug me affectionately. Not recognizing her, I let her leave without learning her identity. We must have been together in some other prison, I thought. Then another woman came over whom I did recognize. Even though she was terribly thin, I was certain it was Blasa Rojo. We hugged warmly. We'd known each other for many years.

"And Mari?" I asked, referring to her sister.

"She's over there on her sleeping mat sobbing because you didn't pay any attention to her."

"Is Mari really here?"

"Yes, you hugged and kissed her, but she says you didn't pay any attention to her."

"But I didn't recognize her."

I went with Blasa to where their sleeping mats were and for sure, it was Mari, but who would have known that creature who had been so darling. But it wasn't only Mari; all the women looked like her. The prison was a hell hole. We women from Santander looked as if we'd been eating in a restaurant every day.

From the first day in Amorebieta we had to be lined up and recounted before breakfast, if you could call a ladle of flavored hot water breakfast. Later on we were ordered to line up in the patio with a spoon and plate for another recounting. If someone was missing the officials went up to see what was wrong with her; if the woman wasn't running a fever, she was punished for being absent—no mail, no visitors. I remember one poor old woman who hadn't been down to the patio for several days because she couldn't stand up. She asked repeatedly if there was any mail for her. Finally one day they called her name to notify her that she had mail down below in the patio. One of the other prisoners offered to get her mail, but the nun in charge insisted the old woman herself go downstairs.

"So, granny," she asked, "why don't you go down to the patio?"

"Because I can't, sister. I'm so sick I can't stand up."

"Oh, no, you don't have a fever; there's no reason for you to lie there on your sleeping mat. Do you understand? You've received a letter and I think there are even photos of your grandchildren in it." And out she pulled a letter and some photos. "Now," she said, "you won't get to see your grandchildren or read the letter from your children." And she tore the letter into four pieces.

That first day in the patio of Amorebieta was terrible for us. We saw how the women who had been there for some time spent the whole day just seated next to a wall, too weak from hunger even to walk around the patio. The time came for our ration. The food tasted good. We hadn't had food like that in any other prison—tasty and well prepared. The problem was not with the food but the quantity; the ladle wasn't of regulation size. After those two spoonfuls I felt hungrier than before. We spent two days on the watch for what could be done to improve the prison; we began to talk with the women to see if they would support a petition for a ladle of regulation size and to have more than just hot water in the morning. It was difficult for those women to complain because they were totally cowed, but at last one morning we succeeded in persuading most of them not to go near the pot for hot water.

The prison was in an uproar; there were threats, many threats. We thought a delegation should be named to meet with the director about a regulation ladle and a better breakfast. Three women went as delegates; one woman was a lawyer, another had been imprisoned for her activity in Freemasonry, and the third was one of the sisters. The director's only reply was to throw them in solitary confinement. We responded in turn by persuading the women to refuse all food. So began our hunger strike. The strike didn't last long because it was just too difficult to sustain it in those miserable conditions. The director walked through the halls warning us it wouldn't be hard to put all of us from Santander in the patio and cut us down with a machine gun. He wouldn't have to answer for the act. It was clear that the women from Santander were responsible for stirring up the mess; before our arrival order and discipline reigned in the prison. Our demand for a ladle of regulation size was granted, and our delegates were released. But the food that came with the new ladle was awful, and it wasn't long before we too were turning yellow.

Not a week went by without one or two women dying of hunger. No wonder we called that prison "the cemetery of the living." One day when the woman who had been imprisoned for Freemasonry was in the patio, she began to feel ill and asked to go to the infirmary. As she was going up the stairs, a dead woman was being taken down. The woman swore that she had seen the corpse move and she yelled right out that it was a crime not to let the woman die in her bed and to take her away for dead when she was still breathing. The director punished the woman by sending her to the "rabbit room." That's what we called the little house at the other end of the garden where they kept rabbits and chickens. That's also the place where they stored the corpses until the following day when someone would come with a box on a wheelbarrow to take them away. As punishment this woman had to spend the whole night in that room with the dead woman. The next day after the body was hauled off and she was brought back to the hall, the director asked her in the presence of the priest: "Well, did you have a good night?"

"Yes, very good. You can repeat this punishment whenever you like.

I was pleased to serve as my companion's family in keeping vigil over her. I wasn't frightened at all. I enjoyed being with our companion."

Then she told us about one of the guards who was passing through the garden and saw something in the window of the "rabbit room" move. He thought the corpse had come to life and ran to get another guard. He didn't know a live woman had been put there for punishment. The guards told their superiors what had happened and refused to go near the "rabbit room." The director was so provoked that he put the woman in solitary confinement again, this time for fifteen days.

Whenever we saw a companion being taken to the infirmary, we were sure we wouldn't see her again. There were women in far worse shape than I, but still my weight had dropped to forty kilograms. Luckily Elvira and Elena received packages from their family in Santander and they shared with me as they could, but not much because they also took care of their own countrywomen who had no other extra food, as well as the older women and the women with children.

One day I had a wonderful surprise. I had been corresponding with the family of the young man I loved who had died with the International Brigades during the Ebro campaign from July 24 to November 18, 1938.[1] When his family wrote to friends in Portugalete that I was in Amorebieta, they came to see me with a package containing a large loaf of bread filled with fried sardines. I shared the bread and sardines with my countrywomen who were most in need. Gloria Nolasco also received packages, from her mother, but we wouldn't let her give away even one cracker. Gloria needed extra nourishment because her lungs were diseased and she often coughed up blood. At night when we were lying on our mats, she would get up, cover her head and eat chocolate and crackers and sip milk from a hole she'd made in the can. I'll never forget the smell of crackers and chocolate; I, too, covered my head—to keep from smelling that delicious food. Gloria and I were in that prison for seventeen months and I cried from hunger every night when I smelled crackers and chocolate.

It was painful to see the begging that went on everywhere in the hall. When someone was about to eat an orange, seven or eight women would cluster around asking for the rind. Sometimes the woman would keep the rind to eat later; other times she gave it away. If she secretly threw it away, someone was always there to retrieve it from the garbage. The same thing happened with bananas. I was hungry, but I never begged; my eyes might follow the woman who was eating a banana or orange, but I never begged.

My friend, Elvira, had the job of delivering packages in Amorebieta. One day she came up to our room very upset and red in the face. "I wonder what's happened," she said to her sister, Elena. "The girl in the office told me she'd heard my name and something about Tabacalera when the officials were talking. And there was a letter they tore up. I know something's happened to my husband. Our friend in the office promised to retrieve the pieces so we can put the letter back together."

Elvira's husband was still in Tabacalera under sentence of death. I don't remember if he was from Torrelavega, but I think so, and I remember that he lost a hand. At last the woman in the office was able to collect the pieces of paper; they were so small that it took us several days to piece them together. At times Elena and I worked alone. Seated on the sleeping mat with a board and sheet of transparent paper, we put the letter together piece by piece. As we were picking up loose words, we realized it was a farewell letter, a beautiful letter to Elvira from her husband, encouraging her to continue the fight to liberate our Spain. We found out later that he had been shot.

I often think about Amalia Morales whom I called my prison sister. Poor girl, what bad luck she had. She lived under the death penalty for a long time before it was commuted. We met in the prison at Santander at a time when her mother and husband already had been shot. Later she began to correspond with a young man who was in prison, and after they both were freed, they married. I met her in Madrid later. She had a little boy and was very happy. Unfortunately, her husband, a mason by trade, fell while working on a job and was killed. Someone told me she left the country with her child, but I don't know for sure. My last memory of Amalia is an afternoon we spent together in the shack her husband had built near the Manzanares river in Madrid. She gave me a photo of herself and her child, which I still have.

Amalia embroidered beautifully, and wherever she was the opportunity arose for her to work with those hands of hers. Her embroidery work was so marvelous that it looked like a painting. The nuns in Amorebieta wanted her to complete a very large order for table linen to be done with cross stitch and filled with embroidered pansies. The order included twenty-four place settings, twenty-four napkins, a table cloth for eight places, and a tea cloth with six settings and matching napkins. She said that she couldn't finish such a huge job in the time specified without help. So I and two girls from Toledo with experience working on fine Toledan linen were chosen to help Amalia. The nuns put us in a separate little room because the work was too delicate to be done in the patio or the hall. The cloth was white, very lovely, and the work turned out to be truly beautiful, all of the linen filled with pansies in a rainbow of colors. The four of us spent nearly two months on the project. During that time our health improved because we received a double portion at one of the meals. But we also left our eyes there.

We were paid 1,000 pesetas for our work. I thought it was a fortune because I had never made more than ten or fifteen pesetas from time to time doing handwork. As much as we were thrilled to share in that money, we were furious later when we heard that the marquis who ordered the linen had paid the nuns 5,000 pesetas.

Following the orders of the doctor at Santander, I would show up at the infirmary for calcium injections, and once in a while I was selected. I don't know how it happened but once when they gave me the injection, I got an infection. Because we had no doctor in our prison, the doctor from the prison in Bilbao was asked to come and look at my arm; he never came. When our nurse, a handsome and courageous Asturian girl, saw how badly swollen and discolored my arm was, she asked me: "Do you trust me?" I told her to do what she thought was right.

"Look," she said, "either we make an incision in that arm and drain all that filth or you'll get gangrene. But I don't have any anesthesia."

When they opened up my arm, the infection filled up a whole basin. The nurse had no medication; all she could do was apply sterilized gauze and change the bandage daily. She managed to heal the infection. According to her, if she hadn't made the incision and drained the arm, at the very least I would have lost an arm.

One episode at Amorebieta started as tragedy and ended up a comedy. A certain mother from Toledo was in prison with two very young daughters. The husband was free at home taking care of the younger children. One day the woman was reading a letter from one of the children and just as she was about to finish the first page, the words "father has died" jumped out at her. Crumpling up the letter, the woman gave in to her desperation. She and the little daughters, the misfortune that had befallen her, her husband dead, the children alone at home, what was going to happen? All the women from the area around Toledo and almost all the rest of us came by to offer words of consolation. That afternoon one of her friends asked: "Did the children tell you the cause of your husband's death?"

"Well, I didn't finish reading the letter."

"But, woman, now that you're calmer and recovered from weeping, read the letter."

The woman opened her hand, smoothed out the letter, and read the last words "father has died." She turned the page over and read "a 350-pound pig." The letter continued: "We did the slaughtering and when the sausages are dried, we'll send you a package." Since the words "ha muerto" could mean either "has died" or "killed," depending on the context, she had assumed the worst.

The conditions in Amorebieta were so harsh that we decided to send letters to the Ministry of Justice denouncing the prison. And in fact we did manage to get our letters mailed. In the meantime the woman lawyer who had been a delegate during the hunger strike had been released from prison but before leaving she promised to go to the Ministry of Justice in Madrid and expose our living conditions. One day when visitors were allowed, she came back to find out if the situation had improved as officials at the Ministry had assured her would happen. We had to answer that we were going from bad to worse: women still were dying and we were getting skinnier and skinnier and more and more yellowish. By now I weighed less than forty kilos. She promised to make yet another trip to Madrid and insist on improvements. This time we did receive news that they had paid attention to her: the director of prisons, Carmen de Castro, was on her way to inspect Amorebieta.

Carmen de Castro and her secretary came in person. Through the prisoner who worked in the office we found out which day she was due to arrive and prepared a surprise for her. According to custom we were lined up in the halls to receive her. In the first row we put many women she had known in the prisons of Barbastro and Gerona; the poor women had come into Amorebieta in the same condition as we had, but now they couldn't even stand up. Some women were beauticians who used to do Carmen's hair; others had cleaned her room; others took up her meals; one even prepared her meals. All these women we placed in the first row. When Carmen de Castro entered the hall, we had to shout "Franco, Franco, Franco" and sing hymns—"Cara al Sol," the Requete, the national hymn, and shout "Franco, Franco, Franco." Normally we detested singing these songs, but this day we sang with real gusto. As Carmen walked in review, the women called out to her as they had been prepared: "Doña Carmen, what a pleasure to see you here."

"Who are you? Do you know me?"

"Yes, of course. Don't you remember me? I'm the one who fixed your hair, the one who was in Gerona and went up to comb your hair every day."

Carmen waived her aside with her hand. Then one after another the women spoke up. Finally Carmen de Castro recognized one of the women, though she couldn't remember from which prison.

Then she and her secretary inspected the toilets, which were hardly enough for 800 women, and the wash basins that didn't have running water. When she turned on a faucet and nothing happened, she asked: "Why are there so many wash basins if there isn't any water?"

That day we discovered there was another toilet. The hall was shaped like a U with two toilets and six basins at one end and nothing but a door at the other end. We had often seen the mandatas going in that door, but we didn't know why. When Carmen de Castro came to the closed door and asked what was behind it, the mandata said: "I'm not sure but I think it's a toilet."

"Ah, and who uses it?"

"It's always closed."

Carmen kicked the door so hard it almost broke. "I want to see this toilet open at all times," she said. Highly indignant, she went to the office and began to give orders and tell them how to run the prison. She even gave the order that we were to go out to the garden because the patio, with its high walls and lack of ventilation, was unhealthy. And when smoke from the kitchen and laundries filled the patio, we had more smoke than ventilation. In spite of her orders, all that Carmen de Castro said to the director as she left was: "Well, look, don't make any changes. I'll handle this myself in Madrid."

We soon found out what her words meant. Within a few days three expeditions were named: one for Saturrarán, another for Barbastro, and the third for Madrid. The women were chosen for Madrid on the condition that they could sew overalls. Try outs even were held. As sick as she was, Gloria Nolasco volunteered for the try outs. If she could just get to Madrid, her mother in Guadalajara would be able to help her. Daniela Picazo also wanted to go to Madrid to be near her family. Consuelo Verguizas was among the women left behind in Amorebieta, but she was freed soon after because she was a septuagenarian. I passed the test for making overalls.

What I remember most vividly about Amorebieta was the hunger. Either you swelled up or you were nothing but skin and bones. The surest thing was death, which came almost daily. Perhaps one day the archives will reveal the names of the women who got out of prison only by leaving the "rabbit room" in a wheelbarrow. One thing I do know for certain: Amorebieta deserved its name—"cemetery of the living."

*How many living dead there were at Amorebieta, I don't know. But from the hundreds who suffered in that "cemetery" I offer this testimony by Pilar Pascual Martínez, who was not a Communist but a Socialist.*

# CHAPTER 11

# *The Socialist:*
# *Pilar Pascual Martínez at Amorebieta*

*Years later, in 1976, a year after Franco died, we returned home to Spain with legal status. At the Christmas holidays in 1977 we received telephone calls, letters, and some bottles of good wine from Yecla in the province of Murcia in southern Spain. They had been sent by a comrade living in Barcelona. One day this comrade came to visit us along with another man from the town. This other man turned out to be the son of my friend, Pilar Pascual. He encouraged me to go to Yecla to speak with his mother for he was sure that she would be delighted to give her testimony. I go to Yecla in 1978 and I find Pilar just fine, living with her daughter and family. I spend two very pleasant days with Pilar and her children, and this is the testimony she gives me.*

My name is Pilar Pascual Martínez and I'm from Yecla in the province of Murcia. I joined the Socialist Youth when I was eleven or twelve years old, before it merged with the Communist Youth. I've been active in the party since then. I was arrested on March 30, 1939, taken first to the commander's office and then to the Court of Justice. There were at least thirty of us together from Yecla. At three o'clock in the morning they moved us to the prison for women. Two days later I was led to the Court of Justice to make a statement, one soldier walking in front of me, the other behind, both with guns.

The first question they asked was: "Are you the one who wrote the article in the newspaper?"

I had no idea what they meant. "No, that's not true."

"Yes, it is," they answered. "Do you want us to show it to you?"

"If you want. What importance can that article have? It was simply a defense of humanity. I didn't offend anyone."

No response. Then the judge came in and began to take my statement. I told him I'd only answer questions about my activities and not what other people had done.

"All right," he said, "take her away. Tomorrow we'll see what's to be done with her."

After a few days I was taken out at three in the morning to make a statement to some men who probably were from Yecla, though I didn't recognize them. I repeated: "Ask me about my activities; don't ask me anything else because I know nothing." When they got tired of questioning me, they said: "Okay, take her out to the little hill tomorrow and put four shots in her and be done with her." I acted as if nothing bothered me. "What? You're not shedding a single tear? Don't you have children?"

"I have two."

"Aren't you even going to cry for them?"

"When you have a clear conscience, there's nothing to cry about."

"Back to prison with her."

For thirteen days they kept me in a cell with only four little fingers of light and space for just one body. I couldn't sleep because there wasn't room enough to lie down. When they took me out after thirteen days, I was half dead. Again I was to make a statement. My answer was always the same: "Just ask me about my activities. I've been president of a women's group and I've helped with artistic stagings for young people. But don't ask me about anything else."

"You mean you don't know so and so or such and such?"

"No, sir, I don't. I was only active with the women."

On June 13 they transferred me with a group of women to the prison at Murcia where some forty or fifty of us were confined in a very small area. From there I left for a military tribunal. I wasn't beaten but they did insult me verbally. And of course those thirteen days in the prison cell had been a kind of torture. Like everyone who went to the military tribunal, I came back sentenced to death. I lived for five long months under the death penalty. Finally one other woman and I had the penalty commuted, but we were the only ones out of that group.

I managed to have the death penalty commuted because none of the accusations against me was signed. The lawyer who met with me before I appeared at the tribunal assured me my chances for commutation were good. Ah, those accusations—everything the town gossips wanted to say but no one would sign! Imagine this—they accused me of killing the mayor's cat. Obviously my accusers were running out of charges.

One day during the war when my sister and I worked in the hospital, we noticed on our way to work a crowd of maybe 300 or 400 people angrily heading for the old folks home run by the nuns. When they got to the door of the home, I was already there.

"Well, where are you going?" I asked.

"We're here to evict the nuns."

"Look, most of all you need to have trustworthy women who'll treat the old people well. If there are problems, there are committees to handle them. The people on the committees are the right ones to decide if the nuns must leave."

That evening we had a meeting with the appropriate committee and the people; the nuns were allowed to remain because the committee knew they were good with the old people. Every day I went to see those nuns, and they always treated the old people well. In those days the nuns weren't allowed to wear their habits; they wore the ordinary clothing of country folk. When Yecla fell to Franco's forces and the townspeople wanted to have me executed, those nuns spoke to the prison officials in my defense.

So the lawyer succeeded in defending me because of unsigned denunciations and witnesses, especially the nuns, who testified for me. I even have a copy of my proceedings that one of the prisoners who worked in the office was able to make.

About forty of us women were taken by train from the Murcia prison to Amorebieta. We had a sympathetic Civil Guard who bought us bread with the money he had been given for his own food. That night we stayed in the Ventas prison at Madrid and the next morning left from the North station. We were about to climb into a car used for transporting pigs when we heard a voice say: "Don't squeeze in here; we've had to do our business in that corner because there's no other place." There were other women prisoners in that car. When the guard climbed in to check the condition of the car, he was thoroughly disgusted. "If you give me your word not to move from here," he said "I'll take you to a heated mail car." Of course, the guard was looking out for himself so he wouldn't have to travel with us in that horrid car. "We give you our word," we replied. "We won't move from here." I don't know where the guard went, probably to get authorization from his superiors and the station masters, but we were transferred to the other car.

The next day we reached Amorebieta. It was the Christmas season of 1939–1940. As we got off the train, accompanied by the Civil Guard, some little kids came up to look at us. I heard one of them say: "Hey, they told us there were prisoners but look, they're just women."

The first day we had a big hunk of bread and a plate of food at noon. After that, nothing for three days. By that time we were so weak we could hardly get up from our sleeping mats. At the word *food* no one could even move. Then the director showed up. I have his image nailed in the retina of my eye: a fat character, dressed in black. He planted himself at the door and yelled: "Don't you want to get your food? There's nothing else. Now let me tell you something. I'm going to put a machine gun here right this minute and not one of you will be left alive. One signature on a piece of paper and it's over for all of you."

When the prison of Amorebieta was closed, some of us were trans-

ferred to Madrid to work in the shops at the Ventas prison making overalls. My release from prison life happened this way. It was the feast of
the Ascension and they called us earlier than usual so we would have
time to attend mass. I refused to get up. The woman we called "Aunt
Poison" came for me.

"Are you the one who's not getting up?"

"I don't feel well today."

"Well, as soon as the doctor gets here, you have to go."

When all the women left for mass, I got up and dressed. I was just
finishing rolling up the sleeping mat when I heard the call: "Pilar Pascual."

"I'm here, who's calling me?"

"There's a letter for you."

Since the usual punishment for not attending mass was to tear up
any mail you might have received, I answered: "I don't know how
you're going to give me the letter when you know I didn't go to mass."

"Come out."

As I went out, some of my companions said: "You're going free."

"Don't waste your jokes on me," I snapped. "I don't like it."

"But it's true."

When I reached the iron grating, the director was standing there.
"Good day, what's your name?"

"Pilar Pascual Martínez."

"And your parents' names?"

"Lucas Pascual Gil and Juliana Martínez García."

"All right, go back to your cell and get ready. You're going free."

My cell mates—there were seven of us—packed my suitcase and
helped me get everything ready. Singing, they followed me as I left. I'll
never forget it. "Good-bye," I said with my heart, too filled with emotion
to say anything with my lips. When I reached the prison door with my
suitcase and purse, I asked myself: "Where am I going? I've never been in
Madrid before." Then I remembered a girl from Madrid who'd been with
me in Amorebieta before her release. "If you get out some day," she'd
said, "go to such and such a street and ask for María Dorado."

So I went to the address and yes, I found María. She went with me
to another address I had, that of Pili's mother. At her home I was able
to telephone my children in Yecla. When they heard my voice, they
shouted with joy: "When are you coming home, Mommy?"

"As soon as I get my papers tomorrow."

My son and daughter were waiting for me when I arrived home in
Yecla. Since my husband had died before the war, my children had been
without a mother and father for years. Thank goodness I had very kind
sisters who took them in.

Life in Yecla was hard for me after I got out of prison. I took whatever work I could find to support my family. And I had to endure gossip that was still going around about me. One rumor was that I had had a child in prison. That rumor got started because one night when I had been taken out to make a statement, I was put in a room with fourteen or fifteen men and had to spend the night there. What a terrible rumor when those men were such good and generous companions! The only place to sit or rest was on a stone bench, which the men insisted was for me. Even today, so many years later, people talk about me behind my back. I know. I see them looking at me and murmuring. But I take comfort in what our Prime Minister Largo Caballero once said: "When people look at us it's because we are interesting; we make them uncomfortable."

*While I am with Pilar we go to eat in a bar; we have toasted bread with anchovies, wine, and a coffee. We reminisce about the good times and the bad and relive the hunger and misery of Amorebieta, feeling once again the fury and impotence that had filled our days in that prison. We visit the park and end up having a snack in a bar-restaurant that served as a prison long ago. This is the first time Pilar has been in the bar since she was detained there in April of 1939.*

*In 1981 I learned that Pilar had been hit by a car in a street in Valencia. I attended her funeral.*

# CHAPTER 12

# *Solidarity and Compassion: Ventas and Segovia 1943–1944*

We arrived at Ventas after three days of travel. At first we were thrown in with black marketeers, thieves, and women of the street. There was the usual coming and going of the prostitutes who paid their fines right away. During the first days we women from Amorebieta were scattered around the room wherever we could find a spot, but little by little we found room together.

After twenty days in what can only be called a dungeon we women who had been selected to work in the shop were transferred to the first gallery on the right. Unfortunately, work in the shop lasted no more than a few months, thanks to the maneuverings of Mother Serafines. That woman was a fascist through and through. She hated Communists. She would go over the records of all the recently arrived women to identify the Communists; then she isolated us in the third gallery to the right and denied us work in the shop.

The prison at Ventas was different from the others where I'd been. Perhaps the reason was that Ventas was located in the center of Spain, in Madrid, while the others were far away and out of political contact. In Ventas there was a true sense of community that bolstered morale for all of us, and especially for the little old women. This solidarity was the consequence of political organization rather than a reaction to a particular condition such as the scarcity of food in Amorebieta. Another difference between Ventas and other prisons is that we knew what was happening outside; we received almost daily news about the war on the various fronts. We were convinced, foolish women, that we would be released when the allies won the war and fascism ended.

It was interesting to see two tendencies develop in the party; one reflected politics of the party outside of Spain, the other, politics within the country. Coming from prisons in the north where the party was not officially organized, I was unable to give opinions on issues of the day. But I remember the heated discussions about the position of Heriberto Quiñones who advocated party leadership from within Spain and a national union to include Republicans and even Monarchists. But his ideas were opposed by the party leadership in exile. And I remember how divisive the issues raised by Quiñones were.[1] What I see clearly today is that the party itself was not free of sectarianism and that comrades suffered recriminations. I believe that regardless of their political opinions within the party, our comrades who gave their lives before an execution squad or in the dungeons of police stations deserve reconsideration and rehabilitation.

Friendship continued to be precious to me in Ventas. Friends like Gloria Nolasco and Daniela Picazo had come with me from Amorebieta. Gloria Nolasco was dying of tuberculosis. We knew that in Amorebieta when she vomited blood and fainted. In Ventas they put her in the infirmary, but except for occasional calcium injections she received no medical treatment. Much later, after I had been transferred to Segovia, I found out that she had vomited a great amount of blood during a visit with her mother. Desperate and almost crazy with concern for Gloria, her mother personally went to the Ministry of Justice, screaming for them to listen to her. Eventually she got a hearing and as a result Gloria was examined. The doctors concluded that she had only days to live. The mother managed to take her daughter home in an ambulance where she remained in policy custody. She died a few days later with her mother, a mother whose courage freed her dying daughter from Ventas.

Daniela Picazo, the woman from Guadalajara I called "aunt," was close to eighty years old; she lived in the gallery where all the old women—and there were many of them—were kept. I visited her twice a week, washing her clothes and writing letters for her, which the old woman couldn't do because her hand was partially paralyzed. I also used the opportunity to lift the spirits of the other old women by telling them about allied advances and assuring them the war was soon to end with the defeat of Germany and fascism. We exaggerated the news sometimes to give our older friends a few moments of hope and happiness.

Among my new friends were the Alicias, so named because both the mother and daughter were called Alicia. Their family had been a comfortable one: Alicia's husband was a fine dentist. The couple had three children, two boys, one a dentist and the other a medical doctor, and the girl. The daughter had grown up to be very delicate, with a small defect in her spinal column; she had always been cared for by this closely knit family. In the summer of 1936 the mother and three children had gone on vacation to La Granja, I think, that little town where well-off families from Madrid and the environs vacationed in the summer. The father had had to stay in Madrid working. The uprising caught the mother and children in La Granja. The boys, who had belonged to the Communist Party for some time, were arrested by the fascists after they fought with the local people in defense of the Republic. Alicia the mother was also arrested; Alicia the daughter was detained for twenty-four hours. When she couldn't get back, she stayed on with friends in La Granja.

The girl was able to see her brothers in prison and she knew they were being brutally tortured. Knowing that death was imminent, the brothers made her promise not to say anything to their mother. They didn't want their mother to suffer knowing that her sons were dead. Alicia the daughter was arrested again, this time in Segovia in 1938, and after being sent to several prisons she was tried in Madrid in 1940 and confined in prison until her release in 1941. The mother and daughter were separated until the parents were united; then the three were arrested again in 1943. All this time Alicia the mother was unaware that her sons had been executed.

Alicia the daughter suffered intensely when her mother spoke about what good sons she had and how she would see them when the war in Europe ended, provided they hadn't been killed. At times the daughter would get up and go to the cells of friends to avoid hearing her mother talk about her sons fighting some place or living in exile.

The Alicias still hadn't been tried. When Mother Serafines broke up what she called the "gallery of the Communist Party" by sending the women to different prisons throughout Spain, the Alicias were judged and sent to Barcelona. I don't remember if the sentence was for twelve years, but I know that later, in 1945, I met the two of them in the prison of Barcelona where I recalled a charming story about our stay in Ventas. The moment they caught sight of me in Barcelona, Alicia the mother said: "You see? You see now what I told you about the Germans not ever winning the war?"

This is the story. I don't know where she got it, but Alicia the mother had a map of Europe that showed the advances of the allies. One day I said to her: "Alicia, why don't you show the advances of the Germans?"

"Because the Germans aren't going to win the war. Why would I want to mark the advances if I just have to erase them later?"

Her answer amused me, so later when I met her in the gallery in Barcelona I asked: "Alicia, what marks have you put down? What advances have been made?"

"Well, well, life goes on!"

"But have you put down any marks or not?"

Then she realized what I meant.

"Look, get along with you girl, go take a walk. I'm too old for you to pull my leg."

We got along very well and I liked her a lot because she was a warm, affectionate woman, always hanging around us younger ones.

"I'm not very worried about having to spend these years in prison," she would say, "but for you, so much younger than I, to spend the best years of your life locked up, that does cause me pain."

Many years later I met Alicia the mother for the third time.

Our famous Communist leader, Dolores Ibarurri, dedicated these words to Alicia the mother: "Alicia Martínez . . . how many emotional memories this name evokes. On one occasion she said that memory may fail but the heart never will. And the name of this extraordinary family is profoundly etched in my memory. I hadn't met them yet when one day in the prison for women in Madrid I was summoned to the room for visitors. A woman with an eight- or nine-year-old girl was there to visit me, me a prisoner whom they personally did not know but whom they esteemed because her sons, Wilfredo and Daniel, who were later shot by Francoism, had spoken about me. Not once in the long months of my incarceration did this marvelous woman fail to visit me. At the time I could not imagine that that admirable woman, the wife of one of the finest odontologists in Madrid, Daniel Martínez, would have to suffer the terrible Calvary to which Francoism would condemn her as the mother of two young Communist men. It is difficult to evoke, with deepest emotion, the life and fate of this exemplary family who sacrificed everything defending the cause of democracy and socialism."

In Ventas I was able to write my family and have visits from them because they lived nearby. I remember that only my mother and brother came at first. When I asked them about my father and sister, they explained that the whole family couldn't afford to come at the same time and that my father and sister would come the next visiting day. I thought it was strange that my father hadn't come first, but I didn't give the matter too much thought. Gloria, too, had a visitor—her mother. After the visit Gloria came up to see me.

"How's your family?" I asked her. "How is everyone? How's the child?"

"Well, the child is very handsome, but listen, Tomasa—Mother says your father died two years ago."

The news chilled me. I put my head in my hands. I don't know how much time passed. I only know that when the meal came I realized I hadn't opened my mouth or cried. My companions looked at me pensively, feeling my pain; clearly they were concerned about how I would react. But I got my food ration and then, as if nothing had happened, ate it up as I did every day. There was no taking back my father's death. What else could I do except resign myself to the fact?

To me my father wasn't just a father; he was a friend and a companion. He had been a strong man; I'd never seen him sick. The two times he was confined to bed were due to accidents. When the war ended he suffered terribly. First they threw him out of work merely because he had let a daughter become a Communist. I didn't feel responsible for his death. He agreed with my thinking. But that business of spending hour upon hour at the prison door, going to the cemetery walls every morning, seeing his neighbors arrested, friends he'd known since we had come to Guadalajara, all that undid him, nothing else. He was one more victim of Francoism.

Mother Serafines was intent on making life impossible for the Communists in the third gallery to the right. But she didn't succeed in breaking us, which was her objective. Our morale remained high. So she decided to break up that nucleus of Communists by dispersing the women to other prisons. Since I was taking a series of calcium injections because my health was so poor, I was chosen for the prison at Segovia where one pavilion had been equipped for tubercular prisoners.

It was almost night when we reached Segovia and snowing so heavily that we couldn't manage our sleeping mats and had to leave them at the station. By the time we reached the prison it was late at night and the snow was up to our knees. They put us in a pavilion with no lights or blankets. When we tried to stretch out a little on the floor, we realized the place was nearly flooded with water. Hungry and cold, we huddled together in one corner of the pavilion. When it began to get light we understood what was going on with the water: after the tubercular prisoners vacated that room, handfuls of lime had been thrown on the floor and left there puddled with water. We were obliged to clean the floor in the morning, but first there was the compulsory sermon. Our sleeping mats arrived in the morning, but we weren't allowed to rest until night in accordance with the prison schedule. Two days later the medical examinations began. Granted a woman here or there was shown from the X-rays to have tuberculosis, but the majority of us were there at the whim of Mother Serafines.

Not many days elapsed, however, before sick women from other prisons came to this place that officially had been named the Anti-Tuberculosis Penal Sanatorium for women. We were astonished to see them bring in little beds for our room; what a stupendous night we spent sleeping in a bed after such a long time sleeping on the floor. But the treat lasted only a short time. When the doctor began to examine the sick women, more rooms had to be equipped. If we weren't sick, we were separated, leaving the beds for the sick women. Once again I found myself sleeping on the floor.

For the first time during all the years I'd been in prison I met a religious woman who was truly religious and humane. An older woman, probably more than seventy years old, Sor Juliana's concern for us was evident from the first moment. She would say to us: "Poor women, how much you are missed at home if your husbands are in prison and you have little ones with no one to care for them, poor children abandoned to the mercy of second families or hospices." She was genuinely sorry for us, and she expressed her sorrow to make us understand that she was on our side and that she truly regretted our captivity. Sor Juliana actually put us in contact with the men prisoners. In the pockets of her habit she brought us news from our male comrades, news about the course of the war and even material from the party. I don't know how Sor Juliana managed it, but in the comings and goings of the doctor from our prison to the men's prison in Cuellar, something for us women always appeared. I don't believe the doctor collaborated with the nun but inadvertently he became the special messenger between the men and us women. We came to hold Sor Juliana in very high esteem.

One of the girls in our room became seriously ill with meningitis and other complications. The doctor advised the priest that the girl, who was only seventeen or eighteen years old, was near death. When the priest tried to administer the sacrament for the dying, she refused to let him even near her bed. She hadn't done anything, she said, and besides, the priest in her village had killed her older brother and father, her mother was in another prison, and the younger children were with other family members.

"You're all assassins," she shouted. "You killed my family and destroyed our home."

The Mother Superior was an evil woman. When she saw that the girl refused to confess and was insulting the priest, this nun refused to administer the prescribed medication and treatment. Because the sick girl was burning up with fever, the doctor had told them to put a rubber bag filled with ice on her head; neither the bag nor the ice appeared. At that time there was some construction going on in one part of the prison and the workers came from outside the prison. Sor Juliana took the risk of speaking with some of the workers about bringing in medicine, which they did. Hiding in the toilet we heated a little syringe in a can used for condensed milk and gave injections of medicine that those men at great risk brought from the town pharmacy and gave to Sor Juliana. It was very cold, and in the mornings the little puddles in the garden would be frozen over. Sor Juliana would go out for pieces of ice, put them in rags and then place them on the girl's head. But the girl's fever was so high the ice melted immediately. At last Sor Juliana dared to ask a worker to buy a rubber bag.

The poor boy Sor Juliana turned to for help thought it was an emergency and he was to bring the bag as soon as possible. So right after work he brought the bag to the prison door and asked to have it delivered to Sor Juliana. Sor Juliana realized she had been discovered. Right there, in front of the workers and prisoners, the Mother Superior and the prison director tried to find out who in our room had ordered a bag that wasn't officially authorized. Sor Juliana defended the boy, who by this time was under arrest; she said he was not to blame because she was the one who had asked him to get the bag and had not told him the purchase was unauthorized. The proof of his innocence was that no sooner had he left work than he brought the bag to the front entrance and asked the portress to give it to Sor Juliana. Her words saved the boy from jail though not from losing his job.

When we saw that Sor Juliana was going to be severely punished—the way the superior threatened her in front of the prisoners was shameful, not acting like a religious woman at all but like some old hag—all of us together, forty or more of us in that room, said it wasn't true, that we were the ones responsible, that we had secretly undertaken the plan, that Sor Juliana had absolutely nothing to do with us. When the officials began to gather names in order to try us for illegal activity inside the prison, Sor Juliana swore before God that our story wasn't true; that the prisoners wanted to come out in her defense but that she was really the one responsible because she didn't want the girl to die without being in a state of grace; that she had acted as the Catholic and religious woman she was; and they could do what they wanted with her but we women and the boy weren't to blame.

The matter didn't go beyond this. What the officials didn't discover is that the medicine was coming in with another worker who was more clever and devious than the first boy. And we were saving the girl. Naturally the officials thought it was a miracle that she was improving without medication. How shameful it was to see the priest bothering her every day to confess and how heroic the young girl was to maintain her position that she wouldn't confess. We were proud to be able to save her.

Yes, they did punish Sor Juliana. They sent her to the laundry to wash the clothing of infected people. But that woman didn't wash clothes. We fixed up a little brazier for her by putting some embers in a can that some friends brought in from the kitchen. That way she stayed a little warm while she sat in the corner of the laundry. Some of the women kept watch in a corridor outside the room while others of us took turns washing the clothing. We couldn't let that woman who was already elderly and who had risked everything to save our friend's life have her hands stuck in water that was so cold it froze you to the heart.

One day when Sor Juliana was in the laundry watching us wash clothes for her, she said: "I don't know if I'm condemning myself or winning heaven, but I must ask your help. I have committed robbery."

We stopped and stared at her.

"Calm down; nothing will happen."

Sor Juliana explained her robbery. She had accompanied some sick prisoners to the tuberculosis sanatorium for prisoners in Cuellar. Some of the men, she told us, didn't even have underwear, so she'd taken advantage of her transfer to the laundry to have some sheets disappear from the closet. Since the sheets already had been recounted, she couldn't replace them.

"What am I to do?"

"We'll make the underwear," we offered.

"Thank you, my daughters, that's what I wanted to ask you. Sending them will be my job."

Of all the nuns we knew in the prisons, Sor Juliana was the only one who reached out with compassion to help the prisoners.

Meanwhile decrees were being issued, sentencing people to maybe six years or six years and one day or twelve years or twelve and one. I was given thirty years and then proposed as a candidate for release. When I signed my release papers, I found out that the sentence had been revised to twenty years. The conditions of my freedom were the following: they asked for three reports from my home area— one from the Falange, one from the Civil Guard, and one from a neighbor. With three good reports, I could go home; with two good ones, I would be exiled three hundred kilometers from the place of arrest and trial; with one good report, I would be denied freedom. This was the usual procedure for all prisoners. If no good reports were sent after three months of initially sending the telegram to a prisoner's home area, the administrative council of the prison could propose you for release to the Ministry of Justice and the Ministry could grant you freedom or not. At least a prisoner had the right to another request for release. In my case two good reports were sent; therefore, I was to be set free, but with exile. So my name was forwarded to the Ministry of Justice.

During my five years in prison all my clothes and shoes had worn out. My friends from Portugalete had sent me some rather good-looking slippers that looked like little shoes; I'd kept these to wear when I went free. But I didn't have a decent dress to wear. So Gloria Cueto, who was in charge of the showers, and I came up with a plan. Since it was spring we were using light-weight blankets. One of those blankets happened to disappear. Gloria secretly dyed the blanket using hot water in the showers, and the two of us made a presentable dress. I wore that dress when I left prison, exiled to a strange city. Where and how I would find support in Barcelona, I didn't know, but I was ready to move ahead.

*With Ventas and Segovia this part of my prison odyssey ended. But my prison days weren't over. Clandestine work for the party was to be dangerous and bring its share of horror in police headquarters and prisons. But for now, those times in Ventas and Segovia bring to mind friends like Josefina Amalia Villa and Antonia García who give us their testimonies.*

# CHAPTER 13

# Reflections on Prison Life for Women: Josefina Amalia Villa at Ventas and Segovia

*In the prison of Ventas in Madrid, during the years 1943–1944, I met Josefina Amalia Villa, a great comrade and friend. She was always a model Communist; proud and rebellious, she showed impressive dignity before her enemies. At times she paid dearly for her dignity. It was through another old friend from prison that I renewed friendship and contact with Josefina. This is how it happened. In 1961, eighteen years after our stay in Ventas, I went to Burgos to visit my husband who was imprisoned there. There I happened to meet Manoli, this old friend I mentioned. Manoli was also in Burgos to visit her husband in prison. I immediately recognized her Basque face. It turned out that Manoli had kept in touch with Josefina in Madrid and knew where she lived. Later, in 1978, when I was visiting Manoli in Madrid, she invited Josefina to have coffee with us.*

*I use this opportunity to take her testimony. At this time she lives alone with her two big dogs. She uses a cane and takes the dogs out for a walk in a nearby park. Like many other companions, we know what Josefina suffered, how they tortured her in the government dungeons, but she doesn't want to talk about that. The following is the testimony she gives me.*

Before I speak about my experiences in Ventas and Segovia, I would like to explain that prison life for women was no different than for men. When a woman was arrested, she was treated the same as if she were a man; she ran the same risks as the men. Because only older women and children remained at home, the arrested woman could expect no help from outside. In the first period of arrests at the end of the war, women and men were denounced and convicted for absolutely everything and anything. It was enough for someone, anyone—a neighbor, a colleague at work, a widow or the relative of a person killed by the "Reds"—simply to appear at the police station or the Civil Guard or Falange headquarters and denounce a person. That denouncer might not have any specific ideas about the beliefs or actions of the woman for her to be arrested, tortured, and left to rot in jail.

How she fared later depended on chance. If the denouncer persisted and if reports gathered in the neighborhood—which were always sought from people on the right—confirmed not the act but merely the ideas of the woman being denounced or even of her family, most certainly she would have to appear before a military tribunal made up of military personnel without any particular legal training. The defense attorney was often some obscure law clerk that the prisoner saw for the first time when she appeared before the tribunal. His participation was usually so pathetic that the most you could hope for was that he wouldn't be confused with the prosecutor for what he said. Then it was back to jail to wait. Most of the time people returned to jail without knowing what they had been asked or what the sentence was. It happened in several cases that a woman wouldn't realize she had been condemned to death until she found herself in the gallery reserved for women awaiting execution by shooting. By the way, I don't know any cases of execution by *garrote vil* among the women executed in Madrid.

There is compelling evidence that convictions were arbitrary and excessive. When the government began to review the cases of women with the death penalty, all of the sentences were commuted for lack of sufficient cause. Obviously, there was no chance of review for the women who'd already been shot.

Normally women stayed in prison for four to six years for problems arising during the war, but women condemned to thirty years or whose death penalty had been commuted spent far longer in prison, between twelve and eighteen years. With respect to the women arrested for postwar activities against the government, they all knew that their clandestine work would incur exceedingly harsh sentences. That's why their mental attitude was different. Women denounced for wartime activities had the illusion of being treated justly, but women arrested later didn't expect justice or mercy. Women who had done no more than act as messengers, without even knowing the content of the letters that passed through their hands, these women were sentenced to as many as twenty years or even to death.

Another pain that sharpened with the years was seeing our youth pass by, a youth that in many cases had scarcely been lived at all. How sad it is for a woman to be aging and to know instinctively that she disappears as a woman when she ceases to be desirable. I saw a woman about to go free after ten years in prison weeping with uncontrollable bitterness; she realized that menopause had deprived her of the desire and hope to have children. But it doesn't do a woman much good to think about how she is to realize herself as a human being. For such a plan to have a real content she must have choice in her life; she must be able to choose her role and not have it imposed on her in some implacable form.

It wasn't only the tenacious struggle to survive that dehumanized us as women. There were the close quarters, the uninhabitable conditions, the impossibility of having a single minute to yourself, the lack of mental stimulus.

Ventas was a new building with red bricks and white-washed walls. Originally its six galleries held fifteen individual cells with large barred windows and a good-sized room with wash basins, showers, and toilets. There were workshops, a school, stores in the basement, two infirmaries, and a pavilion for public functions that was turned into a chapel. Each cell held a bed, a small wardrobe, a table, and chair. In 1939 there were eleven or twelve women in each cell and no furniture at all. There were mats or straw mattresses for the women and nothing more. All trace of the original purpose of the rooms had disappeared. The place had been transformed into a gigantic storehouse, a storehouse of women without food, water, or sanitary assistance. How could they provide meals twice a day to the many thousands of women heaped in there when the kitchen had been designed for a maximum of 500 people?

When the expeditions to the prisons slowed down and the number of prisoners decreased, they organized the school and workshop. Still, there were beds only in the infirmaries and the wider areas of the gallery where the old women gathered. The school and shop eventually lent a kind of rhythm to life, but at the bottom of everything hunger still lurked. And even though the offensive smells that characterized prison life in 1939 and 1940 gradually went away with the zeal for cleanliness, the vague smell of people not well enough washed, of cold food, and of disinfectant lingered.

During my imprisonment in Ventas there was no intellectual stimulation at all. Books were nonexistent. The prison library had suffered attack by successors to the Inquisitor Torquemada.[1] Among the books they burned were the *Episodios nacionales* by the nineteenth-century novelist, Benito Perez Galdós.[2] Nothing more need be said about the ruling state of mind. But, of course, there was no room to hold books in that crowded prison, nor any place where we could organize classes or people to teach. Truthfully, we were too hungry and too cold to find the energy for study.

I want to pay homage to the first gallery to the right that held the women condemned to death. Here Matilde Landa, herself condemned to death, struggled with a group of courageous companions to help, within the bounds of military law, the some 189 women who occupied the so-called gallery of death. Matilda was a well-educated woman with connections to the director of the prison, Carmen de Castro. Matilde's father had been one of the founders of the Free Institution of Education in 1876,[3] and Carmen had been a student there. So Matilde asked the director for permission to set up an office in the gallery for the purpose of preparing formal requests for review of cases. The director gave her a cell for an office and typewriters that she and the prisoners who helped her could use.

As soon as a condemned woman arrived, Matilde would advise her of her rights and make a request for review according to the laws of the Republic, which Franco had not abolished. Of course no judge dared utilize these laws and the military tribunals simply disregarded them. But Matilde did see the possibility of recourse. And it is true that she saved many women from the firing squad. Matilde also inspired hope in the condemned women and their families. After all, of what use were lawyers? We only saw them at the trial and then they were useless; sometimes they even pointed out things that hadn't occurred to the prosecutor.

Matilde also succeeded in getting permission for the prisoners to see visitors face to face rather than through bars. Visiting hours were from eight to half past eight in the morning. Matilde prepared the requests for visits and told the families where to go and what they must do. What comfort it was for families to be able to visit a loved one condemned to death, something that was not possible in any other prison, only in Ventas. Yes, Matilde was a great woman. But I think she came to a strange end.

In the early years we had little information from the outside world, but we did know about and discuss the problem of the German-Soviet pact. Paradoxically, World War II helped us organize; we managed to get propaganda and study material, which gave the women a clearer idea of events and created a close connection between us and the outside organization. We became aware that in spite of their discontent people outside continued to mobilize themselves and maintain their sense of struggle and indomitable fighting. Regardless of desertions, personality conflicts, and personal ambitions—and there were many of them—the spirit of struggle and self-denial was kept alive.

I had been transferred to Amorebieta by the time World War II ended. What emotion we felt on hearing about the liberation of Paris and the end of the war! What emotion there was in Amorebieta, where we lacked all human contact with the outside, when the director, who was a good person, had us lined up to hear the news that the Soviet troops had entered Berlin and a peace treaty had been signed in Europe!

Fearing the reaction of the oblate nuns, who were ferocious functionaries in the prison, the director ingeniously asked us to pray the "Our Father" for those who had fallen on both sides.

When we learned in Amorebieta that Franco's position had been consolidated by international support, all of us women, whatever our party, felt a heavy weight on our hearts. We knew that we would have to complete our sentences unless there were changes inside Spain. But we also thought that the foreign governments supporting Franco would do what they could to see that he lived up to his name as the so-called sentinel of Christian civilization.

From Amorebieta I was sent to Segovia, which was a central prison. Here they managed to have books available, usually simple novels that the priest carefully censored and some work or other of history. At least we could read in groups while our hands were busy with the endless needlework that brought in a little money to buy toothpaste, cotton for sanitary purposes—though many young women didn't menstruate because of their hunger—stamps so we wouldn't lose contact with our families, who were the only ones authorized to write us, and a little food, poor in quality and high in price, which turned out to benefit the prison officials more than the prisoners.

The situation in Segovia was very tense, however. The living conditions were impossible. Then suddenly on January 16, 1948, we were informed that the office was expecting the imminent arrival of a Chilean woman who was writing a thesis on penal systems throughout the world. This woman had friends among Spanish intellectuals in exile, and apparently there had been discussion about whether the spirit of Don Quixote[4] was still alive in Spain and whether the Spanish people truly accepted Franco's regime. The exiles had told her: "Try to see the prisons. You will discover how many quixotic spirits there are in Spain."

When the woman came to Spain, she presented the authorities with evidence of her visits to facilities in other countries and asked to visit women's prisons in particular. The Ministry granted her permission to visit one prison for an entire day and to talk with the prisoners without interference from the officials.

We found out that she was due to arrive because on that day they gave us sheets, which of course we never had, cleaned up the infirmary, and even took off the bedspreads that hadn't been washed for months. The authorities tried to give us uniforms, but we refused them; the sheets we took, thinking, "Man, these are ours." We didn't believe that the visitor would be allowed to spend the entire day with us so we agreed to have a spokeswoman ready in each room to answer the woman's questions. We tried to have well-educated women like lawyers and professors set to speak for us.

But the visitor didn't come alone; the prison officials, the doctor, and the priest were with her. First she was taken to the hall for common criminals, then to the area that held the old women; the functionaries wanted to convince her that the rest of the prison was the same, but she insisted on seeing the other halls where the political prisoners were. When they came into the third gallery, all of us were lined up in orderly fashion. The visitor stopped in front of Merché Gómez, a self-possessed young woman from Madrid. Merché began by explaining that she was a prisoner whose death sentence had been commuted. To the visitor's first questions, Merché responded that it wasn't possible to speak frankly about the prisons because the visitor had come with the backing of the fascist regime. Then she said: "But I'm ready to talk. Ask what you want and I'll answer you with no thought for what might happen tomorrow."

The woman asked her many questions about the system in prison, and Merché explained everything: how they gave us injections without boiling the syringes; how we had to dry our clothing by piling it up on a railing; how there was no running water and only two toilets for all of us women; how the sheets on our beds were given us just this day to impress her. Merché went on and on talking about prison life, and then she told the woman that, please, if she wanted to know Spain, she ought to visit the suburbs, by herself. The woman remarked that from what she had seen the people didn't live so badly and she didn't understand why there was still armed resistance against the Franco regime. Merché answered that she herself took part in guerrilla activities in the city; that the prisons were crammed with women arrested for clandestine activities; that people feared for their lives because the repression was brutal; that even though government control made full-scale resistance impossible, the spirit of resistance was still alive; and that even though the threat of incarceration was ever present, many people made sacrifices that kept the flame of rebellion alive in Spain. Merché invited her to visit ordinary people and gave her the address of a sister of hers who lived in the ghetto in Tetuán de las Victorias in Madrid; there the Falange had constructed a fence around an area where people were left to live as they could in collectives—families had only one room to themselves and shared a dining room, wash room, and kitchen. There the visitor would see people who had no place to live because their houses had been destroyed by bombs. There, Merché said, the woman would find the spirit of the people, not in the company of María Topete, the daughter of marquises and a Falangist to her bones. By this time the priest was furious: "In a Communist regime they would shoot you for what you're saying."

Merché answered: "And we don't know what will happen this afternoon when this lady leaves."

By now the Chilean woman was visibly unsettled. She asked the director not to take measures against the prisoner; after all, she was just answering her questions. Assured by the director that no sanctions would be taken against the prisoner, the visitor hurriedly left with the officials, but not before she quickly gave us some directions: "Please, if something happens to you, I'm in such and such hotel."

In spite of the director's words we knew that the matter wasn't closed. At improvised meetings of Communists and other parties we agreed to prevent at all cost the expected punishment of Merché Gómez. We would take collective action. Merché had spoken for all of us and either all of us or none of us would be responsible.

Merché was summoned to the director's office. We prisoners became nervous. A little while went by. Then in the profound silence that reigned throughout the prison we heard a door close, a door to the cells on the first floor. Those were the cells used for punishment.

Within four hours of the woman's visit the order came: as an example, Merché Gómez was to be shot in the patio the next day.

Every woman, whether she was Communist, Socialist, or Anarchist, agreed on a plan: we would all go up to where mass was said in the patio, surround Merché and say that if they shot her they'd have to shoot all of us because what she said was what all of us thought.

Officials from all the prisons around Segovia, including the men's prison, arrived. They beat us with whips and clubs. Bunched together, we tried to protect our chests and heads. Women vomited blood. We agreed to go back to our cells, but we weren't done. We called a hunger strike for four days in hopes that Madrid would hear about the terrible happenings in Segovia. Many of the women were already so worn down from lack of nourishment that the strike almost killed them. They had to be carried to the infirmary and revived with glucose. When the medical inspector, a Dr. Botija from Ventas hospital, made his report, he wrote that the smell of acetone was noticeable, a clear indication that the women were living on their last organic reserves.

As further punishment for our actions, the officials took everything out of our cells: mattresses, clothes, everything. Some women were left in those empty cells for three weeks, others for six, while some were kept in isolation until September. On Friday, the twenty-eighth, Dr. Botija went in one of the cells. There wasn't even one light or a peephole in the door; the women were locked away in absolute darkness. The doctor was so upset he almost fainted and had to go outside to a small bar facing the prison for a cognac.

In spite of this harsh treatment we felt we had won: Merché got out of solitary confinement at the same time as the other women.

So now the question is whether there is any compensation for our suffering. For the loss of our youth. For the sadness and the loneliness. What would be our sincere reply if each one of us were to ask the question that Joaquina, one of the minors who were condemned to death, asked. How horrendous it is to hear a twenty-year-old girl sentenced to die ask, "Is the suffering worth it?" I would like the reply to be, "Yes, the suffering was worth it."

I have faith that something positive survives from the sacrifice of those men and women; from the prisons of Franco that were never emptied of political prisoners. We keep the torch of rebellion flaming, paying the high price of lives destroyed not only by death but also by the weariness and bitterness of those long years, by the loss of the human aspect of life that slipped away between our fingers. And the reply is, "Yes, the suffering was worth it." Let me end with the words a man uttered before the military tribunal that condemned him to death and ordered him shot: "In spite of everything Spain will be reborn!"

*I'm told that the three companions, Josefina, Manoli, and Petra Cuevas, meet each month for dinner in a Madrid restaurant. They must look like three old witches in their coats, their heads wrapped in kerchiefs, and Josefina hobbling along on her crutches.*

# CHAPTER 14

# The Costs of Sacrifice:
# Antonia García at Ventas and Segovia

*Another companion I met in Ventas was Antonia García. She also came from a prison in the north, Saturrarán. I remember Toni as a sensitive, politically well-informed young woman. I also remember how much her friends respected her. Because of the torture she suffered, especially the electrical shocks that were put in her ears, Toni had cerebral attacks that left her unconscious. I came into contact with Toni again through the party's clandestine work before Franco died. I saw her again in 1978 and took her testimony. She lives in Barcelona, is married and has two grown children. She gives body massages and beauty treatments in her home. That's where I get her testimony.*

The Falangists arrested me several times, and all together I spent eleven years in prison. Since it takes a long time to tell my whole story, I'm going to paint it in large strokes. My story starts when I was a little girl and my mother took me with her to clean the Civil Guard barracks. The truth is I almost grew up in those barracks. I remember how fond the older guards were of me and how they would hold me on their knees. I wasn't even eleven years old when my mother died. The day she died she told me many things I've never forgotten; one thing was that she trusted some of those men even more than some family friends. She assured me the men would always help me and that I should do what they said. So I did become very close to them, spending lots of time at the barracks from the age of eleven to thirteen. At that age they thought I was old enough to work for them.

My job was to copy the duty sheet in the guards' room and then clean the room after they left. Following their instructions, I locked the door from the inside while I worked and never told anyone, not even my grandmother, that I saw people being tortured at the barracks. My situation was somewhat strange. On the one hand I was very friendly with the guards; while they were making their rounds they would stop by the house where I lived with my grandparents to play cards and have a cup of coffee. On the other hand I wanted to join the Communist Youth;

whenever the guards returned with political posters they had confis-
cated, I'd secretly return them to my friends. But I never joined the
party. At first, I was afraid to go against the orders of my friends, the
guards, even though I was involved in political activities that would
have gotten me in trouble. Later, a membership card just didn't matter.

The first time I was arrested, the guards went to the police station
and got me released. Later on they couldn't help me and I was finally
arrested for good. I was taken to the police station on Núñez de Balboa
street and stuck in a dark, dark dungeon. I couldn't see anything but
after a while I realized from some groaning that someone else was there.
After what seemed like a long time, a light switched on and six or more
men along with a woman and young boy were brought in. The police
began to beat the boy so hard that blood streamed from his mouth and
nose; then they stomped on his testicles and left him limp as a rag. All
the while his poor mother was crying "My son, my son." Unable to bear
the sight, she turned her face to the wall and in desperation threw herself on one of the men and scratched his whole face. The men pushed
the woman away and she fell so hard against a stone bench that one of
her eyes popped out.

I wasn't even eighteen years old when I witnessed that horror. From
that moment on I vowed that no human being would ever suffer because
of me. No matter what was done to me, I wouldn't say a word. When I
was taken out to make a statement, I was tortured until my tormentors
grew weary. They put electric currents in my ears that made me crazy
with pain for years and years. Still I said nothing. I wouldn't open my
mouth. That infuriated my torturers. They questioned me nonstop—
what had I done, where had I been, who was so and so and such and
such? But I didn't even consider making up stories. I simply refused to
talk. Whether it was from trauma or shock, I'm not sure, but I remember with absolute clarity that only one thought was in my mind: I don't
have to say anything. They tried to put electrical currents on my nipples
but I was too young to have any so they put them in my ears again. My
eardrums burst. I lost consciousness.

When I came to I was in the prison infirmary. For a month I suffered blackouts and was half out of my mind with pain. According to
doctors, the brain's neurons are always moving and if one stops, a
blackout results. I am aware that I have these blackouts, which in itself
is psychologically very upsetting.

I'll never forget the first day I spent outside the infirmary in the hall.
After the women were counted, they fell to the ground right where they
were standing, just to get a place. I was stuck next to the wall along with
many more women and that's where I stayed all night, unable to move.
I awoke to a frightening view of the life that awaited me: the place

looked like a picture of demented people with women picking lice and others scratching at their mange. "We're being changed into beasts" was my first thought.

I was placed in the room set aside for the minors, thanks to the efforts of Doña María Sánchez Arbos, who had been an administrator at the Free Institution of Education where our director, Carmen de Castro, had studied. Carmen de Castro was very moved to see this outstanding educator in the prison. Doña María refused special treatment and asked Carmen, as a human being who respected her, to treat all prisoners on an equal basis. Carmen couldn't guarantee equal treatment for so many women, but she granted Doña María's request to have a gallery set aside for the children to keep them apart from the rest of the prisoners; there the children would have a little better food, more room, and a different schedule from the other prisoners. Doña María also asked for a separate room for the many minors so as to keep them away from the large number of prostitutes.

I was one of the minors who had been arrested for opposing Casado's policy near the end of the war. After several of our friends in leadership roles were arrested, a group of us turned to clandestine activities. The *casadistas* got hold of the files of the Provincial Committee in Madrid that held information about the members of the Socialist Youth. So it was easy for them to find us. Twenty-four of us from my neighborhood were caught. All of us were minors, sixteen, seventeen, eighteen years old at most. These were the minors whose cause became notorious. In the first round of arrests about seventy-five minors were killed, including the thirteen girls made famous in this poem written by Rafaela Fernández "Rafita" on August 5, 1939, the day the girls were executed:

I

When the stars die
Green, green water . . .
A sky of blue fish
The stars have died!
Shrouded roses among the white rushes
of the dawn! The whiteness of maidens!
Ay! Green, green water . . .

II

The stars have fallen in their flight,
three stars, red
blue and yellow,
and the earth is covered with currants,
and white roses and little bells
for the stars have died . . . !
Ay! Green, green water . . .

### III

Thirteen stars have died,
thirteen vestals
from the temple of freedom
Virgins!
Who in a white cortege without uttering a cry
in the arms of death move toward infinity
Ay! Green, green water . . .

### IV

You course silently among the lichen
and nourish the fields and the garden
with eternal essences
verdure of spring!
of purity!
of grace and beauty!
Thirteen roses have rent the eternal rose garden
Ay! Green, green water . . .
Goddess of nature!

Their execution caused such a scandal that leftist groups from all over Europe organized to intervene. Their actions were grace for three of us. On August 12 twenty-four of us were sentenced to death; in September three of us had our death penalty commuted.

The authorities had granted the minors permission to study and have classes, but I wasn't able to participate because the electric shocks had left me with excruciating headaches. My ears rang, I was sick to my stomach, and my eyes hurt as if knives were being stuck in them. So I spent only a few months with the minors before I was transferred to a prison that had been set up in Quiñones for crazy people. The authorities considered us crazy if we had those splitting headaches. It's true the pain was enough to drive us crazy but we certainly weren't out of our mind.

So began years of being shuffled from one prison to another: Palma on the island of Mallorca, Amorebieta, Saturrarán, Ventas again, Segovia. So many memories, so much pain. Some are little memories but significant in their own way. There was the time we left Madrid. Our families had found out we were leaving and had come to the station to say good-bye and give us what food they could. My poor old grandmother gave me some food along with a mysterious little package. As the train pulled out, I peeked in the package: three candles and a box of matches! Why did she put these in? Didn't she know we weren't allowed to have matches and why the candles? Did she think they'd let us loose on the island? On the day they took us to Palma in the hold of a stinky, beat-up boat full of lice and every imaginable bug, a terrible storm came up. Suddenly the lights went out and we fell over one another. How frightening! Thanks to the little candles and matches my grandmother gave me, well, look, those of us who weren't as seasick as others held the candles so at least we didn't fall on each other. Ah, poor grandmother, who was going to tell you how helpful your little gift was?

It was in Mallorca that I saw Matilde Landa again, the woman who had done so much for the prisoners in Ventas. I have mixed feelings about Matilde. I was immensely grateful to her for all she had done in Ventas to get my death penalty commuted. But as a working woman I didn't understand Matilde. Oh, I knew she was intelligent, cultured, and politically idealistic, but she wasn't treated as we were. She certainly wasn't tortured like other women. Her own secretary, María Guerra, was beaten to death in a cemetery. Matilde Landa knew how to act with the police in such an intelligent way that they let her talk and were ashamed to employ certain methods with her that they applied to the rest of us.

But Matilde was considered to be dangerous just because she was intelligent and cultured with connections in high political places. So she was transferred to Mallorca. There the prison officials pretended to treat her as an equal so as to get her on their side. But she saw through their game. The fact is that you were either for them or against them. She was against them but she wanted to be their equal. For that she was brought down.

Two days before she died, the officials let her leave her cell and spend some time with us. Matilde said to me: "What do you think, these people want to baptize me, but I'm not going to be baptized."

A lady who was president of Catholic Action[1] in Palma had befriended Matilde. She spent a great deal of time with Matilde and gave her things to ease her life in prison that Matilde then passed on to the children and old people. The day they wanted to baptize her, Matilde told me she would like to make the Catholic lady happy because she was a good person and Matilde had become very fond of her. "Look, Matilde," I said, "I'm an uneducated woman, but if I were you, I wouldn't even talk with that woman. Leave her in her place and you in yours. You can't be friends in this place, truly you can't. You're going to find yourself in a dead-end street. You're very intelligent and probably what I'm telling you is just nonsense. Who am I compared to you? Nothing."

The next day Matilde Landa threw herself out the window. At least that's what the officials said. No one saw her do it. She could just as well have been thrown out. Who knows? What I do know is that Matilde was an emotionally stable person. She wouldn't have lost her mind. I think that at the last moment she preferred death to renouncing the principles she had fought for.

In Palma and later in Ventas we were able to earn a little money for extra food and books by doing handwork. Catholic Action had organized an office with some prisoners and a nun who had connections with the outside. The specialty in those days was knit items. We were paid by the skein. A certain percentage of what each of us earned went to our "family," which is what we called the group of women who shared money and packages. While the rest of the women sat in a circle knitting, one of us would read the books we were permitted to buy. The best readers read for two hours each day, taking turns every half hour. After the reading we would discuss what we had heard. Our library was what you could call ambulatory. We even had a librarian who kept a record of who had which book. When a book had been read by all the prisoners, it was raffled off; in that way each prisoner had her own book.

Study was important to us, and we organized classes for the women who couldn't read and write. We wanted all the women to be literate. Our program was successful because there were well-educated, professional women among the prisoners. Some of the prisoners went so far as to take examinations for careers.

When I returned to Ventas, the workshops that had made military clothing were being converted to civilian use. Accordingly, the prison officials set up shops in the prison basement and used prison labor to make money. But we managed to use the shops to our own advantage: we smuggled articles of clothing out for the guerrillas.

We also used our wits in the matter of social service. Supposedly all women under the age of thirty were to do social service. Falangist ladies were in charge of this social work and they would take us to work in their homes everyday. We decided to resist in a novel way: we'd act like dummies. When they tried to teach us to make little figures out of felt, we ruined meter after meter of the material. So they tried us with paper . . . failure again. Then it was sewing; I don't remember how many handkerchiefs I ruined trying to learn the hemstitch. The only thing we did well was discuss politics. We would ask the Falangist ladies to explain their politics and then demonstrate why they would never achieve the revolution according to the Falangist agenda or how they were nothing more than Franco's puppets.

When employment in the prison shops came to an end, we were able to arrange embroidery work through a certain Swiss man. The items we embroidered using all kind of stitches were of invaluable craftsmanship. One day when the truck from the man came for the work we had done, some of the Falangist ladies happened to come by and see our work. "Who made these items?" they asked.

It turned out that the women responsible for the exquisite handwork were all from the gallery of Communists. Those ladies almost went crazy when they realized how we had mocked them. But look, we had women who had been seamstresses for Balenciaga, a woman who had specialized in embroidering evening gowns, others who had held office in sewing and tailoring unions. Spain's best seamstresses were in our prison. That's why the Swiss man had come our way.

I wish I'd had a camera when those ladies realized how we had pulled their leg. At the expression on their faces, we asked innocently: "Has the regime fallen?" Then we gave them a lecture.

"It's clear to us that you came here thinking you would teach us. But you forget that we are people of the working class. We're workers. We know how to cook and sew and embroider. These are our jobs. Most of us are here in prison precisely because we have a history as workers who have been outstanding in our jobs since before the war began. Those people stood out because they knew their profession and enjoyed respect from other people. Here we do first-rate work and earn something to help ease the misery of prison."

That same day they brought out a Santa Claus doll that was a full half meter in size with its pocket filled with felt dolls. The woman who created it already had won two international prizes and had received many, many commissions. And she was one of the prisoners who didn't know how to make even a felt poppy! The ladies were speechless. We continued: "You've offended us because you presumed to teach us. It's possible you can teach us other things, but to work like workers, certainly not. Maybe you think you wouldn't have found out if it hadn't been for the Swiss man. Oh, no. We'd been planning to bring you a sample of our work after our social service was over. We needed to teach you that you don't know the women you label 'Reds' and that even when you're around us, you don't know us. So you see—it's ignorance that keeps this regime afloat. You do what you're told and nothing else."

After the hunger strike I was held incommunicado for six months. During that time news came that my request for freedom had been granted. But the local officials refused to release me because I was being punished. So I had to put in another year. Apparently a relative of mine had been responsible for the many, many telegrams and telephone calls that the disciplinary committee received. The director called me every two or three days telling me to make a written declaration that I repented, but each time he called, I said: "Look, I've been unjustly imprisoned for eleven years and I'm not going to dishonor myself now by repenting, not even if you ask me fifty times. I've spent all these years thinking that the only thing you couldn't take away from me was my dignity. I'm not going to lose my dignity now just so you'll set me free. I'm not going to sign that document."

During the many years I spent in prison, I've seen all kinds of women on both sides: directors who were hypocritical, violent, or gross and prisoners with nothing but revenge in their hearts. But I never wanted anyone to have to suffer as I did and others did. I have always thought it was my duty to combat a regime that would persecute its citizens and that I could not stop struggling for one moment to bring down that regime and create a different society. But we should never do to them what they did to us. I am in complete agreement with the politics of reconciliation. I have agreed to speak about our experience so that it may serve as an example to others and help them realize the fascist nature of this dictatorship.

I am ready to be a living testimony. What I ask of young people is for them to do whatever possible to make sure that the horrors of the past are not repeated. I have seen so many women die; I have seen so many brave people disappear; I have seen the sacrifice of marvelous people who dedicated their entire life to changing society. Now it's not a matter of weeping for those who died or avenging their death. No, but in the name of all these men and women I ask each and every person who realizes the need to change society to rise up and take the place of those we lost. We will succeed when the absence of those lost in battle is no longer noticeable.

*Toni died in 1991 or 1992.*

Tomasa Cuevas and Mary E. Giles collaborating on the English version of the text in Tomasa's home in Vilanova i la Geltrú, Spain.

The young Tomasa, first row, right, with companions in prison.

Rosario Sánchez Mora, the "Dynamiter," as she appears much later in Barcelona.

María del Carmen Cuesta, second row, fifth from left, and companions present an artistic production at the prison in Gerona.

Pilar Pascual Martínez, second row, far right, is with friends in the prison of Amorebieta on a rare "holiday," or day of grace.

Over a good lunch, Pilar Pascual and Tomasa recall the days in Amorebieta
when breakfast was dirty water.

In the top row on the far right, wearing a white blouse, is Antonia García with a group of her companions whose death sentences had been commuted. Taken in the prison of Palma de Mallorca in 1940, the photo also shows Matilde Landa, third to the left from Antonia, the woman who worked on behalf of the prisoners at Ventas.

In the prison of Les Corts are Tomasa, first row, second from left, with her prison family, Mercedes, Adelaida, and Victoria, second row, third, fourth, fifth from left, respectively.

From left to right, Angelita Ramis, Victoria Pujolar, and Adelaida Abarca, enjoying the fruits of freedom in Toulouse after their escape from Les Corts.

Years later in Burgos, Tomasa, María Valés, and Soledad Real recall the long fight for amnesty for political prisoners.

Tomasa's friendship with Victoria Martínez (now dead) continued after their days in prison as the two women traveled the same road to Burgos to visit their husbands who were imprisoned there.

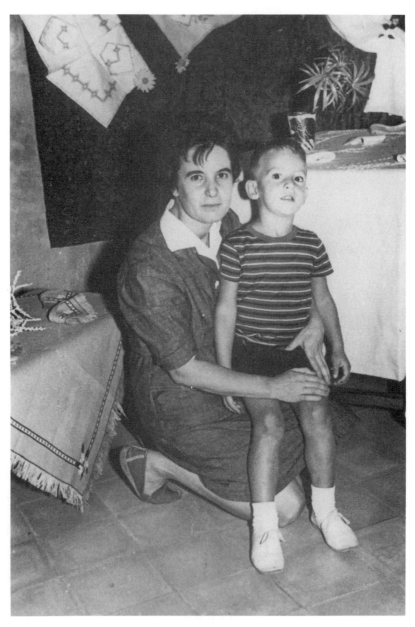

On the rare day that visitors were allowed Esperanza Martínez enjoyed the company of a nephew.

A typical workshop in prison where women worked as their only means to reduce their sentences.

# PART 2

# *Resistance and Prison*

Map by Robert Richardson, California State University, Sacramento

# CHAPTER 15

# A Stranger in a Strange City
# 1944–1945

My appearance in Barcelona didn't make waves. After I left my miserable suitcase in the checkroom at the station, I went to the city center and walked all around to orient myself as best I could. With only thirty-five pesetas in my pocket, I couldn't afford to spend money. Most of the day I spent looking for work. At last at a fruit stand in the Boquería market in the Ramblas I was given the address of a house where they needed help. I found my way there and spoke with the lady of the house. Apparently I made a good impression. She offered me a job and I accepted the salary.

The woman told me to come back the following day at nine in the morning. But I insisted several times on starting right away; I wanted to stay there that night. By then it was after six o'clock. The lady asked if anything was wrong and I explained that yes, I had run away from home. I told her I was from another town—I don't remember if I said it was Toledo or some other place in Castile—and that my family wanted to marry me to a cousin just for the sake of combining the small lands the families owned. I continued with my story that the family couldn't force me to marry against my will because I was of age. I had left home and now I found myself without a place to stay in Barcelona. Good Catholic that she was, the lady crossed herself and said: "Oh, my poor little one, so that's why you want to spend the night here. Well, yes, my child, but don't you have anything, not even a bundle?"

"Yes, mam, I have a little suitcase at the station."

"Well, dear, run and get it, go on, but come right back. Barcelona has turned into a bad place and I don't want you to get mixed up with some of the girls around here."

That night I slept under a roof, happy to have found work. It's not that I liked hiring out for housework, but I didn't worry. I knew I would do well in the housework and later we'd see. Gloria had given me addresses of people in Barcelona who might be able to help me get other work.

Bene, my friend from prison, continued to be a worry to me. I didn't know what had happened to her or how to find her. So the next day I found an excuse to leave the house and go to the police station to see if she had checked in with them and given her address. The police weren't very helpful: so many people had presented themselves that the police didn't even know which list she might be on.

Some things are incredible but true. After two or three days of housework that involved ironing and lots of washing and mopping the house and the owners' leather goods store with lye, my hands developed awful sores. The boy who cleaned and greased the locks early in the morning saw me mopping the store one day and noticed my bleeding fingers. He knocked at the grille of the door and asked in a low voice: "Did you just get out of prison?" I said I hadn't, but he answered: "Look, my sister got out recently and she's got hands like yours from doing housework. So you can't fool me. Besides there's another very young girl at the corner bar who was just released."

The incredible happened: the girl turned out to be Bene. We managed to spend Sundays together. I would tell my employers that I was going to mass and then I'd meet Bene and we'd go for a little walk. Bene explained that when she was released in Segovia, she asked permission, just as I had done, to stay over in Guadalajara in order to visit some aunts and uncles. But the authorities had denied her request because permission had to come from the Barcelona police. So Bene continued toward her destination, a destination without family or friends or anyone, to a large city she didn't know—all this for a girl who had never been separated from her mother until the moment she was transferred from Ventas to Segovia.

When Bene appeared before the police and they asked her for her residence, she answered that she had no family and no place to live. They took her file and suggested she go to the large market in the Ramblas where she probably could find housework. Bene followed their advice. She went from place to place. But she didn't find a job. And she didn't have a place to spend the night. Night surprised her still out on the street.

Fortunately she met a kindly night watchman who gave her protection in the concierge room. The next morning he found out on his rounds of the bars in the neighborhoods of Barcelona's old quarter that a girl was needed with a family on Baños Nuevos street. He himself took her there. When her employers discovered that she was just out of prison, they agreed she should go to the police station with her address. The police advised her to appear at the station on the first Sunday of every month. I had found out earlier that we were in the precinct of Ancha street. I persuaded Bene to change from the station on Vía Layetana to the Ancha one because I'd heard horror stories from Catalan comrades about the tortures they had suffered at the hands of the Creix brothers, Poloco and Quintela,[1] at the Vía Layetana station. Antonio and Vicente Juan Creix belonged to the secret police in Barcelona and were responsible for the torture of prisoners at police headquarters. So were Eduardo Quintela and Poloco, or Polo, who were both commissars in the hated Political-Social Brigade.

So many exprisoners had to appear at the same time each month that there were long lines of men and women waiting to sign their names in the appropriate book. It was especially painful to see the men because they had fewer opportunities for work than we women. At least we could start out with housework. But when the men who applied for work at factories and for construction showed their papers with the words "libertad vigilada," which was something like parole, they wouldn't be hired. Weakened from hunger, poorly clothed, desperate, some of the men even said that they preferred prison to exile. One day a certain boy failed to appear with the group of us waiting to check in with the police. We found out he had been arrested for stealing food. One of our comrades said furiously: "That's what these assassins want, to evict us from our homes, close the doors to work, and force us to steal. Above all else we're political people and we have to defend our rights." He told us we didn't have to be criminals because that's what the authorities wanted us to be. The man's cadaverous face lit up with this truth. How well I remember that face. I don't recall his name and I don't know what happened to him, but whenever possible he would gather people around him and tell them it was better to die of hunger in the street than be sent back to prison as thieves. If we died in the streets, he said, people would realize that we were being thrown out of prison with no rights at all, left to die of hunger or steal and be imprisoned as common criminals.

During that period of four weeks all of us women who had housework would take something from our employers' kitchens, a little can of preserves, chunks of bread, tobacco, anything we could get away with, for the men on the streets. We women would meet to pool what we had taken and then on Sundays on the way to mass we'd meet the men some place and give them the little packages. Bene was able to get away with lots of little things because there were always appetizers left over in the bar: croquettes, little meat pies, sandwiches, things like that. It was a nightmare for us whenever we sat down to eat in the kitchen.

In the meantime I made friends with a marvelous woman who worked in the house opposite my employers'. Carmen was a wonderful person and she offered to share her shanty on the Diagonal with Bene and me. So Bene and I moved to Carmen's shanty. Bene quit her job and I started work at a tailor shop that a friend in prison had recommended.

The drawback was the owner asked me to join the union so that he wouldn't be fined and have his shop closed. I knew party members weren't supposed to unionize and that the party had ousted members for joining unions. I preferred to leave the job until such time as I would find the party. So on Monday I phoned the shop with some excuse and didn't go back to work there.

Then I looked up a friend of a countryman of mine who owned a shop that made and sold children's underclothes.

"Here you have a job," he said right away. "Come whenever you want."

"This very day."

That very day I did begin work. There were several electric sewing machines as well as two pedal ones. I used a pedal machine. I worked twelve hours with fifteen or twenty minutes off for rest and a sandwich. I was anxious to get in extra hours. The first night I took home a big package with clothing for Bene to sew little bows on.

Our health was improving, but life was mainly work, work, and more work. I remember that just seeing people lined up at the movies stirred me to rebellion. I would think about the prisoners and friends I'd left in prison, about the people they would shoot or had shot already that very morning, about the police stations where our companions were tortured. And seeing people dressed up in the evening for parties, I wondered how Spaniards could live like that and why they weren't capable of fighting and thinking about the thousands and thousands of prisoners all over the country. At that time there were so many prisons stuffed with prisoners that I couldn't understand why people didn't fight on their behalf. I thought about how much good the money wasted on movies could do for the prisoners.

After one of the girls in the shop got married, I was changed from the pedal machine—I had done a lot of pedaling in my twelve hours of work a day—to a motorized machine and one of the apprentices inherited my old machine. The apprentice was a young girl, only fifteen or sixteen years old. She was the only person I had contact with at work. I found it difficult to become acquainted with the Catalans; they're more serious than Castilians and they spoke a language I didn't understand. It really hurt when we left the shop in the evenings and the other women went off in a group. They never said to me, "Let's go have a beer," as they did to each other. Perhaps I couldn't have gone because I couldn't afford such luxuries, but it would have been nice just to be invited. Now I realize that when you do become friends with a Catalan, she'll do anything in the world for you. But until she knows you and offers her friendship, you feel like a stranger in a strange land.

I didn't hide the fact that I had been in prison. Nor did the shop owner; he'd been imprisoned, too. One Saturday after this young girl had discovered I had been in prison, she drew me aside and invited me to Sunday dinner with her sister and brother-in-law. I told her I'd let her know in the afternoon. I didn't know whether to accept the invitation or not. I hardly knew her. But I finally decided to accept; perhaps I'd meet a comrade.

I wasn't wrong about that. The brother-in-law turned out to be a comrade in the party. He didn't get to the heart of the matter right away but talked with me first. He wanted me to tell him about prison, how we had lived and how we were getting along now. Finally everything was out in the open and he asked if I would be ready to do something for the party. I asked him why he had risked talking so openly with me when he didn't know who I was. He answered that he did know who I was because several Catalan women who had been arrested in Barcelona had been imprisoned with me. Most of them had been with me in Ventas but one, Catia Alonso, had also been in the Segovia prison. When Catia was released, she spoke to them about me. It was pure chance that his sister-in-law had gone to work in the shop and met me. I told him I was ready to do anything to work with the party. It was agreed that the girl would let me know the day and time for my meeting with a contact person.

By coincidence there was a terrible storm the very day and hour when I was supposed to keep the appointment the girl had relayed to me. In spite of the storm I hurried to the place. I even remember what I was wearing: a pleated percale skirt and a little white blouse. I was to meet the contact person on the Diagonal at the corner of Aribau. I waited and waited. All the while rain poured down and the wind blew furiously. I couldn't let go of my skirt or it would have blown over my head. After half an hour I was soaked to the skin. No one ever came. Finally I went home.

During the following days the girl didn't say a word to me in the shop, nor did I mention anything to her, even though I was furious at the effort they had cost me. So I chalked up the failure to unreliability on the part of my comrades.

The next Sunday Bene and I were in the streetcar on our way to Carmen's when Bene noticed a young woman in the streetcar. "Don't you know that girl?" she asked me. I had difficulty recognizing the girl but Bene knew who she was. "It's Pura. Don't you remember Pura?"

Bene recognized her immediately because she had spent more time with her in prison than I had. Bene and I agreed not to get out until Pura did. We went past our stop and got off with Pura. We set off walking behind her. Then Pura realized she was being followed. She turned around and recognized Bene. "You, here, Bene?"

She was slow to recognize me. But she did, and then the three of us chatted for a while. It was clear to Bene and me that Pura was in a better position than we were. She invited us to have a snack in a nearby cafe and get out of the rain. She and I agreed to meet another time. That's when I told her about the failed meeting. "Don't worry," she said. "I'll find out if that contact was really from the party. At any rate, if you like, you can work with us."

Of course, I had no doubts whatsoever about Pura's reliability. A few days later we met again and Pura told me not to worry: the contact had been certain I wouldn't be able to make the appointment because of the storm. So it was that in September I finally found what I had been looking for since May.

Life was very difficult for Bene and me during the last months of 1944. As party work increased, I worked less and made less money. But Bene knew nothing of my clandestine activities; I wouldn't compromise her by telling her anything. I made sure she never missed a meal. Even though we were very poor, I was happy because I could carry my head high: my work was honorable.

On December 24 I didn't go to work. My comrades had commissioned me to carry food packages to the prisoners in the Model prison. They gave me an address where I was to pick up the packages. Seeing how many packages there were I asked one of the men: "How am I supposed to carry all this? Do you think I'm a pack mule? I can't carry these packages, not even on the streetcar. I'll have to use a car or pay for a taxi."

"Well, my girl, I don't have money for a taxi and I don't have a car."

We began to discuss how I could take the packages. Perhaps I could make several trips to the prison. What to do? Suddenly he had an idea. Another comrade who had gone to bed very late after attending a meeting just might have taxi money. He hated to wake the fellow up but he had to.

"Antoñito, Antonio," I heard him say. "Wake up. There's a woman here who's supposed to take the packages, but there's just one problem. She can't take all those packages by herself. She'll have to pay for a taxi and I'm broke."

I heard a voice from the room: "Hold on, I'm coming."

A young man came out, not very tall but not short either, very thin, with curly black hair, and very good looking. You could say it was love at first sight. I remember he was wearing tattered pajamas with a hole in the shoulder. But he made a tremendous impression on me.

"Comrade," he said, "I've known you for a long time. I've seen you several times from a distance at some of the appointments you've had.

Besides, my comrades talk about you, especially Moises."

Taking out money for the taxi, he told the other man to help carry the packages to the door. When we were about to go down stairs, "Antoñito" asked: "Hey, Peque, you don't have anyone here?"

"No."

"No family?"

"No."

"Well, what are you doing tonight?"

"Nothing, I will stay at home with the friend I live with."

"So is there someone with you?"

"Yes, a girl who got out of prison and is living with me in the shanty."

"Good, well tonight the two of you won't be alone. You'll eat with us."

I accepted—I liked that fellow.

That evening we were having a very good time when the blow struck. I had taken a real liking to that boy when I saw him in the morning with his tousled hair, sleepy-eyed, and in torn pajamas. That night in between all the customary toasts for democracy, liberty, socialism, the family, and on and on, they also toasted his sweetheart. "For Maruja, may she get better and may you be able to join her one day."

I felt as if a bucket of cold water had been thrown on me. So he had a sweetheart. But we still had a pleasant evening. Among the many things we talked about, aside from singing, laughing, and telling jokes, was my situation. This young man was truly concerned about everyone. He asked how I was getting along financially; he thought I was too thin, very pale, and sickly looking. I told him I wasn't sick but I was worn out and didn't have enough food to put on weight. I was working for the two of us; Bene made very little money sewing bows on little shirts. Bene and I stayed the night there and in the morning as we were leaving, he said: "Okay, I've spoken with my companions and you're going to have one less burden. Bene will live here. She'll be one more family member. She can help with housework. They can't pay her, but she'll have food and we'll take care of her clothing needs."

The truth is that they did take a load off my shoulders. Seeing that he was a person with whom I could speak candidly about my worries, I told him how disgusting my situation at work was because the owner had been trying to get me to go out with him—and he was a married man! He promised to do all he could so I could quit the job.

Toward the end of December the shanties were torn down. Fortunately, Carmen secured through her employer's influence one of the residences the unions were building in the Meridiana. We moved between Christmas and New Year's. The utilities weren't hooked up yet, there were puddles everywhere, and the street was full of ditches. But the place was a palace compared to the shanty.

In January of 1945 I quit my job in the tailor shop and started work in the Cottet factory assembling glasses. I worked there until April. I was able to do more and more party work now that I didn't have the worry of Bene and could limit my work day to eight hours. I was a contact person between the party and the guerrillas. It was risky business. I knew that if I was caught I would be tortured and could get the death penalty or at the very least thirty years in prison.

In the early months of 1945 with the Allied advances there was intense contact between the party and the guerrillas. So many Spaniards were fighting with the Allied forces to destroy Nazism that we were sure those Spaniards, thousands and thousands of them armed, would cross the border and liberate us too. The guerrillas in the mountains were preparing for that event while the party was working within the country.

I remember one trip I made in this effort to the province of Gerona. I went to the city by train and from there I took a bus for a little village. The bus stopped at a small pension in that town. I got off with my big bag. The first thing I was going to do was get a room for the night; the bus wasn't scheduled to return to Gerona until the following day. But when I got off the bus I noticed a man who didn't seem to be waiting for any of the passengers; he stood looking at me in a most interested way. I asked for a room in the pension. They gave me one with a window facing the street. I looked out the window. I didn't see anyone. My suspicions about the man must be wrong. I went outside to walk to the address where I was to identify myself with the password. As I turned the corner of the pension, I saw the same man I'd seen when I got off the bus. Bad business. I walked around and around the town. I went in a market and bought who knows what. I went out. There he was again. I went in a dairy and drank a glass of milk. I went out and met him again. That bothered me so badly that I went back to the pension. At supper time I went out again. I walked around the town. I didn't see the man. Then, making some moves that we used in clandestine work to make sure no one was following us, I went to the house designated for the meeting. Imagine my surprise when the person who opened the door was the very man who'd been following me. I must have changed color, for he said: "I made a serious mistake. I realized that you were on the verge of not coming, so after you went in the pension for the second time I left so you could make sure no one was following you. We are cautious to the point that I had to verify whether you were alone. But all I accomplished was raising your suspicions that I might be the police. Forgive me. It won't happen again. This has been a real lesson for me."

That evening the friends gave the heavy bag I'd been carrying to a young guerrilla from the mountains. This house was the support point for his group. The next day I returned to Barcelona.

Whenever I traveled by train, I tried to sit in the car with the Civil Guard. I would pretend to be very naive and ask them if I could sit in the same car with them because I was traveling alone and would feel safer with them. They would puff up like roosters with their hens. "Yes, yes, of course. Sit down, sit here." They would offer to put my bag in the baggage compartment, but I'd say: "No, that's all right, it's fine here." Then I'd put the bag on the seat next to me, leaning my arms on it, or on the floor next to my legs. So I traveled around under the protection of the Civil Guard.

I was very worried about living in Carmen's house with her daughter because if something were to happen with the work I was doing, Carmen would be in danger too. I couldn't go to the police with the truth about what the woman meant to us, how she had opened up her home to me, and that she knew nothing of my activities. She would end up in prison and maybe her little girl, too, who was only fifteen or sixteen years old at the time. Because "Antoñito" was the party member I knew best, I asked him if he would please inquire among his comrades about finding me another place to live. That's how I came to rent a room on Sepúlveda street from Antonio del Amo's sister. But I didn't tell Bene where I was living because I didn't want to put her at risk. Still, she managed to find out.

The stories I could tell about underground life! Some of them are even funny. I remember one night we were sticking posters on walls, trees, wherever we could. We were in the act of pasting one on a wall when the night watchman appeared. I put my back to the poster, which was already up, and my companion got real close to me, as if we were lovers. The watchman passed close by, looked at us, and said: "Huh, if you were my daughter, I'd give you a little spanking, out on the streets at this hour of the night, you shameless girl."

In March there was a small number of arrests. "Antoñito" had to leave the house where he stayed. I was asked to pick him up and take him to Carmen's boarding house. Carmen and I had become close friends, and she was aware of my clandestine work. I trusted her enough to tell her that a boy was coming to live in the small vacant room she had, but I didn't explain who he was. I was supposed to meet him on Muntaner at the corner of the Gran Vía. I saw a man crossing the street. By the way he walked I knew it was "Antoñito." I looked again. No, it wasn't. I kept on walking. By this time the man had caught up with me. He grabbed me by the shoulder: "Where are you going? Weren't you expecting me?"

"Me? Expecting you?"

Then I burst out laughing. I recognized his voice. But in the few days since I'd last seen him he had let his mustache grow and with the hat and the strange glasses he was wearing I didn't recognize him. His own mother wouldn't have known him.

March was drawing to a close. In spite of all our precautions we didn't realize that some of us, including me, were being followed.

# CHAPTER 16

# *The Exile of Prison:*
# *Les Corts 1945–1946*

April 4, 1945. I worked all day at the factory so I didn't know anything about the arrests and shootings in the street. Returning from work, I was just about to go in the door when I realized there was someone by the tree in front of the door. Then I saw another guy in the entrance where the shoe repairman worked. Just as I went in the door, the man in the entrance hall came out with a pistol in his hand and stuck it in my cheek. The one on watch by the tree put another pistol in my back.

"What is this?" I asked, turning sideways.

"Come on, take us to your flat."

"Flat? I don't have a flat. I've got a room."

"Whatever!"

They began to search the pockets of my jacket.

"What do you think, that I'm carrying bombs?"

"You're mixed up in this business."

"Me, mixed up with bombs? You're on the wrong track."

They told me to be quiet and go upstairs. I went up to the mezzanine where I lived and knocked at the door. Creix opened it. He and another policeman were already there, their guns on the table, sitting with poor María. They asked me where I was coming from.

"From work, from the factory."

"Show us your room."

When we entered the room, there was another policeman, sitting on my bed. "So why did you ask me where my room was when you'd already invaded it?"

They began a thorough search. Fortunately, they didn't find anything. There was an armoire that was always locked.

"This armoire?"

"It's not mine; it belongs to the woman who owns the house."

"Call her and tell her to open it."

"María, bring the key to the armoire. These gentlemen want to know what your brother has inside it."

I knew the armoire belonged to her brother, Antonio del Amo. He kept his materials for developing photographs there. Antonio was a fan of photography and movies. During the war he had made films for the Republican Army. Afterward he was imprisoned by the Franco regime. Since his release he had been a cinematographic director. There was a knock at the door. I intended to open it, but Creix said to me: "No, no, today you've got servants to open doors for you."

He himself went to the door. My blood turned to ice when I heard Bene's voice.

"Who are you looking for?" Creix asked.

"I'm sorry, I made a mistake."

I breathed a sigh of relief. It didn't last long. Creix was too astute. He kept asking her questions and harassing her until he got her to admit that she had come looking for me. He grabbed her by the arm and pushed her into the room. My first impulse was to deny that I knew the girl. On the other hand, I thought it might complicate matters even more. I immediately thought about the comrade she had in her home. I didn't know whether the police could get to him through her and then use him to find the others. In short, I was afraid I'd risk everything with a lie. That's when I noticed Bene was carrying an empty milk can.

"Why didn't you bring the milk? How are we going to have break-fast in the morning?"

The men looked at one another, saying: "What, what's this?"

"Since I get home late from work, it's her job to buy milk."

"Well, where does she live?"

"Here, with me."

I had a double bed in the room so two people could have slept there.

"So she lives here with you?"

"Yes, certainly, the two of us live here."

María looked at us very surprised.

"Listen, mam," Creix said to María, "does this girl live here?"

"No, she doesn't live here and I don't know her."

"Ah, so she doesn't live here and you don't know her?"

I looked intently at María: "But don't you understand that these men will treat you the same whether one or two of us live here? You know very well that we both live here."

"You're lying," Creix said to me. "We'll see about this at head-quarters. Let's go."

And the three of us women were taken to the Vía Layetana police station. My intention was to gain enough time with the story about Bene living with me for my comrades to find out about her arrest and vacate the house. I succeeded—but at the cost of severe beatings. They put us in the same office, separated by a couple of meters, and questioned us, one after another. To Bene: "Where do you live?"

"With her."

"Where do you live?"

"I said with her."

Then they would come to me. "Where does she live?"

"With me."

Fortunately, they didn't touch Bene because she was such a thin little thing. But they hit me so much I thought my temples and ears would burst. They would ask María: "Mam, tell the truth, do the two of them live with you?"

And pointing to me she would say: "No, she's the only one who lives with me."

I would look at her and say: "But why do you say that? Of course the two of us live with you."

Then they'd hit me again. I remember Polo. He was so small that if the two of us had hit each other with our hands free I don't know who would have won. He grabbed my head between his hands. I still remember his white shirt stained with the blood running from my gums where a tooth had been broken out. My lips were bleeding, my nose was bleeding. He kept on hitting and hitting. He was obsessed with where Bene lived. She kept answering the questions with "I live with her, I live with her."

Hour after hour went by. I think it was about nine o'clock at night when we reached headquarters. At one in the morning, or even later, we were still in that office and he was still hitting me and asking the same three questions. To María: "Do the two of them live with you?" To me: "Where does she live?" To Bene: "Where do you live?" Bene's answer: "With her." María: "This one lives alone." And I: "She lives with me." On and on. Nothing changed.

My head was spinning. There were moments when I thought I was going to faint. They hit me in the ribs, kicked me on the shins. Thank goodness they didn't touch the other two women. Once they lifted Bene out of the chair where they held her and Polo cornered her: "Look, girl, if you don't tell me right now where you live, I'm going to pull your tongue out by the roots."

He slapped her twice. She gave the name of the street and the number. I heard her perfectly, but the man who was taking down the statements on a machine didn't. He was further away and with the noise of so many policemen in the office, he couldn't hear clearly. He asked them to repeat the address. I was near him so I repeated the number, but I changed it slightly. I put a one in front of the two numbers she had given.

They stopped beating me and took us down to the basement cells. It was two in the morning, maybe later. Obviously they went to the number that had been written on the statement. They must have combed the floors from top to bottom trying to find someone who knew Bene, but they were a hundred numbers too far up the street. It was probably five in the morning when they returned and made the two of us go up to the office again. This time they didn't bother María. They asked Bene where she lived and she gave them the address. By now I wasn't worried because I was sure our comrades had escaped. They took her down again to the basement and left me. They verified with the man who was taking statements by machine that I had taken advantage of the confusion in the office to change the true number the girl had given.

I paid dearly. The police knew I was trying to gain time for friends to get out of the house where Bene lived. This time they beat me with real fury. They threw me to the floor. They picked me up by my hair. They kicked me in the ribs and kidneys. I was supposed to tell them who lived there.

"Look," I said, "you've made a mistake with me. It's true I said that girl lived with me but that's because she's sick. I lied to save her from ending up alone and out of work."

I insisted that had been my only lie and my arrest was a mistake. How could they have followed me for several days and then arrested someone who was completely different from the person they'd followed? Then they said: "So you're not the one who was with the light-hair man on the Rambla de Cataluña?"

"I don't know what you're talking about. I don't know any blond man on the Rambla de Cataluña."

"And you don't know the man in the dark red hat either? We've seen you with him more than four times."

"I don't know what you're talking about. You've arrested the wrong person. I'm not the one you're looking for. The only thing I do is go from home to work and back home again."

During one of the interrogations Antonio Creix said to me: "Look you're a fool. After five years in prison you get out and instead of finding a nice friend and living a better life you hook up with your party again."

I thought about that exprisoner who would say when we were standing in line to check in with the police: "These people exile us, the men back to jail, but this time as common criminals, and the women, to the streets, without a soul in the big capitals, without families and out of work. But we should die of hunger before these people call us common criminals." Those words went through my mind as I answered Creix: "Yes, certainly, you exile us so that later you can arrest us for turning to prostitution out of hunger and misery. But the party is in my bones. I came from my mother's womb a proletarian. I've worn myself ragged working. Leave me in peace. You've made a mistake, arresting one person for another."

Their only response was to give me details of the seven days that according to them I had been watched. But my denial was stronger and stronger. I didn't know anyone. I never had a meeting with anyone. I didn't know anything about anything. All the policemen who had taken turns following me came in, and all of them said, "Yes, certainly, she's the one." I kept on saying no, and they kept on hitting me from head to toe, everywhere on my body. I was prepared to leave my skin in the hands of those murderers before I'd reveal a name, an address, or anything that would give away my companions. Confessing doesn't free you from beatings. No, they always want to get more and more out of you. If you give them just one little clue, they keep hounding and hounding you to confess everything you know.

The second day after arrest they carried out a test. They went to Bene's previous employers and tried to find out where we'd been in Barcelona since her release from prison. I had told them the two of us had done housework on Baños Nuevos street, she in number one, a bar on the corner of what street I don't know, and I in number two, opposite her. The owners of the bar knew perfectly well that Bene had been in prison and had arrived at their house under the circumstances I've already related. And they knew I worked at the house at number two, Baños Nuevos. But I hadn't told them the truth about where I'd come from. The police's reply was that here was one more lie, like the one I'd already told about Bene living with me. They insisted we had made contact with the party before we ever got out of prison and that the party had support and a place for us to live. In this respect, they were surely wrong. I quickly made the point that they should prove what they said.

"Why don't you take Bene to the bar and straighten it out? That's right where the night watchman took her when she had no place to stay. They'll tell you the truth about whether she arrived with a contact already set up or with only the sky and the earth and four pesetas in her pocket."

That's what they did. They took Bene to the bar, but that son of a lying mother must have been a brutal Francoist. He denied even knowing the girl. The police returned to headquarters. The blows rained down on me again. I was the one who deceived them, the one who was holding out. Whatever it was I had done I was hiding something and either I confess or they'd kill me. I insisted I had told the truth. Why didn't they take us there? I would go to the house of my exemployers and to the bar; they knew me at the bar because on our days off I would go there looking for Bene. The police agreed. You could see they were bent on knowing where my statements were leading. First they took me to my employers' house. When those people saw me with the police, they asked: "What has this girl done?"

"Nothing, just tell us if you know her, that's all."

"Of course we know her. She worked here. We wish she hadn't left. She knows we were ready to increase her salary if she stayed. She's a good girl, a hard worker and very honest. We're very surprised to see her with the police."

"It's not a question of theft or anything like that," the police explained. "She's been arrested for political reasons."

Even though those people supported the Franco regime, they still spoke on my behalf: "We have nothing to say about her except that she is a very fine person of complete integrity."

Next we went to the bar. The owner of the bar refused to recognize me. But I had my own proof. When that guy assured the police he didn't know me, I said to him: "How can you say that? You turned your back on Bene but you'll not do it to me. Behind that door is a circular stairway that leads up to the room where Bene stayed. Do you want to test me? I'll prove this guy is lying."

I pushed past him and went up the circular stairway to Bene's old room, which another girl now occupied. The owner had to admit that, yes, the night watchman had brought Bene there, but he really didn't know much about her.

We went back to headquarters. Now they wanted an accounting of my life from July first until December. I told them about living in the shanty on the Diagonal. They couldn't prove me wrong about living there because the shanties had been empty since December. The rest of the time they knew about; I was living at 172 Sepúlveda. So we got Bene released.

The nights in prison were terrible with women and men being tortured. Days were horrible too. I was held apart from the political prisoners, thrown in with common criminals: the usual black marketeers, thieves, and street walkers. Some days fifty women were crammed into a cell that could barely hold half a dozen.

One night, or more precisely, one dawn, they took me up to the offices and resumed their interrogations. They were obsessed with finding out where I went on Saturdays and Sundays. They didn't ask me about the man with the dark red hat because they had arrested him already. They'd already arrested Pinocho, the one they called "the walking professor" because he walked along the streets reading. He had been my comrade for some time, since I'd begun clandestine life in Barcelona. Poor Moises Hueso, he'd been beaten so many times that an old wound in his lungs had reopened and he'd had several hemotypses.

That dawn Polo put me in a corner against a wall and began hitting me. One of the times he hit my head against the wall I felt such a searing pain in my neck and down my whole spinal column that I could hardly breathe. I thought I was going to faint. As if in a dream I heard them say, "She's going to faint and we've got to stop her." They grabbed me by the shoulders and sat me in a chair. Leaning his hands on the back of my chair, Creix put his feet on mine and leaned all his weight on my toes. The pain in my spine was excruciating. I didn't lose consciousness. I knew I had to continue denying everything. I remember how Polo looked at me and said: "You will talk, you will talk."

"Assassin, you son of a wolf."

He hit me again and again.

"Look, you don't have a mother because if you did, you wouldn't hit a woman."

That made him hit me so hard with his fist that I fell from the chair to the floor. They picked me up by my hair. By then I couldn't stand up. My only thought was not to lose consciousness. I thought about my comrades. I thought about the responsibility the party had given me and which I had to fulfill. I thought that day was the last day of my life, but I felt proud they couldn't drag anything out of me except "no," "no," and "no"—not even if I had to leave my life in the hands of those assassins in the dungeons of the Vía Layetana station!

That dawn they finally took me down to the dungeons. But not before they made someone else suffer too. The police had hidden Bene in one of the halls so she would have to see me go by, bent over, barely able to shuffle.

"Do you see what shape your friend is in? Well, if you don't tell us the names of comrades you know, you'll have it even worse tonight when you go down to the dungeons. So get on home. But we'll come looking for you. I think you're going to talk now." I didn't find out until months later that the police had threatened her.

I remember going down the stairs after the interrogation. After the first flight there's a landing with a door leading to the guard corps of the Armed Police. Just before reaching this flight I heard a policeman say: "This woman is falling." That's the last I heard. I don't know how much time went by. When I opened my eyes I found myself stretched out on a bed used by the guard of the Armed Police. The sergeant came over. "Don't be afraid," he said. "You're with us. Don't worry. Nothing will happen to you now."

After a bit a policeman came with a glass of cognac and some sugar cubes to revive me. When I was a little better, he said: "Good, now get up and we'll go to the cell. We can't keep you here any longer."

But I couldn't move. When they put me on the bed, I was completely bent over. That's how I was and that's how I remained. I couldn't put my feet on the floor. The pains in my spinal column made me scream. A big, strong man picked me up and carried me down to my cell. They put me in a corner. There I lay for days and days, unable to move. My legs were as dark as burnt wood from the kickings and beatings. I could hear my comrades begging and begging: "A doctor to the first, please, a doctor to the first." The first was my cell. Finally they got a doctor to come down. But what a doctor! I was stretched on the floor. He drew near, with two policemen.

"What's happened to you?" he asked.

I didn't have time to reply. A woman in my cell accused of black marketing sneered: "What do you think happened! They tortured her and threw her on the floor."

The doctor did nothing for me. Fortunately that was the last time I was taken up to be tortured.

I found out that "Antoñito" had been arrested. The arrest had come about because of a companion of his who had been with him in the Ocaña prison. The two men had been like brothers. When that man was arrested in Madrid, he didn't resist torture. He took the police to arrest the man who had been his prison brother. One morning a policeman told me to come out. Opposite the first cell was the door to the stairway going up to the offices. I stopped there waiting for him to open the door, but he signaled, no, that I was to go toward the hall. I remember that he cornered me in the wall between the fifth and fourth cells. Then he opened the fifth cell. Out came "Antoñito." Of course he was unrecognizable. His face looked like a monster, all swollen and discolored. He put his hands on my shoulders and out of the corner of my eyes I saw that his wrists were swollen and bloody from the handcuffs by which they'd hung him. But seeing him helped me with my declaration; now it was safe for me to give the address of Carmen's pension where I spent Saturdays and Sundays sewing and ironing. My interrogators were surprised when I finally gave them the address. They asked me why I had refused for so long and suffered so much.

"Because you treat everyone alike. That lady has done nothing but good things for me, like giving me work, and I'm very grateful to her. I was afraid that if I gave her name and address, you would arrest her and she's a person who had nothing to do with my life. She's a widow with a daughter and she earns her living by running the pension. I would never have forgiven myself if you had connected her with me and arrested her, leaving her daughter out in the street and her work abandoned."

But I had to go up to the offices one more time. When they arrested us they heard Bene as well as María calling me Toni, and when I left the house the doorman had said to me: "Good evening, Antonia." That's how they put the name of Antonia Gutiérrez on my file. And I hadn't felt like revealing my true name. When that file reached central headquarters, my real file was sent to Barcelona—my finger prints had betrayed me. Then they brought me up again and with joking little laughs, said: "So, you tricked us here too or you tried to trick us. What did you think, that we weren't going to find out who you are?"

That was the last time I went upstairs until they transferred me to prison. I was down there forty-eight days. At that time—today the situation is different—but at that time they only gave you a little hunk of bread toward eleven o'clock in the morning, that's all for twenty-four hours. There weren't any mattresses and they didn't allow me to have a blanket brought in because I was being kept incommunicado. When I was able to stand up a little, I cleaned the cell with water and disinfectant. The Armed Police that served in the dungeons had to threaten the prostitutes to get them to help keep the cell clean.

I had been there for more than twenty days when a woman who was forty or forty-five years old came over to me.

"I know you," she said. "I don't know from where, but I'm sure I know you."

I looked at the woman. I remembered her face perfectly well.

"Yes, you saw me every morning going down to the University metro at half past five on my way to work. You were selling black market tobacco on the stairs."

"Well, yes, that's possible. That's right where I station myself when people go to work."

"Yes, there's no doubt it was you. You saw many people go down the stairs, but we who were using the stairs saw only you and so I remember you perfectly."

That woman treated me very well during the twenty-four hours she was there. She said to me: "But my girl, how can you stand being here for so many days without even a blanket, just that little jacket to lie on?"

I told her I was being held incommunicado and that the authorities had refused to let me have the blanket that friends had tried to bring me. Carmen, from the pension, tried to send me food and a blanket, but even after I gave the police her address, they didn't allow it.

"Tell me where to go to find you a blanket," she said. "I don't have one to give you, my dear, but I could pass one along to you."

I told her that it wouldn't do any good because the police wouldn't give me the blanket.

"Yes, they will," she answered. "Look, this woman"—and she went to find a woman over in the corner—"this woman is going to stay here because she's been told that she can't pay the fine until she's been here forty-eight hours. They're not going to take her to prison so she'll be here for sure. But I'm leaving today. So tell me where I can get a blanket and I'll bring it for this woman and she'll know that it's for you."

And that's how they sent me a blanket from María's house.

One day they brought in a young girl who came over to me when she realized I was a political prisoner. She stood looking at me.

"But aren't you Peque?"

"Yes, and you, who are you?"

She told me her name. Then I remembered her from the prison at Durango. We had been separated when we left Durango. She had gone to other prisons and we hadn't seen each other again until now.

She explained that after moving through the penitentiaries of Spain she finally was pardoned for the twenty years still on her sentence. Even though the paddy wagon used for thieves and prostitutes had brought her in, I thought she'd been arrested for political reasons and that perhaps there had been another general arrest in Barcelona.

"What's happened? Has there been another general arrest?"

Her head drooped and she started to cry: "No, no, they didn't arrest me for political reasons but because I'm a *piculina*"—that's what we called a prostitute in those days.

I stopped in my tracks.

"How could that be? How could you have fallen so low?"

She explained that when she got out of prison and reached Barcelona, she wandered around the city with hardly any clothes or money. One day as she was looking at clothes in a shop window, an older man approached her. "Look, daughter," he said, "if there's something there you like, I can buy it for you."

That was her first fall. Afterward she continued in that life. As she related it, she had been arrested many times. I thought again about the comrade who spoke to us when we were waiting in line to present ourselves on the first Sunday of the month. I repeated his words to her: "That's what these people want, for us to fall, some by robbing, others by turning to the street. Isn't it true that at some time or another the police threw it in your face that you had once been a Red and now were a whore?"

She wept even more bitterly because that's exactly how the police had taunted her time and again. I assured her she was young and still had time to change her ways. In spite of the sorrow she showed on seeing me in those conditions, she still answered—which infuriated me—that for the time being she intended to continue as she was: the old man supported her well and she was working now to save a little money. She would quit her life later on. Her reply repulsed me so much I think I insulted her. I left her. We didn't speak again until they paid her fine and she went free. She huddled in a corner, crying with her head down, not daring to look at me. When they called her after the fine was paid and she was free, she came over to me and said: "I wish you much luck. I envy you and am ashamed of how I am, but now there's nothing to be done."

In general the Armed Police treated us well. I remember that one older guard said I reminded him of his daughters. He truly did feel sorry for me. At the time of my arrest I was having my period. The beatings made me hemorrhage so much that I flowed constantly for fifteen days. I hadn't been allowed to bring any sanitary materials from home. But this good man secretly passed me packages of cotton. Every time I asked him to please bring me another package of cotton, he would say: "But my daughter, are you still like that?"

He would shake his head and then bring me what I asked for. He also brought me a toothbrush, toothpaste, soap, and a fine-toothed comb used for getting rid of lice, which we had in abundance. Thanks to that fine man I was able to enjoy a little personal cleanliness. I'm sorry I didn't find out that guard's name. Here was a man who in helping us prisoners ran the risk of becoming a prisoner himself.

I was in the basement prisons of police headquarters when World War II ended. The Allied victory filled me with satisfaction and joy. We prisoners had been expecting that the end of the war would bring coordinated intervention from within and without to crush fascism in Spain. The day we heard the news of the Allied victory was wonderful, a time of hope. Most of the police didn't come to headquarters because they also expected changes in Spain as a result of the war's end. But our illusions crumbled at our feet. Our men had sacrificed everything in war and thousands had died in the trenches, guerrilla activities, and German concentration camps. Once the war was over and our men were disarmed, fascism in Spain did not collapse.

On the forty-eighth day of confinement in those cells, I was taken out and put in a paddy wagon for transfer to the prison of Les Corts. Les Corts was an old convent, a convent-reformatory, I think, for girls on the street. There were no cells, just naves, a patio, interminable halls and stairs, with everything divided by those well-known barred doors with bolted locks. When a woman entered the prison, she had to spend a thirty-day period of observation, for disinfection and other things. My clothes were filthy. I asked them to let Adelaida Abarca—we called her Deli—know I was there. I knew her through the party and the Montoya sisters, but not personally. Deli immediately brought me clothes of hers to wear until mine were disinfected.

There were only four of us political prisoners in the room for observation. The rest were prostitutes, thieves, girls who'd had abortions or killed their newborn babies. Through the efforts of Deli and Estrella I had a few days taken off my observation period. Deli and I and later Victoria and Mercedes, we formed a prison family.

Here, as in Ventas, I found some "special" little groups, as I used to call them, groups of friends who had risked their lives in our struggle. Many of them were arrested twice, first for their war activities, then for their clandestine work after the war. We did lots of handwork, especially making linen table centerpieces. We burned our eyes out on that work but it sold very well at first, even though the nuns took their percentage. One time we refused to take the centerpieces down for sale because we'd found out that the nuns had replaced the prices we'd put on the items with their own prices. Eventually the centerpieces came back to us because people couldn't afford the high prices the nuns asked. We responded by attaching a little piece of paper to the centerpiece with our asking price. The nuns were so upset at this they wouldn't allow us to take centerpieces down when we had visitors. At that time people would come on visiting hours just to buy our handwork. Finally we reached an agreement with the nuns; we would give them a certain percentage of our sales.

My stay in the room didn't last long. I was suffering very badly from damage to my spinal column inflicted during torture, and the pains in the nape of my neck were so excruciating I would even lose consciousness. One day I fainted when we were lining up for our twice-a-day counting. They took me to the infirmary where I spent the rest of my days in Les Corts. The prison doctor diagnosed a blood clot in my neck, brought on by the beatings. The reason I lost consciousness now and then and had such terrible pains was because the blood clot was drying up and rubbing on a nerve. The best solution was an operation.

I didn't feel as abandoned in this prison as I had during my previous five years of incarceration. That's because I received a beautiful package every week—from whom I well knew. I also had a visitor every week. Through him I could let my friends with the party know about the doctor's offer to send me to a hospital for the operation. My friends advised me not to accept the offer because it looked as if all of us would be released before long and then I'd be able to consult a good specialist. They didn't want me to go to a hospital as a prisoner and have my life in the hands of a doctor we didn't know. I was told to refuse. At any rate I was getting better even though I was in almost constant pain.

Without leaving the prison I began to lead an almost normal life. I would go out to the patio to be with my friends, take part in the artistic representations, and do handwork. Sometimes when I went to the patio I chatted for a little while with the Alicias, mother and daughter. What a joy it was to see them! I respected and liked them so very much from the time we'd been in the same gallery in Ventas. Alicia the Mother was an astounding woman, so enthusiastic. She loved to speak about the years of the Republic and her friendship with Dolores Ibarruri, better known as "La Pasionaria," from their time together in prison. Alicia often said about "La Pasionaria": "Ah, if we were worth only one fourth of what she is worth." I also came to enjoy a family with three other women. I think it was in the month of July when three girls were brought in; two of them, Victoria Pujolar and Mercedes Pérez had been beaten very badly. Mercedes was black and blue all over; she'd been slapped and hit so much that her face was misshapen for the rest of her life. Victoria looked like some hunched over old woman because they had stomped on her kidneys; but she was young and strong and recovered quickly. She was even able to play basketball later on, as was Mercedes. As the youngest of all, Deli was also the most serious. She worked in the prison offices. The four of us, Mercedes, Victoria, Deli, and I, were so close we called ourselves prison sisters.

As I mentioned, I liked to chat with the Alicias in the patio. I often found Alicia the Mother talking with a woman named Pura de la Aldea. Pura's story was extraordinary. I had known her by name in Ventas where, amazingly, she had served as a prison official during the period of the Republic and the war. She had worked in the prison when Dolores was a prisoner there.

I remember Pura de la Aldea as a very friendly woman who never had a harsh word for the prisoners. She did her best to help the prisoners and make their life in prison somewhat bearable. She was a sweet, affectionate woman, and all of us who knew her will never forget her correct and courteous behavior. Possibly it was the comportment of the Communist prisoners that persuaded Pura de la Aldea to join the party. When the Republic was defeated, Pura de la Aldea, like so many democratic women, was arrested, sentenced to thirty years and tortured with the brutality that the fascists usually employed. The memory of Pura de la Aldea as a woman of great dignity and fine character lives and will live among those of us who knew her.

In their conversations on the patio Alicia the Mother and Pura de la Aldea always got around to talking about Dolores. The affection and respect Pura had for Dolores was reciprocal. Later, when I got out of prison, I found out that Pura, by now an older woman, had been released and was living with Enriqueta Montoro. The two women had been very close in Les Corts. To earn a living Pura worked as a dressmaker in private homes. Their house was a gathering place for the party leadership in Barcelona. The two women were arrested again in 1958, at the same time that Miguel Núñez was tried. I didn't see the women again until 1967 when Miguel got out of the Burgos penitentiary. Then the two little old women gave us the great satisfaction of spending a day with us in our home.

Later, in 1969, when I was living clandestinely at a support house belonging to José Aymami, his wife, Mercedes, said to me one day: "Today I have an old friend of yours sewing at home. With your clandestine status, it's best not to tell her anything. The woman is Pura de la Aldea."

"I trust her and I'm not leaving without giving her a hug" was my answer.

Our meeting after so many years was very emotional. Her first question was: "What do you know about Dolores?"

"The only thing I know is that she's all right."

"Can it be that I'll die without seeing her again?"

At one time or another I had inquired about having Pura do something for the party that would put her where Dolores was. But that was out of my control, and besides Pura was already an old woman and in no condition to travel, certainly not make a long trip, no matter how much she longed to see Dolores again.

Later I had the joy of embracing Dolores and giving her news of Pura. How happy Dolores was to hear about Pura, the prison official who was penalized when the war ended and imprisoned for having treated prisoners well and supporting the Republic. When we said good-bye after several days, Dolores gave me a letter for Pura and a pretty broach as a remembrance. When I gave Pura the gift, she was so touched that she kissed the broach as if she were kissing Dolores and wept with emotion and happiness. Here is the letter that Dolores wrote to Pura, which shows how the memory of this exofficial from Ventas during the years of the Republic remained alive in Dolores.

To Pura de la Aldea. Barcelona

Dear Friend: It's been several years now since I have had news of you and the news I have received fills me with profound emotion.

I have never forgotten you, just as I have not forgotten some of the friends I knew, whose memory, pleasing or not, lives indelibly in my memory.

You do not know that I searched for you when I found out about the death of your Max, but I could not find out where you lived. Forgive me, Pura, if perhaps I didn't do everything I could have to find you during a time that was so painful for all of us.

I am sending a little remembrance with our mutual friend in the hope that one day, perhaps not too far off, I can embrace you and show you my affection and respect.

Cordially yours, Dolores Ibarruri
July of 1969

*In my clandestine work for the party as well as in the prison of Les Corts I became good friends with Victoria Pujolar, Adelaida Abarca, and Angelita Ramis. Adelaida, Victoria, a third friend named Mercedes, and I formed what we called a family in prison. Their names appear in the next chapter of my story and I include their testimonies among the following chapters.*

# CHAPTER 17

# *From Prison to*
# *Clandestine Life Again 1946*

I remember the Christmas of 1945 that I spent in prison. The packages arrived in the afternoon of the twenty-fourth. Deli came up to get me. Without saying a word, she took me by the hand and ran like a crazy woman to the place where the packages were placed for distribution. "Look, just look at the basket they've sent you!" There was a precious basket with a bouquet of red carnations tied with a darling ribbon. It was filled with stupendous things: roasted leg of lamb, fish in a pastry shell, beef filets in pastry, Catalan cream, nougats, fruit, and a bottle of sherry, the only bottle left by the officials.

We had organized the Christmas party to honor the old women. We pulled together the bedrolls to make a kind of table and used sheets for table cloths. Dressed up with paper or cloth aprons and little paper coifs on our heads, we served the women their dinner. They were so happy and moved by what we'd done for them that they cried with emotion. Two or three times we were told to be quiet, but we had obtained permission from the authorities to celebrate until midnight, so we kept on singing. Afterward we were obliged to attend midnight mass. We had a marvelous evening, and we were especially pleased to honor the old women, many of whom had been in prison for up to ten years. Lots of women came from the fascist zone and had been imprisoned since 1936.

The following day we members of the artistic group acted out *The Little Shepherds*. And that day I had a big surprise. From the time of our arrest I had kept up a wonderful friendship with my comrade, "Antoñito." When he was arrested I learned his identity; his name was Miguel Núñez. He had written me several times from prison. I knew it was from prison because only a close family member could write directly to a prisoner. He was able to have his letters smuggled out and then they would be mailed to me in Barcelona. He pretended he was my nephew, and as he told me later, he wrote with his left hand making lots of mistakes and using incomprehensible words so his writing really looked like that of a boy just learning to write. This ruse meant that it took three or four days for his letters to reach me because the censors had trouble deciphering that writing. However, I had a way of reading the letters the very day they arrived. Whenever the office workers had to go out to be counted or for some other reason, my little sister, Deli, would bring me the letter to read and then take it back with her to the office. That's how I already knew what my little letter said and meant; after all, a person who doesn't know how to write very well can easily understand the writing of someone with similar difficulties.

Miguel's letters filled me with wishful thinking; he knew that I hadn't let my family know I was in prison, that my mother was very old, and that I didn't want to worry her anew with my arrest. That's why I had my letters to my family smuggled out and why I wrote about my work and life outside of prison as if I were in fact living as a free woman in Barcelona. I gave them to understand that I didn't have a permanent address yet.

Since my family more or less knew my political leanings, they assumed I couldn't give out my address. They were content just to receive news of me and know that I was all right. But I didn't get letters from them. So Miguel wrote to his parents and asked them to write me as if they were my aunt and uncle. Their letters I received regularly.

Miguel's sweetheart had died in August of 1945, her death perhaps hastened by her fiancé's detention. Her disease was very advanced and there was no hope she could live much longer, but the news of his arrest didn't help. On Christmas Miguel was already out and his parents came to see him in Barcelona. Maruja's sister, Luisita, came along. Apparently the families hoped the ties would continue.

On Christmas day the three of them came to visit just as I was getting ready for the theatrical presentation. They were allowed to come see me in the auditorium. Since the prison authorities had invited their relatives to the performance, some prisoners, and especially the women who didn't have many visitors because they weren't from the capital, were given permission to have visitors. A choir sang songs and selections from zarzuelas.

The three people were just about to enter the auditorium when someone caught Miguel by the shoulder: "Friend, you're not going in."

"Why not? My cousin and mother are inside."

"I'm very sorry if your mother is inside. Wait until she comes out because you're not going in."

Maruja's sister backed up when she heard this. She didn't go in either. So his mother was inside the prison to watch me act; afterward they let me embrace her. That was my first direct contact with Miguel's family. Apparently it was very difficult for me to go free even though many people from the group I'd been tried with had already been released. I don't know why they were keeping me. In any event, thanks to Miguel, who walked near the Captain General in the company of our lawyer, Mr. Gómez Ponchón, I was granted my freedom.

The day I got my provisional liberty in February of 1946 I was a little under the weather and in bed with a slight fever. As soon as Deli got the news in the office, she flew up to tell me. So it came as no surprise when the official appeared to advise me that the order for my release was in the office and to collect my belongings. As I embraced Victoria and told her good-bye, I said: "Our plan has fallen through. You'll have to find someone else."

I was very close to Victoria. Since I'd already spent five years in prison, I didn't want to spend more time in this prison. And Victoria would have to spend even longer than I since this was her first imprisonment. So Victoria and I had thought about how we could escape. At the time of my release, we'd already hatched a bunch of plans for escape and had decided on the best one.

Carmen from the pension had offered me her home in case I got out; it was no secret to the police that we knew each other and that I often went to her house to sew and wash clothes. But I had resolved not to submit myself to monthly check-ins at the prison and not to expose another person to danger by being with me. I remembered perfectly the street and the number of our old shanties on the Diagonal; that's the address I gave. Of course, I knew that they'd been pulled down and all the area fenced off.

The officials were surprised when I told them my residence was right on the Avenida de Generalísimo Franco, a street that people called the Diagonal whether or not they were from Barcelona.

"Don't be surprised at the address," I told them. "There are just some shanties there that face the Rosaleda."

Those shanties were well known, so the authorities swallowed the bait. What they didn't know was that the shanties had been torn down more than a year before.

Only a few days after leaving prison I received news that Raquel, Mercedes, and Victoria were being taken to Madrid for sentencing. I spoke with a friend—the poor woman is dead now—Maruja Montoya, a fine girl, and the two of us went to the station to see them off. We took a box of cookies and a thermos of coffee with milk. When we talked in prison about escape and how to pull it off, I told Victoria it would be easy to escape during transfers just by distracting the Civil Guard a little. Victoria remembered my words.

When the three women reached the station, they weren't wearing handcuffs, something very unusual for the Civil Guard. In a moment when the guard relaxed his vigilance, Victoria got away. By the time we arrived, there was a tremendous uproar all through the station and out in the street, with both the police and Civil Guard involved.

"Victoria's escaped," I said to Maruja.

"You're crazy. How could Victoria escape?"

"I tell you she's escaped. Look at the confusion here and look over there where the guards are—there's just Mercedes and Raquel. No Victoria."

Just then someone called out to Maruja; it was Victoria's cousins.

"Don't come near," they yelled, "Victoria has escaped. We were here spying and realized what happened. We don't want to get close."

Maruja stayed back with them, but since I could clearly prove that it was only a few days since I had been released and that Mercedes was a friend from prison, I went up to the guards and told them I was taking a thermos of coffee and cookies for my friend.

"Which friend? Victoria Pujolar?"

"No, no, Mercedes Pérez."

"Well, get it to her and then leave right away."

I thanked them, went up to Mercedes and without giving her a kiss, handed her the coffee and cookies. As she embraced me, she whispered that Victoria had gotten away.

I left them and went to join Victoria's family. I told Maruja that it would be much better for us to get away from the family because someone who knew them might come up to ask about her. We moved away from them but lingered at the station watching what was going on. The police were frantically running around and searching for Victoria, but she didn't appear. We saw an aunt of hers, a little old woman, with a package for her niece. She and the other relatives didn't see one another. The woman went up to the guards asking about Victoria. We felt badly for the woman because she was old, but at the same time we admired her nerve. Dressed in her little light-weight coat, she gave those guards a hard time: "Where's Victoria? Where's Victoria? Of course, you've got her. I've come to see her because they told me she was being transferred and I know you're taking her."

"She escaped. Don't you know she got away? Tell us where she is."

"You tell me where she is. I just came to give her a little package. I don't know anything."

"What do you mean you don't know anything?"

"I don't, sir. If I knew something, I wouldn't have come."

We waited until we finally saw men and women boarding the train and our two friends being taken to the train. We left, thinking: "Where can this girl be? Where did she go?"

I continued to visit Deli in Les Corts. At the time she was having trouble with her ears. Since the prison administration trusted her so much, they decided she could go to the Hospital Clinic for treatment.

She got word to me when she was going so that when she was taken out, I caught the same streetcar and accompanied her to the clinic. The prison officials certainly didn't show the trust they professed to have in Deli: she was taken, handcuffed, by two Civil Guards. Delia had the face of a little girl. In spite of her twenty-one or twenty-two years, she didn't look older than sixteen or seventeen. She was very blonde with rather long curls and she still wore short socks. It pained me to see her handcuffed between two guards. More than once I heard people commenting: "What could that little girl have done?"

"Nothing," I would answer, "she's a political prisoner. They're taking her for treatment to the clinic because she has ear problems."

"Political prisoner?"

"Yes, yes, political. Besides she's been in prison for more than six years."

Generally her treatment was at the same hour each day and the same pair of guards accompanied her. Deli and I struck up a kind of friendship with those two men. They wouldn't let me in the clinic while she was being treated so I stayed out by the door and chatted with the men. One day Deli said to me: "I have some material for a coat I'd like to have made. How do you think we could arrange that?"

"Well, Juan Bernal's companion, who's in the Model prison, is a dressmaker. Ask the office for permission for her to go in and take your measurements and do a fitting later."

"Yes, but . . . to make me a coat . . . they'd ask why I wanted a coat made."

"Tell them you need a coat when you go to the clinic."

That's what she did, and Joaquina, the dressmaker, went to the prison, took her measurements and left with the material. She also went in for the first fitting. I often saw Joaquina and her little girl, María Rosa Bernal, with her leg in a cast. She was a charming little creature. She had a sealed cardboard box that she used as a money bank and whenever clients and visitors came, she'd hold it out and ask for money for the political prisoners.

One day Joaquina said to me: "Look, I'd like to have another fitting for this coat. Tell your friend to get permission for me to go to the prison again."

I forgot to advise Deli to ask permission. So when she left for the treatment, I told her I had forgotten to let her know that Joaquina wanted another fitting, the last one.

"Confound it! That's a pain."

"A pain? Why? You can ask permission today."

"Yes, but we're going to lose time." (The escape had been prepared already.)

While she was having the treatment, I asked the guards if they would do us a favor.

"Tell us what you want."

"Well, she's having a coat made and the dressmaker told me to ask permission for her to go in to do a fitting. I forgot to tell Deli to get permission. It's my fault. But if you men agree, we could take a taxi to the dressmaker's house and try the coat on in a jiffy. I promise you no one will know. Besides, if someone asks, tell them we were a little longer at the clinic, that's all."

They agreed. We went to Joaquina's house, they stayed at the door, and we told them to go in if it wasn't a bother. They did go up, and Joaquina gave them coffee. But they felt a little uneasy and went back down to the street. We stayed upstairs. The coat fit beautifully. We chatted with the little girl and then left. Not to lose time taking the bus, we paid for a taxi again and returned to the prison. Deli also asked me to look for some shoes in her size. She had such small feet it was hard to find women's shoes to fit her. I finally found some very good-looking shoes.

Deli's situation in the office was becoming more and more dangerous. In her desire to help friends she was doing things that would have cost her dearly had they been discovered. For example, she saw to it that the order for Angelita Ramis's transfer for sentencing disappeared, not once but several times. Angelita ran considerable risk in sentencing; apparently the accusations against her were so serious that the death penalty would be asked for. The party decided that both women, Deli and Angelita, would escape. I was to be the link between the party and Deli.

During my last visit when everything was set, Deli, with her little girl's face, said: "And if it fails, what will we do, without a phone number or an address?"

I was living in a room on San José de la Montaña under an assumed name. Without thinking, I gave her my telephone number. I didn't tell the party because I knew it wasn't the right thing to do. But I thought everything would turn out okay and my irresponsibility wouldn't be discovered.

On the day set for their escape a friend was to go for Deli and Angelita in a taxi and pick them up at a spot close to Les Corts. But a terrible storm came up that day and the girl couldn't get a taxi. So she took a streetcar. She reached the meeting place too late—the girls were nowhere in sight.

*I was especially close to Deli and Victoria in Les Corts. Angelita, too, was a good friend. I've talked a little bit about their escape, but my friends should be the ones to tell their stories of escape and flight.*

# CHAPTER 18

# Escape:
# Victoria Pujolar at Les Corts

*Victoria had been arrested in 1945. I met her in the infirmary of the prison of Les Corts in Barcelona. I left prison with provisional liberty in February of 1946 and Victoria escaped the next month. She went to France where her parents lived as political exiles. She returned to Spain after Franco's death in 1975. She lives in Madrid where she works as an artist for a publishing firm.*

My arrest was the last in an important round-up of members of the JSU in Catalonia in 1945. In Barcelona they also arrested a group of young guerrillas who had recently come from France. Their leader was Francisco Serrat, nicknamed "Cisquet," a JSU member for twenty-three years who had been active in the French resistance and was on the side of Cristino García[1] in the liberation of towns and villages in southern France. The group had performed a "miracle." They had managed to get into Spain with arms. Unfortunately, just when they were at the delicate point of making contact with political organizations in order to join efforts with the guerrillas in the city or with the civil organization, there was a breakdown in communication. Either they contacted a person the police were following or someone denounced them. The fact is that the Political Social Brigade hunted them down right by the house where they'd left their weapons. Along with the guerrillas two girls were arrested, one who lived in the house and another sent by the organization from Madrid with an empty suitcase. I saw those weapons, including the machine guns, some ten days later when I was arrested and taken to the office of Quintela, who headed up the Political Social Brigade. It was there that I was slapped in the face for the first time. Some of the propaganda found in my bag Quintela had difficulty reading because it was written in Catalan.

In our clandestine work we were careful to change the place and time for appointments at the last moment. I was on my way to meet the man in charge of propaganda; our job was to find a safe place for the copy machine that was so essential in our work. The usual procedure was to reach the meeting place ahead of time. I knew that if he hadn't been arrested, he would be there before the designated time as well. Without stopping I walked by the place where we were supposed to meet. I looked in the vestibule but he wasn't there. So I kept on walking rapidly toward the Vía Layetana. But when I rounded the corner two policemen in civilian clothes came running after me like crazy men. They grabbed me by the arm, took my purse and made me take the caramel out of my mouth. But they didn't handcuff me for the short trip to the police station on the Vía Layetana.

The policemen told me they had taken a taxi to the meeting place with the very man I was supposed to see. Just as I rounded the corner, he'd said, "That's the woman." It might have been the truth. It might have been a lie. But the truth is that at the very least my appearance as a girl from the suburbs of Barcelona didn't exactly fit the image the police had of a Communist woman. They probably never would have arrested me if they hadn't been tipped off.

At the police station I was taken downstairs to the cells. They were cramped, dirty, and barely lit. Behind the bars, silhouettes, faces, political prisoners and common criminals, all mixed together. They didn't give us any food or blankets. Whatever we had came from friends and families, unless we were being kept incommunicado; then we had nothing but a piece of bread for the entire day. There were only two cells for women. In the first one I met four young political prisoners, two very young black-marketeers and a fat old French woman who had been denounced by a policeman just so he could keep the place she had sublet him. Later all of us political prisoners were thrown in with the prostitutes in the other cell.

When I was brought in they already had just about finished interrogating the people from our round-up. Most of them had been beaten. When Mercedes Pérez insisted that the only reason she'd come from Madrid to Barcelona was to find work, she was punched so hard that her face was permanently twisted and disfigured. Of course, Mercedes had another reason for coming to Barcelona: she intended to return to Madrid with her empty suitcase filled with arms.

The interrogations went on and on, interrupted only briefly at night. You could feel the fear in the air as soon as the sound of the locks echoed through the cells and someone disappeared up the stairs between two guards. The first ones interrogated were the guerrillas. All of "Cisquet's" teeth were knocked out. When I saw him, he looked just like a baby with his toothless smile. Raquel, the woman from Santander, was beaten repeatedly; they'd found a machine gun in her house. "Cisquet" was our neighbor in prison. Coming and going, or pressed against the bars, we exchanged a few words, even though we couldn't see each other. In this way he let me know that someone had squealed to the police, but it wasn't one of *his* boys. He thought this "someone" just might be Raquel.

On June 24, the eve of the Feast of St. John, the guards down below—they were always more humane that the ones upstairs—those guards opened up the barred cells for a little while so all of us political prisoners could chat. All the prisoners belonged to the Communist Party, the JSU, or the Fighting Youth,[2] which was the youth branch of the National Spanish Union, the national union that the Communists had called for in August and September of 1941. That's when I saw Jesús Monzón,[3] the Communist governor of Alicante, for the second time. I had seen him once before in the hall talking with a girl with curly blond hair, but I didn't know who he was.

Then my interrogations began. The police concentrated on one point—my contact with the party. Since they didn't know or couldn't imagine that I was in direct contact with the party, they assumed I must be in touch with a comrade named Lluis whose undercover name they'd discovered in a letter in my bag. The police became increasingly nervous and irritated. One day they took me to an interior room with hardly any furniture, just an armoire in the back, a table, and some chairs. It was sinister. A long, blood-stained jacket was hanging from a hook. One of the policemen, Calleja was his name, played the good cop: "Look, I have to wear worn-out shoes too. I understand you. You're idealistic, but listen, don't sacrifice yourself for your leaders in Paris—they're leading the life of luxury in exile. It's better if you just speak out. Do you want some coffee?"

"No."

On and on it went. Then a bunch of police headed by the Creix brothers appeared. They stood in a semicircle around me and took turns slapping me in the face while one of the Creix brothers bombarded me with questions, his voice getting louder and louder, coarser and coarser. My alibi was that Lluis didn't exist. Lluis was just the name we used for the party leadership; if we said that something came from Lluis, it meant the leadership said such and such. The blows rained down along with hysterical cries: "You're lying. Lluis is your lover. Confess it." Then one Creix pulled a lead bludgeon out of the armoire; they immobilized me on a chair and began to hit me in the area of my kidneys. They kept on hitting and hitting. For how long, I don't know. But my back turned black and was crisscrossed with nasty welts. I had a raging temperature and terrible thirst. One of the guards brought me some water, something that was strictly prohibited.

One day one of the Creix brothers sent for me and as a joke tried to convince me that he hadn't been the guy who'd hit me. When I told him

I knew perfectly well who had done it, he laughed cynically and said he hoped I wouldn't denounce him if things changed. Clearly he didn't have the least fear that the situation would change. It was a dangerous game of cat and mouse—and the police played the cat!

Seventeen days went by. Our group was transferred from the police station to the prison of Les Corts. I breathed a sigh of relief. No one else had been arrested after I was. Men and women prisoners went together in the same paddy wagon. First we went to the Model prison where we said good-bye to the men. As Jesús Monzón embraced me, he urged us to keep up our solidarity. I got a knot in my throat when I hugged "Cisquet." I was sure I'd never see him again.

I had seen Les Corts from the outside. And I'd been in the visiting room when I had visited prisoners who belonged to the JSU. Now those big, heavy prison doors closed behind me.

Mercedes, Raquel, and I came in with the same group. First we had to undergo quarantine in the transit room, sleeping on mange-infested mattresses. No wonder I got mange. Finally we were put on a normal schedule and placed in the main part of the prison. There I faced the harsh, though fraternal, reality of prison life. Granted, it was no longer 1939 or even the first years after the war, but I saw women there who bore the scars of that previous period. There were women from Catalonia and from all over Spain who'd been transferred to Les Corts just to deprive them of assistance and visits from families and friends. There were even some women still finishing their sentences for "war crimes." Among the Communists, which included women from the party and the youth organizations, the majority had been arrested for "posterior crimes," meaning for activities after the war. These women we called the "posteriors."

In effect, along with the Alicias, mother and daughter, the country women from Toledo and others, there were "posterior" women who had been arrested for organizing the party or the youth organizations and for their solidarity with the men prisoners. The women included Antonia Hernández and her sister, both grossly tortured and violated in their dignity as women soon after the war ended. There was the young woman, Adelaida Abarca, from Madrid, who was part of the group of minors arrested in 1939 on account of their solidarity with prisoners. Thirteen girls from that group had been shot. There was a large group of textile workers, all arrested, I think, from the same factory. And there were many women, young and old, accused of reorganizing the PSUC. Isabel Vicente was in that group.

It was in the infirmary that I met Tomasa Cuevas. She was there because of the problems she suffered with her spinal column as a result of beatings at the hands of the police. Tomasa was arrested as a "posterior" after spending time as a war prisoner in half of the prisons of Spain. Angela Ramis was another member of the PSUC. She'd been arrested with a group of people accused of crossing the border. She lived under the double threat of being transferred to a prison in Africa where others from her group were held and of being sentenced to death. There were many other women whose faces I can still see, but their names have slipped from my memory.

Prison life was a monotonous series of lining up to be counted, morning and evening, singing "Cara al sol" in the patio, cleaning, and doing our official jobs like working in the kitchen or the offices. And there were the annoyances: obligatory mass on Sundays and as always, spoiled food. We tried to earn a little money doing handwork, but of course we weren't the ones to profit; the real money went to the people inside and outside prison who found buyers for our work.

When we arrived, we put more spirit into all the activities. Our morale was a little higher because of the Allies' recent victory over fascism. We reorganized the JSU in prison. We read and discussed clandestine materials that kept us in touch with the party outside. We managed to read the daily press even though it was prohibited inside prison. Our sisters working in the office devised ingenious ways to get forbidden material in and out of prison; food containers with false bottoms were put to good use.

We also took advantage of whatever the administration would permit. We played basketball, performed plays and operettas, held poetry recitals, song fests, and dancing. Both common criminals and political prisoners took part in all these activities. We also had a natural comic among us who improvised on texts with lines alluding to prison life.

In short, we kept solidarity alive. Sometimes solidarity meant raising a woman's morale and being with her in her pain. Low morale could affect a woman's physical condition so that she lost her appetite and became sick. That's what happened to Angela. Angela was always worrying about her trial. She got to the point where she couldn't stand having to clean newly arrived prisoners. She was sick of fleas and lice and disheartened by the moral and physical misery all around her. I tried to get her to eat some of the food her mother brought and which she insisted on dividing among the other prisoners. I tried to convince her to escape—Tomasa and I sized up all the possibilities for escape and came up with a plan. I was in a position to falsify a safe conduct across the border that either Tomasa or I could use. It was agreed that the safe conduct would go to the first one summoned to a tribunal. As it turned out, I was that person.

Meanwhile, we received some news that turned our hearts to stone. "Cisquet" had been taken summarily to the military tribunal and condemned to death. We drew up a letter of protest to be sent to the embassies of the western nations in order to have our position on record. Without exception, every political prisoner signed the letter. We got the letter smuggled out and a copy sent to Miguel Núñez, who was responsible for the party in the Model prison.

A year in that prison had gone by when I and two of my companions from our original group, Mercedes and Raquel, were notified that we were being transferred to Madrid to appear before the military tribunal. The day before the transfer I entrusted Mercedes with a letter of recommendation for the organization at the prison of Ventas. Mercedes looked at me and hugged me. She understood my intentions.

At five o'clock in the morning, after saying good-bye to all the political prisoners, we left Les Corts. On foot and without handcuffs, we set out for the Model prison where the pair of guards escorting us was supposed to pick up a common prisoner who also was being transferred. Walking slowed us down. When we left the Model prison, the guards suggested taking a taxi so we wouldn't be late for the train. But we had to pay for it. We got in a taxi with one guard while the other guard and prisoner set out on foot. When we reached the Francia station and got out of the cab, Mercedes paid the fare while we started for the stairs up to the station. When Mercedes complained that we'd been over-charged, the guard went over to see what was going on. As Raquel and I reached the top of the stairs, Mercedes joined us. Just then, at that very second, I made a decision. I put down the packages and sped down the other stairs. Two memories stand out clearly in my mind, the one of sound, the other visual. The first memory is Raquel crying "Victoria, not now" and Mercedes saying "Yes, Victoria, yes." The second memory is seeing the Civil Guard out the corner of my right eye running up the stairs two at a time while I was going down the other stairs.

I dashed through alleys and streets until I reached the Post Office. There I went down to the metro. The ticket vendor shouted after me that I'd forgotten my change. I got it. The metro came. I found myself protected by the crowd on its daily way to work. I got out at a station that was beyond the reach of radio. I went into a cafe. I remembered the phone number of a friend I'd known for years. I called him. The rest was easy.

I waited for my friend outside in the splendid sun of that wintry morning. By the time he got there I had made a decision; I couldn't stay in Barcelona. As soon as possible I must go to France. He had the same idea and arranged a meeting with the organization. That same afternoon I had a train ticket for Figueras.

Isi, from JSU, and her sister, Marujilla, came looking for me. Marujilla had been waiting with Tomasa since early in the morning at the

Francia station to say good-bye to us. When they didn't see me, they knew I was trying to escape. They took me by taxi to the home of some sisters from Madrid who had also been in prison. They dyed my hair and used makeup to change my appearance.

A few hours after my escape I returned to the Francia station, this time in the company of the women from Madrid and with a first-class ticket. I was on my way to Figueras and the Madrid women were saying good-bye. What could be more natural?

When we reached the border zone, I was asked for my safe conduct. I showed it to the authorities. We reached Figueras at one o'clock. I only knew Figueras from the time of the retreat in 1939 when we had been under full air attack. But I found Angela Ramis's house from her descriptions during our chats in prison. Angela's mother opened the door. She recognized me from her prison visits and pulled me inside.

A few days later I crossed over to France with the help of a professional guide, a contrabandist. It took two days and nights of tough walking to cross the Pyrenees.

I reached Toulouse and my parents' home safely, only to read in the newspapers that Francisco Serrat had been executed by *garrote vil* in the patio of the prison. They had murdered "Cisquet!"

# CHAPTER 19

# Through the Gate to Freedom: Adelaida Abarca at Les Corts

*Adelaida, or Deli, was one of my dearest friends in Les Corts. After her escape, she went to France, but from the 1950s on we kept in touch through clandestine party work. Like Victoria, Deli returned to Spain after Franco died in 1975. I got her testimony in 1978–79 in the same years that I saw Victoria. Deli lives in Barcelona, is married, and works for an insurance company.*

During the war I joined the JSU and like many young people was active in the organization. After the war and in spite of the atmosphere of repression the JSU began to organize secretly and all of us who knew one another regrouped. We began by organizing aid for those who were arrested. By the beginning of May in 1939 the arrests began. I was sixteen years old when I was arrested, right in my own home. I was hiding a JSU comrade the police were looking for because of her activities with the Bureau of Military Investigation.[1] Her parents had been arrested already, and we had looked in vain for her mother in police stations and in the prisons at Ventas and elsewhere. She was left completely alone.

It was a group of Falangists with guns that invaded my house. questioned us about this friend's activities, and searched everything. The Falangists took me away along with Paquita Rodríguez, the girl who was staying with me. They escorted us by foot down the street until we reached a house in a vacant field on the outskirts of Madrid. The house must have belonged to farmers; there were just a few little windows with bars and only straw on the floor. There they locked us in and left us, not saying anything except they would be back. We took advantage of the time before they returned to make sure we were alone and no one was around to hear us. Then we agreed on what we figured would be their line of questioning and planned our answers. The Falangists appeared about midnight or a little after, took us out, and walked us through the empty field. I didn't recognize where we were. They led us to a house in a large field where there were stables for horses and a hangar. They separated us. Paquita they took to one side and me to the other. In a room with twenty or so Falangists, including men and women, the first interrogation began. They threatened me with insults and vile words, demanding the names and whereabouts of our leaders. They threatened to get the information by force; they knew I was a member of the Provincial Committee and assumed I knew where the leaders were and where the propaganda and weapons were stashed. The interrogations went on and on. I hardly had a moment to breathe.

Because I didn't say what they wanted to hear, their threats became harsher: they would cut off my long hair. They grabbed some scissors and started to take my hair in their hand and snap the scissors. Each time they asked me something and I didn't answer they cut some more hair. So it went for quite a long time, exactly how long I don't know because I was too nervous even to guess. A Falangist raised his fist to hit me but one of the girls objected: "No, leave her alone; she's very young." At least there was one person among them who didn't agree with their brutish behavior.

I couldn't breathe. I was very thirsty. I asked for water. They brought a pitcher but I didn't trust them. When they saw that I didn't dare drink they took a glass and put water in it for me. Then another girl took a glass, filled it with water and drank first. So I decided to drink. They kept on cutting my hair and the interrogation turned nastier and nastier. But they were getting tired of the whole business. One of them got up, grabbed the scissors from the other and threw them down. That's when I realized that what was on the floor wasn't my hair but hair from a horse's mane. I shook my head. No, they hadn't cut my hair. Meanwhile another man had arrived and asked if they had finished. They were done, they answered, but they hadn't got anything out of me. Now they would work on the other girl.

They took me out and went to find Paquita. They put me in a stall with two young Falangists. There were horses there too. While those two guys were guarding me, they continued the interrogation using more subtle methods. They said that Paquita was telling them everything. Besides, there was another man, they said, who was locked up in the dungeon. He'd spilled the beans and told lots of things about me. When morning came, they told me they were sending me home. They opened the corral gate. "You can go now."

I didn't know where I was. They showed me more or less where to go. I left, but I was very careful in case someone was following me. I made lots of turns so I wouldn't meet anyone I knew. In fact I did see people I knew, but we didn't speak. They understood I was being followed. Finally I got home. My family and friends thought the trouble was over, but the next day a knock came on the door. It was the secret police.

They took me by car to the police station on Núñez de Balboa. There I met Paquita. The Falangists hadn't released her but had brought her directly to the station. There we found many others who had been detained. Núñez de Balboa was a hellish police station. Interrogations were conducted late at night and before dawn, under blinding and bewildering lights. Whenever we were summoned, they made sure we had to see the person they'd just tortured. If we didn't answer their questions, they warned, we'd end up like one old man I saw—he couldn't stand up or even raise his head. When we were taken away after the interrogation, they'd show us to the young people waiting their turn, as if to say: "Do you see what happened to these girls; well, the same to you if you don't act right." But we'd look at the prisoners with signs of encouragement not to say a word.

During one of the interrogations we had to go by a hall where they had hung a prisoner upside down by his legs. One of the policemen told me to wipe up the blood on the floor under the man. Another time when the police beat a man to death during an interrogation, Paquita and I were ordered to take the dead man's clothes to his family who were waiting at the door. On the victim's undershirt were blood and pieces of his skin. We went to the entrance and gave the man's wife the bloody underwear. Paquita and I were unable to utter even two words, but that woman realized what had happened.

After a few days in this station we were taken to the Ventas prison. Ventas already held an incredible number of women prisoners. Paquita's mother was there. When she found out we had arrived, the poor woman came running, frantic to find out where her daughter was. She was in prison because Paquita hadn't been found. She hadn't heard anything about her daughter for many days. This woman was both happy and sad at her daughter's arrest. She only calmed down a little bit when she learned that Paquita had been arrested because of me and not for anything she had done.

I was given the job of taking the children from their mothers and handing them over to their relatives who then took them to be weighed. Too often the little ones had no care whatsoever in prison; by the time they were taken out of prison they were dying or so sick they never returned. In my job I managed to get messages back and forth between prisoners and relatives. I had to trick the officials who would undress the children to see if anything was being smuggled out with them. To avoid being detected, I would carry the child in my hands along with notes prisoners had given me, and as I handed the child to the family member, I would slip my hand under the little coat or cape and give them the messages. When the family came back, I did the same thing, in this way getting messages to the prisoners. These children had a horrible life in prison. With childhood illnesses, epidemic, and no care available, the children died, little by little. Every day six or seven little ones died. The corpses were taken to a room and put on little marble tables. There the mothers had to keep careful watch over the corpses because of the rats. How frightful it was to see those awful, hungry animals coming to eat on the squalid little creatures, their bodies no more than skeletons, reduced to nothing. Gradually the majority of children without help from relatives outside disappeared from our midst.

One day I happened to meet the director of the prison, Carmen de Castro. Rather severely she asked me what I was doing there. When I told her that I'd just been brought there, she called me into her office where she questioned me about my age and why I was in prison. Then she said she was going to conduct an investigation because at my age I shouldn't be in prison. I replied that if it wasn't right for me to be there, neither was it for many other women. So she took Paquita and me to the room for minors.

When our trial was near, some forensic judges came to question Paquita and me; they isolated us in a room for interrogation. Pura de la Aldea didn't trust the men; she asked to be in the same room with us. Her action was reassuring because we had been frightened just thinking about why these men were here and how they'd gotten entrance to a prison that usually was off-limits to everyone. The forensic judges came to verify our age and ask several question; they looked in our mouths as if we were horses and filled in some papers. Their certification undoubtedly played its role because it was read on the day of the trial after the sentencing. We were in the same process as the "thirteen roses" who were shot on the fifth of August. We were all members of the JSU, and the accusations against us were identical. The "thirteen roses" were tried on the third of August and our trial was on the fourth.

Our trial took place with open doors. There were many people in the room. We were accused of every kind of crime; we were even called depraved women. I didn't even know what the word *depraved* meant. They insulted us in every imaginable way and concluded by asking for the death penalty. After asking for the death penalty they read the certificate from the forensic judges and went out to deliberate. The sentence was for thirty years. That same day we signed the sentence for twenty years, not thirty. Returning to prison on August 5, after being sentenced, we found out that the minors had been taken out to be shot. Our arrival was very dramatic because the women in prison didn't think we would return. The door had hardly opened when we were met by such an avalanche of women, including Paquita's mother, that the officials were helpless to stop it. The women took us everywhere. I only saw heads, haggard faces, sunken eyes, and heard questions and more questions.

No one could believe that we hadn't been condemned to death. They all thought we would be shot too, if not the following morning, then at least within forty-eight hours, as had happened to the "thirteen roses." It was very difficult to convince them we hadn't been sentenced to death. Our companions in the galleries feared we would be shot from one minute to the next and for forty-eight hours they called out night and day for news of us.

In May of 1940 we were transferred, first to the prison at Tarragona for several days, and then to Gerona. I spent four years in that prison, until it was emptied of political prisoners so it could be used for prostitutes. At that time they had begun to arrest and imprison prostitutes in an effort to curb the epidemics that resulted from the increase in prostitution. The prostitutes would undergo a special treatment to prevent the spread of disease. The officials left behind a group of political prisoners to do office work and care for the patients. We political prisoners didn't want to stay on. I protested loudly. I went to the director several times, telling her I wanted to leave with the women who had been arrested with me. My protests were in vain. I was part of a team forced to work for prostitutes.

Some 400 prostitutes came. We had to work among women sick with venereal diseases. tuberculosis, and other contagious illnesses. We had to learn how to draw blood, give injections, administer medication, and take care of personal hygiene. We had to do everything. It was very hard for me to learn how to draw blood and give injections. The first time I felt the blood going through the syringe I almost fainted.

The nun in charge of the medicine dispensary was a smart but evil woman. When the patients were dying, the nun ordered us to give them injections and call the priest to confess them and administer extreme unction. When the poor women saw the priest arrive, they imagined their last moment had come. They would try to get out of bed. Many times it happened that they would fall as they were trying to get up and die right there on the floor. I couldn't stand the situation. I wouldn't be an accomplice to this cruelty. So when I saw that a woman was at the point of death, I didn't give her the injection and I didn't advise the priest.

That nun told me indignantly that I was responsible for the woman going to hell and that I had the devil in my body. Then she would grab a bottle of holy water and douse me from head to toe to rid my body of the devils. Besides, she forced all of us to pray the rosary in the medicine dispensary. Every afternoon I sat there with the others as a discipline. Not seeing me pray she would ask: "Well aren't you going to pray?"

"Yes, sister, yes I do pray, but it's that I . . ."

"I don't see you move your lips."

"Well, I am praying, but I do it within myself." My words didn't convince her. Finally, some days later she looked at my lips again. "Don't you hear me? Pray with your lips."

The treatment of women who were less seriously ill took effect. They didn't lack for what was needed to be cured. But we didn't have the right to treat ourselves or take medicine because everything that arrived was for them. Little by little they improved with treatment and were put out on the street again. The prison was emptied. That is, once the mission was accomplished with the prostitutes, the convent was returned to the nuns of Gerona and we were sent away, each woman to a different prison.

When we had to be transferred, the nun who had behaved so badly with us felt the need to say good-bye.

"My daughter," she said to me, "I am so old now that I won't see you again, but I am confident that one day we will meet in heaven."

I couldn't help but answer, "If I knew we were going to meet in heaven, I would rather commit a crime than see you there."

They transferred me to Les Corts and on the recommendation of the director at Gerona I was assigned to office work. My assignment gave me the opportunity to do many things on behalf of the prisoners. Sometimes when the mail arrived and was put on a pile on the table, I sneaked out letters addressed to prisoners from friends in other prisons and made sure they ended up in their hands and not the waste basket, as usually happened. Other times I collected bits of letters from the waste basket and got them to the addressee to piece together. I was also able to help in some cases where the punishments could be very serious. If the notice for a proceeding arrived asking if such and such a person was in our prison, I would answer yes, register the letter, and set it aside for mailing. But after the director signed the letter, I would tear it up. Months would go by and I would get another letter insisting that a request had been sent before for information about such and such a woman. Again I would answer and then tear up the letter. That happened three or four times, I don't remember exactly, but I do know that even the director finally asked me what was going on—hadn't I answered the letter? I would show her the registry and tell her yes, the letters had been sent. I couldn't understand why those letters hadn't reached their destination!

The day they came to get Victoria Pujolar, Mercedes Pérez, and Raquel Pelayo, I went down to the office to prepare their documents for the guards. This was another of my jobs. It was a day when we didn't have any light in the prison because of power failure and we were half in the dark. Since the transfer was public knowledge, almost the entire prison was up very early that morning to tell the women good-bye. Their departure was very emotional. All the women prisoners gathered where Victoria and the other two women were to exit, and dressed only in nightgowns or wrappers and with their candles lighting the way, they accompanied their friends right up to the door, bidding them good-bye.

Meanwhile I was speaking with the guards and telling them to treat the women well because they were good people. At that moment the guards had no way of knowing whether I was an official or a prisoner. I handed the documents to the guards, making sure they didn't realize I hadn't taken the women's fingerprints. Then I telephoned from the director's office that the expected number of prisoners was just leaving. The women were taken to the Francia station. That's where one of them managed to escape.

After her escape I was under suspicion. Many nights when the officials came by to check on the prisoners they would touch me to make sure I was in my bed. There was an atmosphere of suspicion even in the office. The rumor was that I might be removed from my job; that prospect worried me because then I wouldn't be able to help the prisoners as I'd been doing. Because I kept the records of visitors, I was able to tear out the pages with the names of people who had visited the prisoner who escaped. When I realized that I might not be useful any longer because my activities would be limited, I started planning how to get out of there before something happened to me. I was able to communicate with the party. They agreed I should escape, taking all possible precautions.

A friend who was due to appear before the military tribunal to petition her death penalty planned the escape with me. I took advantage of the time left me in the office. The usual procedure was to hand over the release papers signed and sealed by the director to the guard at the garden door. Since prostitutes went free every day and at no set time, I could arrange for their release at any hour and have the director sign and seal their papers. I would arrange for two prostitutes to be released.

One of the precautions that had to be taken concerned the dog that was at the entrance and belonged to the nuns; that dog knew me. So a third person had to be involved to shut the dog in the office so we wouldn't be endangered. When the time came, on March 8, 1946, Angelita and I left with the greatest precaution. It just so happened there was a rain storm that day and the guards were in the sentry boxes. We went as far as the garden door where the sentinel was, handed him our signed release, and went out the gate.

# CHAPTER 20

# Crossing the Border:
# Angelita Ramis at Les Corts

*I met Angelita Ramis in Les Corts where she worked disinfecting the new prisoners. We corresponded for years. She went to live with her husband in Budapest, Hungary. That's where I met her again; the party had sent me to a special hospital in Romania for Communists from all over the world. I was there for treatment on my fractured spinal column. Since I was in Romania and close to Hungary, I asked for a passport to visit Angelita. When I see Angelita she is in very bad shape and depressed because of her husband's death. I interview her in her home. She doesn't even perk up when we go out for a walk. But here is the story she tells me.*

As soon as the war ended, we began to organize within the party. I made crossings from Spain to le Perthus in France. Another comrade I had contact with went to Ceuta. He must have given something away in our correspondence because the general arrest originated in Ceuta. But I didn't know what had happened in Ceuta so I continued making crossings. Unfortunately I was caught in le Perthus. I told the police I was engaged in the black market, but of course they didn't believe me. I spent eighteen days in a police station, along with nine young people who also belonged to the party.

I never told my mother about the beatings in the police station. I was questioned under harsh lights they kept on night and day, and they threatened to shove my head right through the wall. But I didn't say anything that would compromise the party.

After eighteen days we were sent to the Model prison in Figueras. While I was there a military tribunal met with the commandant and a lawyer and questioned me about my activities. I insisted that I had gone to France only to get food to sell on the black market. They sent me to Les Corts in Barcelona.

In the meantime there were efforts to have me transferred to Ceuta. The first time my transfer orders arrived, Adelaida grabbed the papers and said: "The order for your transfer is here. But look, now it's disappeared."

The party managed to send me a false form, one that was used for rationing and didn't carry a photo. If I had a chance to escape at the station or some other place I could use that form. But since Victoria got her transfer order for Madrid before I received mine, she was the one to use the form. The party sent me another form, but it turned out I didn't use it because my escape happened in a different way.

Adelaida made the documents disappear a second time after the transfer was requested. Now it was too dangerous for her to use the trick again. I was working with a prison official at the little window where we received packages and mail. Joking around, I would pick up her door keys, one a regular key and the other one with a bolt. For a long time she didn't trust me and she would try the door to make sure it was securely closed. Since she always found the door locked, she gradually came to trust me and didn't watch me so carefully.

On the day we had the preparations made with our friends outside, I was to give two turns, one to open the door, and the other to close it. That is, there would be two sounds. But I didn't push the bolt in the whole way on the other side so the door was left unlocked. The guard who was supposed to be at the door had gone to the office for the meal that had been brought to him from home. Meanwhile Adelaida had prepared two false release documents for prostitutes. At eight o'clock, the time when they counted the prisoners, I was counted in the hall. After that I went to my job of disinfecting newly arrived prisoners. I went down the stairs that led by an area where the nuns had their living quarters. The nuns saw me go down. I didn't say anything to them, acting as if I were going to work. They probably thought some prostitutes or political prisoners were arriving. At any rate, they had no reason to be suspicious.

Down below I met Adelaida. At the very moment when we went to open the door, we heard some steps. We ducked behind the door where there was a sign for the deposit of cadavers. We stayed there until we didn't hear anything more. Then, quickly, very quickly, we slipped the bolt out and went into the room where packages were. That morning we had put a package there with our most necessary things. We loosened the light bulb. In case someone heard a noise, she wouldn't be able to see who was in there. We escaped through the little window used for receiving packages.

I had been hoping for rain all day, and there it was, rain! The guards were inside, leaving only one guard outside in the sentry box. We gave him the papers Adelaida had prepared with the false names and out we went. We walked down the street and turned the corner where a car was supposed to be waiting for us. We found a car with a man sitting behind the steering wheel. José or Pedro, I'm not sure which was the name we were supposed to give. But the man took us for prostitutes and said something or other to us. We left quickly. Then we saw another car on the other side of the street. Surely that must be the person we're supposed to meet. We gave him the password but he behaved very badly to us. Later we learned from Tomasa that the person who intended to pick us up had missed us by just minutes. She said the party knew we had escaped because all the lights in the prison were ablaze, a sure sign that they were counting the prisoners.

We decided to get out of there. We started walking along the Diagonal, walking and walking. Finally we reached a house that belonged to an acquaintance of mine. We got a warm welcome.

This was a rooming house for students. My mother had stayed there when she came to visit me in prison. That's why I knew the address. They gave us coffee with good hot milk; it was heavenly. After we got there, Adelaida said she had to make a telephone call. I didn't know who she was calling until I saw Tomasa. Adelaida had kept the number in her head and said nothing to me except that she had a number.

Tomasa came and took us to a very pretty house in San José de la Montaña belonging to some lady. I don't think she knew who we were. We spent the night there. The next day a man named Fernando came. Later, much later, I found out he was Miguel Núñez. We were there all day. The following morning a car picked us up in the Sanllehy Plaza and took us to the little town of Corvera Baján where we stayed for maybe three weeks. We stayed in the home of friends. Adelaida passed for my sister-in-law and since she was small, young, and very cute, we said that she was rather delicate and was there to benefit from the mountain air. They told the people in town that we were roomers. We stayed until the party told us that Adelaida would remain in Catalonia to work while I was to be in Madrid. Later the party thought better of it and ordered us to France. We were advised to go in disguise.

They brought me the long, black skirts of an old woman and one of those bodices that country women wear and a black kerchief. They dyed my hair blonde and Adelaida's black. They cut my long hair and dirtied it with shoe polish to resemble an old woman's hair. Since my hands weren't those of an old woman, I put them in a flower pot and got my nails and hands all dirty. But there was no way my face was an old woman's, even though I dirtied it a little bit and put on dark glasses and stuck some cotton in one eye.

We reached Gerona dressed like that, neither of us talking to the other. I had told Adelaida to follow me so that if they caught one of us the other would get away. When we got off the train in Gerona, I recognized the road because I'd often been there with my mother. I knew where we had to go. On our way we passed by a pretty furniture store owned by a friend of mine from Figueras who had married a man from Gerona. The store had large show windows. I could see Deli beside me, but I didn't see me! I didn't even recognize myself. We reached the home of Catalina Brasera who had given shelter to Maruja Montoya when she got out of the Gerona prison. When the mother opened the door, she said: "What does that gypsy want?" I gave her a big push and in we went. She was very shocked and called her daughter. By the time the mother and daughter came into the room, I had taken off my gypsy disguise.

"So, where's the gypsy?"

"I'm the gypsy."

"But, look, it's a young girl!"

We told her we had escaped from prison. We spent the night there. The father spoke with some railroad men who were taking people to France by train. But our luck was bad. The man who had been taking comrades to the border had come under suspicion and had been relocated to the machine shop. Our passage to France looked impossible now. I suggested we go to Figueras and arrange for a crossing through my parents and friends.

There was a train leaving at half past six in the morning with workers who went every day to the border. I put my rags on again and we left early in the morning. It was a cold, cloudy day, raining a little. We reached the station, me with those dark glasses and a cotton patch on my eye. Right there were two Civil Guard, some soldiers, and two rural policemen.

"There they are," I said to Deli. "There they are. Leave it to me."

I went up to them and in a pitiful voice asked, "Oh, mister guard, where's the train for Figueras? Right in front of me? Oh, excuse me. I've got a bad eye and don't see very well."

"So where are you going?"

"I'm going to an eye doctor in Figueras that I hear is very good. I have such a bad eye that I can hardly see. I've got to get there."

"So you're going on the train? Well, there it is, right in front of you."

"Many thanks, mister guard, many thanks."

With Adelaida behind me, we got in the car, without papers and with just a form. But when we reached Camallera, which is where the control began, two guards went along one side and two on the other, asking for papers. I was sitting by the little window with Adelaida seated in front of me. I had a little basket and was eating some chocolate. Through the window I could see the guards approaching. I thought, well, now we're going to see what happens.

Two people were seated beside Adelaida and two by me. The guards began to ask for our papers. Since I had asked where the train was that went to Figueras, they had trusted us a little—they didn't say a word to us. How lucky we were! They made two other women get out and they detained two men without papers. But we made it to Figueras. Imagine what a coincidence when I got out on the platform and saw that there were guards in Figueras too. We had to present our tickets. The man on guard was one of the men who had detained me, but he didn't recognize me.

I told Deli to follow me. We went to the house of some friends of my mother whose son I knew was a member of the party. We got there early in the morning. He had a little umbrella shop, but it wasn't open yet. I knocked and María, the woman of the house, came out. Seeing my appearance, she said: "What do you want? The store's closed." I pushed her inside. Then her husband and daughter appeared.

"What kind of manners are these?"

"Quiet, please be quiet. Don't you know me? It's Angelita." I took off my trappings and we embraced. They went to let my mother know I was home. Meanwhile the family took us to a flat that they were painting and getting ready to rent. That's where my mother came to see me. Later my father came too. How wonderful to embrace them again!

We slept there one night. By the following morning my mother had contracted a guide to take us across the border. She didn't tell him I was her daughter. She only said that there were two women. He'd already taken Victoria across. When Victoria escaped, she'd gone to my mother's house and spent several days there until she could go over to France. When that man took us across, he said: "Oh, Doña Dolores has a daughter in prison. If you could see her daughter! What a misfortune." He spent the whole time talking about Doña Dolores's daughter: "Poor little girl, she didn't do anything wrong, but there she is, in prison in Barcelona. Her family are very good people. But they're scared she'll be shot—she's got the death penalty."

He talked like that the entire way. It was a terrible trip with rain and wind. During the day we hid in a kind of cave he had and then at night walked, stumbling and falling. One of the horrors of crossing the border by foot over the mountains was climbing parts where the bushes were all smoky from a recent fire. Adelaida wasn't very strong so she climbed the mountain by grabbing hold of bushes. When it dawned the next day, we laughed and laughed to see how black she was from those bushes. We spent two nights on the mountain, usually walking but sometimes crawling so our silhouettes wouldn't be seen in the bright moonlight. Finally our guide said: "Here's the border." My mother had given me a ring with these instructions for the guide: "When you reach the border, come back and give me the ring. Then I'll know the girls got safely across the border."

So I gave him the ring, and he said to us: "Look, go down to le Perthus if you like."

"No," I said, "no, not to le Perthus. They can seize us there even though they're French because one side is Spanish and the other French. No, on to le Boulou."

We didn't go on the highway but instead followed a road through the woods. We slept there, cold, soaked, just about undone. In the morning we saw from up above that some men were going to work along the road. We fixed ourselves up a little to go down. We could barely walk because our feet were even more swollen and painful than the night before. When we reached a bridge leading to le Boulou, we suddenly spotted a guard. He said something we didn't understand. There was nothing we could say. He turned away and let us pass.

In the first open store I saw I went up to a woman and asked her if she knew a certain Ricardo Garriga, a cousin of mine who worked in that town.

"Yes, he works in my house."

"Don't you know me? I'm the daughter of Dolores from Figueras."

"My heavens! How wonderful."

We embraced, and she gave us everything they had until there was no more to give. Then my cousin came.

We were there a day or two, I'm not sure, until that woman's son arranged for us to go by car to Perpignan where they were supposed to put us in a concentration camp. Since I could speak French, I said to the man who met us: "Don't leave us in the concentration camp."

"You've crossed the mountain clandestinely, without passports, so you have to go to the concentration camp."

"Don't be like that. Listen, we've got relatives in Toulouse"—I meant Victoria's parents. "They'll take us in once we get there. So why do you want to stick us in a camp?" In short, he was a very good man and let us go on. And since they had given us a bit of money and a suitcase, we could travel decently and a little better dressed.

We reached Victoria's parents in Toulouse where we stayed until we made contact with the party. Since we were coming from Catalonia, we appeared before the PSUC. Joan Comorera, a leader of the PSUC in Catalonia, his son-in-law, Wenceslao Colomer, and another person whose name I don't remember were there.[1] When they saw the three of us, Victoria, so good-looking, little Deli with her curls, and me, now looking a little decent, they said: "What do you mean you're from the party? You belong to the JSU."

Out of sorts, they dismissed us.

"Mother of mine, what are we going to do?" Victoria asked. "We've got to find a contact."

Luckily at that very moment Santiago Carrillo, a long-time party leader, appeared to preside at a meeting. Our story was being checked through the PCE.

"Don't give your names," they told us, "but go to this address, to the Hospital of Varsovia."

But the hospital director also greeted us disagreeably, probably because in those days it was hard to know who was the good guy and who was the bad one. So we had to leave. By that time, however, Carrillo had received the names of three girls who had escaped from prison and probably were in Toulouse. The party in Toulouse telephoned the PSUC: "Well, three girls with those names came here and we sent them away."

Carrillo telephoned us immediately. We went to meet him, and after spending some time together he said that we would have to be checked by Doctor Parra who was the director of Varsovia Hospital. After being examined at the hospital, we were sent to a rest home near Pau. We three fugitives spent a month there.

Afterwards, Victoria and Deli left for Paris with the JSU while I remained in Toulouse. I was told to stay there and work in the Varsovia Hospital. I was there until Felix, the man I'd married in Toulouse, was deported. In 1950 the French government rounded up the Spaniards and deported them to Corsica. Felix was with Dr. Bonifaci,[2] a Communist doctor in Varsovia Hospital. The two of them went together.

Boni's wife, Elvira, and I joined our husbands in Corsica and from there Felix and I sought asylum in Hungary. I buried my husband in Budapest and I myself became seriously ill. In my Spain I no longer have any immediate family to help me or free medical assistance. But the doctor does come each week to see me and I get along all right.

# CHAPTER 21

# *The Guerrilla:*
# *Esperanza Martínez*

*I met Esperanza Martínez in Barcelona in 1968, but not in prison. She had been in the prison at Alcalá de Henares and when she got out our comrades told her to go to Barcelona where they would put her in contact with me. From that time we have kept in touch, even after she moved to Zaragoza to live. She married a man who had also been a prisoner. In 1978 I go to Zaragoza to get Esperanza's testimony. At this time her health is good. She works in a private home and her husband in a factory. They have a son who rebelled against military service and escaped. She tells her story in her own words.*

I first came into contact with the guerrillas through the Montero family. After the father and older son got out of prison, the father found out that his job as a forest ranger had been filled by someone else. With no income, the family lived miserably. My father, Nicholás Martínez, needed help with the summer harvest, so he hired the younger boy, Casimiro, who had experience in the harvest. When my father found out how the family was suffering reprisals because of their leftist beliefs, he helped them in every way possible.

By working at whatever jobs they could the Montero family managed to get ahead a little. But the older son was a restless fellow; he got involved with clandestine activities. Eventually he had to go off to the mountains with the guerrillas to avoid arrest. It was through him that we made contact with the guerrillas.

My father was a widower with five daughters, Pruden, Esperanza, Amada, María, and Angelita. He was opposed to our getting mixed up in any resistance activities. But one night this boy showed up at our house looking for a straw loft or some place to hide; his feet were so swollen he couldn't walk any further. My father hid him and secretly cared for him. My sister and I didn't know about the boy but we did wonder why we were always running out of food. We'd slaughter an animal and suddenly the sausages, blood pudding, and ham would be gone. We'd say to our father: "How can everything be eaten up so quickly?" He wouldn't answer. He was in touch with the guerrillas and was smuggling food and other goods to them through the boy.

One night my sister was flirting with her sweetheart at the window when she noticed some men with a machine gun. She thought the men were from town coming to take reprisals against us again. I was frightened, too; like my sister, I thought the men were after my father. They called for him at the window of his room that faced the street. Then they came in through the corral and met my father. The men embraced. Our hearts rejoiced because we saw that the men were on our side. We didn't know if we should run out to embrace them too; we decided to act as if we didn't know what was going on.

My father didn't say anything to us about his clandestine work. But my curious sister went to the straw loft one time and found the boy there along with some other friends of his.

"Please, Pruden, don't give us away."

"Why would I give you away? Not a word. What do you need?"

"Nothing," he answered, "nothing, don't say anything about seeing us."

He told my father that Pruden had discovered them. "There's nothing to do now but talk with her," father answered. "I'll speak with her and she'll help you and me too."

The situation got more and more complicated. My sister didn't say a word to me and went on working with my father. When I discovered the situation, I didn't say anything either. For a time, then, all of us at home knew what was up but no one said a word. Finally the plot was out in the open and we could all act together as one.

After my sister got married and went to live with her mother-in-law, I began to work with my close friend, Reme Montero, furnishing supplies to the guerrillas. I would leave my house, go to Reme's village, and then the two of us would go to Cuenca to shop and lead the donkey loaded with goods for the guerrillas. We often met the Civil Guard when we were bringing provisions, but we just put on a foolish act so they wouldn't realize what we were doing.

We lived like that for a long time, supplying the guerrillas and letting them stay in our place as needed. I was very idealistic about the work. I knew the guerrillas were Republican soldiers who had escaped to the mountains rather than face jail.

The Civil Guard didn't have any solid information about our activities, but they began to watch the houses of people known to be leftists. When the guerrillas knocked at our windows at night, we answered with the countersign, and if they returned the signal we opened up. Then the Civil Guard got to knocking at the windows to see if we would think they were the guerrillas and open up. But they didn't give the countersign, so of course I didn't respond. I don't know if it was an error or a good guess, but I said to my father: "Look, I think we've been discovered. The Civil Guard were dressed like beggers and came asking for alms to see how we'd react. We have to do something, father, or one of these days we're going to be arrested."

We had a tremendous watch dog; he never barked at the guerrillas but as soon as he smelled the Civil Guard he would alert us.

"I'm going to the mountains," I told my father. "If you want, come with me; if not, stay with my sisters. But I'm going before I get caught."

"Then let's all go," he answered. "I won't let myself get taken either. If they're going to fire a shot at me, better in the mountains where at least I stand a chance of defending myself."

By this time we'd found out that some friends from a nearby village had been arrested and tortured unmercifully; supposedly they'd disclosed the names of people who helped the guerrillas. My sister and her husband, in fact all the family, were helping the guerrillas, so we all agreed to leave that very night. Reme, her father, my father, my two sisters, my brother-in-law, and I, all of us set out at the time and for the place set by the guerrillas. Reme's mother wasn't with us; the family had buried her just the previous day. But that was fortunate because the poor woman was paralyzed and suffered horribly: she couldn't do anything for herself, not even feed herself.

So we set off for the mountains and became guerrillas. For us, being with our comrades and feeling free was the greatest thing in the world. My father had heard about atrocities committed against young people and he couldn't help but imagine what the police would do to his daughters if they were caught: they might rape us or do any number of barbaric things. If they killed us in the mountains, we would die defending ourselves and not like helpless creatures waiting for them to come to our house. In the mountains we would also enjoy camaraderie.

But life in the mountains was very difficult, with snow and rain, lots and lots of problems, and always having to hide from the Civil Guard. One time we had nothing to eat for four or five days because the snow was too deep to get to the aid stations for provisions. All we could do was pick out a book and read.

One night Reme was caught when she went for water. Before we realized what was happening, the guards were on top of the rest of us. We did what we could, but the Civil Guard was everywhere. Three of our people were wounded, and the Civil Guard lost three men. We managed to escape because we were quicker than the guards. The next day we spent the entire time lying on an esplanade covered with rosemary; we didn't dare move until night.

After that Reme left for the city while my sisters and I remained as guerrillas in the mountains for almost two years. Later Reme returned. By that time the guerrillas had decided we would have to leave because they couldn't provide for us. My sisters were to go to the city and Reme and I were supposed to go to France. It was agreed to send our fathers to a quieter sector until a safe place could be located in the city. Our fathers were sent to the seventh sector, but the two men didn't go together. My father set off with another man. They happened upon a shepherd who gave them away to the Civil Guard. The Civil Guard killed the two men, but they didn't finish my father off right away. He was still alive with his pistol in hand, but he couldn't fire it. Since he couldn't kill himself, my father grabbed the guard by the leg and bit him. The guard's reaction was to shoot him. It's clear that my poor father thought it was the only way he would be finished off.

One day my brother-in-law and Reme's father were killed in an ambush by the Civil Guard after some shepherds had given them away. When their encampment was attacked, the men tried to cross the river to safety. But they didn't know how to swim and drowned. When their bodies surfaced, not even the families recognized them.

So time passed. Then the order came for the guerrillas to retreat. But the group didn't dissolve completely; some guerrillas remained along the border and some walked with us to France. They sent my sisters to a specific town, all very clandestine. Nothing was revealed about the plans; we were just told to prepare to leave.

Reme and I were off for France. To leave the mountains we went by different routes. I went with a comrade named Teo to a town in Valencia and from there to Barcelona where Reme and I were reunited. From Barcelona we walked to a specific place in the mountains where other friends were waiting for us to cross the border, going first to Perpignan and from there to Paris. In Paris the party asked if we wanted to work as links between France and Spain.

I left for Spain before Reme did. I traveled to Pamplona with friends I'd left there and met up with others. We made the journey in the usual way. We spent the least possible time in Barcelona and at night we left to cross back over the border, walking as far as St. Jean-de-Luz and from there to France. I made the trip safely, without any problems. No sooner did I return to France than I was asked to go back to Spain because Reme was in danger. That night we made the necessary preparations and the next morning we were underway.

I was to make contact with a man who would help me across the border. I didn't trust that man from the time we reached St. Jean-de-Luz and he asked for a certain address in Bordeaux that the party had given me in case I missed the contact. I told him the address wasn't his business, but finally I did give it to him. That was a mistake.

At night we left St. Jean-de-Luz. Wherever we rested, he treated me well enough, but I didn't like the way he wanted me to carry more weight. And I couldn't understand why he made me go right by a power station and near farm houses with dogs barking everywhere when I'd been trained to avoid light and populated areas. What's more, when people passed near, we pressed against house doors to hide. All this seemed very strange to me.

I was so suspicious about this guy that I was tempted to kill him while he was crossing the Bidasoa in a rubber boat with the knapsack. I had stayed behind with the machine gun waiting for the next crossing. But how would I look to the party if I told them I had killed a comrade because of personal suspicions? Then I thought that my duty was to continue the trip because what mattered most was to save the lives of comrades who were in danger. Still, I mulled over arguments I would give the party for disliking that fellow.

We reached Rentería where we had a coffee with milk for breakfast. Once in Spain he opened our suitcase so we could change into city clothes; he was very upset to see that I had been given more money than he. I told him it was all the same because whatever money I had left over belonged to the party. He asked me to reimburse him for the money he had spent for our breakfast. I was thinking about his strange behavior while we waited for the train to Salamanca. He badgered me about exactly where we were to go in Salamanca and whom we were to meet. I told him not to worry, that I would tell him when we were close. I distrusted him all the more when he spent a long time talking with the man at the window where he was buying our train tickets.

When we boarded the train, he handed me the tickets. He sat in one car and I in another; evidently the police knew the man well and he ran the risk of arrest. When we were well under way I heard loud talking in the next car where he was sitting. After a bit the police came in and demanded my documentation. Then they said I was under arrest until some matters were cleared up. They took the money I was carrying, except for the thousand pesetas I had in a money holder; this I put between the seats for some lucky traveler to find. That was better than having the police get money that I knew they wouldn't return to me.

I think it was Miranda de Ebro where we were taken for a statement and from there we were transported by train to Burgos. Under questioning in Burgos I revealed only the name and job indicated on the documents I was carrying. At noon they asked us if we wanted something to eat; I didn't feel hungry at all but I did ask if they could bring me an orange because I was thirsty. I was surprised to hear my companion asking for a succulent banquet. I imagined they would bring what he asked for and that he'd strike it rich.

The authorities began to ask where we'd come from, what the purpose of our trip was, and what party I belonged to. I answered that I didn't belong to any party and I didn't understand anything about football. I was making a pun on the word *partido* which means both party and football game in Spanish. They didn't find my joke funny. Their answer was to hit me.

They left me. Then they came back to get me. Every two hours they took me out and beat me. I insisted that my name was Consuelo Pallares Olivares and that I worked at such and such a dress shop, just as it said on the documents. The police made a call there and tried to get me to take the phone and talk with the owner. I refused. I told them I had no reason to speak with the woman. I kept to my story. After two days they took me to the provincial prison for men where a group of women also was held. When I got to the prison an official demanded the thousand pesetas that I'd put between the train seats. Now it was clear that my friend was in on the plot during the whole trip.

I was taken back to the police station where they beat me again; the police were furious because I wouldn't reveal my reason for going to Salamanca. When I was returned to prison, my head and body were swollen from all the beatings. The prisoners reacted violently against the police when they saw the shape I was in. The men who'd done this to me were nothing but beasts, they shouted. They protested so loudly that one official even took my side and agreed that the police had no right to treat people so brutally.

On one of the trips to the police station, a couple of men came to see if they recognized me. They walked around me a few times, peering at me from head to toe, taking a few steps here and there. Then they said: "No, it's not Peque. You can take her away."

That "Peque" was Tomasa Cuevas, who had been in the hospital of Pedrosa in Santander as a prisoner; many friends called her "Peque." She had escaped after two years in the hospital and they were looking for her. This I found out many years later.

They took me away when they realized for sure that I wasn't the woman they were looking for. Afterward they took me to the provincial prison where I was for how long I'm not sure. Then Reme and I and some other comrades were put, handcuffed, in a freight car and kept at the point of a machine gun for the trip to security headquarters in Madrid. They put us in some ancient dungeons. If those walls could talk, they would tell of monstruous things they had seen, men and women maimed and even killed by torture.

The cells were very dark by contrast with the place where they took us to make statements. There brilliant lights were played on our eyes at full strength. They put us in the center of a ring and played hardball, giving us all the wood we could stand. At seven in the morning they stuffed my mouth with dirty rags so I couldn't scream. They knew I was in for a rough time. I was ordered to lie on the floor. I refused. They knocked me to the floor, face down. After I had covered myself up, they lifted my skirts and took off my underpanties. Two men, one on each side, hit me with rubber clubs, first one, then the other. When they saw that the beating wasn't hurting me because I had gone numb, they let me rest. Then they resumed their act, always in the same way. "Get down on the floor. Undress." I refused to do anything they demanded. They threw punches freely, from one side and then the other.

I refused to give my true name.

"Reme says your name is Esperanza Martínez," they said. "Besides, we've got letters you wrote and information about you from guerrillas."

"I'm Consuelo Pallares Olivares, not Esperanza Martínez."

How many blows I suffered that way! In the final analysis I could have saved myself all those blows because I ended up confessing that I was Esperanza Martínez. Besides, they had loads of information and photos. I don't remember how long I was beaten. Once the policeman who was playing the good guy took me out in the hall and after going through a large gate and a tunnel he sat me on a stone bench.

"Don't be a fool. Tell everything you know and we'll give you documentation so you can go to Portugal and no harm will come to you."

I answered that I had nothing to say and they should speak with the man who was in charge of the mission.

"That's 'el Largo,'" he told me. El Largo was Eduardo Pelayo Blanco, which was also the name of the man I had traveled with. I answered that I couldn't accuse that man of anything even though I might be suspicious of him. I told the police over and over that I had nothing to say.

Even though the police knew my name, they kept on questioning me about my mission. Then some police from Valencia came and had me transferred because my case belonged in Valencia. So it ended up that I spent an entire month going from police station to police station. In Valencia I found out they had arrested my sister, Amada, who had also been with the guerrillas. She had been arrested just a few days after she reached the town where she was supposed to go. The Civil Guard had granted her provisional freedom with the purpose of seeing whether she would meet up with me.

Our first days in Valencia prison were very hard. Among other things they tormented us by saying we were going to be shot. And we were convinced they would do it. They called us vipers with so much poison in our hearts that we had no feelings. The guerrillas, they said, were nothing but heartless bandits. The police got furious when we women answered that the guerrillas were the most honest people in the world.

I was arrested in 1952. In 1954 I was notified of my upcoming transfer to Madrid. I spent a year in Ventas. Given the situation there, I got along very well. I met some companions in the second gallery who were political prisoners. During this year I began to work in the Ventas workshop. Then I was transferred to Burgos where I was scheduled to appear before not just one but two war tribunals. One proceeding was for helping the guerrillas and crossing the border, the other for communist activities in Valencia. One arrest, but two proceedings.

I spent a year in the Burgos prison and then went before a war tribunal. I saw Eduardo Pelayo Blanco; he was in the same group with me when they took us to the provincial prison. I was put in an upstairs pavilion until my appearance before the tribunal. At the tribunal I was given a list of lawyers. They all sounded the same to me so I just chose one at random. The man I had distrusted so much also was tried; but he had the benefit of a private attorney, who got him off. From the statements he made at the trial I found out how long he'd been a member of the party, his dedication in helping Communists across the border and how he had taken the police to the place where he'd hidden the knapsack, the gun, the clothing, and the documents.

They asked for ten years for me, and I think it was the same for him. But they gave me a sentence of six years to sign and even less for him; and counting the time we had already spent in prison he went free. But the prison director must have been a hateful fellow; he sent that fellow's case to a higher court that condemned him to how many years I don't know. As for me, they didn't give me just six years or even ten but twenty-six years, four months, and one day.

After being tried in Burgos, I asked for a transfer to Valencia to join Reme and my sister, Amada. After four years they judged me again; this time I got twenty years. How could I be tried twice? I still don't understand it. I think they tried me twice for my part in trying to get to our group in Salamanca. That is, after they arrested the Salamanca group they tried me as part of them. Since I was arrested with the guide who helped me cross the border, the two of us were tried in Burgos. But how did they know I had crossed the border? They arrested me in Spain, my documents were Spanish, and nothing about borders crossed my lips. In that trial they sentenced me to twenty-six years with the aggravating factor that when they took it up to the higher court I had signed for six years. After I was tried in Valencia and sentenced to twenty years and already doing time for that twenty-year sentence, they notified me of the judicial action in Burgos that sentenced me to twenty-six plus more years on the grounds of false documents and crossing the border.

Between the two proceedings I now had a term of more than forty-seven years to complete.

My sister and Reme were also sentenced to twenty years, but with credit for time already spent in prison and other considerations they ended up with eight years. I also got some credit on one of my sentences, but not the other; exemptions could only be applied to one sentence. So I spent four more years in prison. In 1967 when I was released, I had spent fifteen years in prison and was out on conditional basis.

The period I remember most fondly was when Margarita Sánchez entered. I consider her one of our best comrades even though she was a little strange to live with. It was her idea to form communes in which we shared equally everything we received from outside. For me the best part of all the prison years was living like a family.

My friends began to leave until one year there were only two of us left, I and an anarchist, a very nice woman. She had been a member of our commune. She and I spent a Christmas all by ourselves, but in good spirits. The following year I spent Christmas completely alone. That's when I started reading lots of books in my little cell. Since the custom among political prisoners was to toast the New Year, I didn't let that occasion go by without toasting, even though I was by myself. I couldn't be a coward. I got into bed to wait for midnight. I didn't have champagne or wine because they weren't allowed, so I took a glass of beer. At midnight I got up to toast happiness for the New Year, for freedom, for so much we had fought for. In those moments I wasn't thinking about being alone, not at all, because as soon as I lifted my hand with the glass, I thought about how thousands and millions of people were lifting their glasses to toast with the same desires and goals for which I had fought and for which so many people in the world had fought. After the toasting I felt comforted, very happy and extraordinarily sleepy.

I continued to expect my freedom. But when José María de Oriol y Urquijo[1] served as Minister of Justice, he made it the rule not to grant provisional freedom to political prisoners. I should have received my provisional freedom six months before it was granted. Thanks to the General Director of Prisons I did get my freedom. It seems that the sister of Mercedes Gómez spoke to the director about me when he was buying a newspaper in her kiosk. I appeared before the council of ministers and on February 25, 1967, I was released.

I had kept current on all the news while I was in prison, but I wasn't prepared for real life. I felt very insecure, as if I were floating. I spent some three years in that insecurity, not knowing little things like intersections with traffic lights, new neighborhoods, different currency, and strange shops.

I went to Manresa to the home of a sister who was the widow of the brother-in-law they had killed with the guerrillas. I spent two years there. Then I began a relationship with my current husband. We wanted to get married quickly and had all the papers in order. But the wedding was delayed because ecclesiastical authorities still refused civil weddings, even though they were legal at that time. As soon as the authorities found out about our plans to marry, they took away Manolo's provisional freedom and put him back in jail to complete the sentence.

Meanwhile I continued with the wedding preparations. Once the papers were finalized, I transferred my conditional freedom from Manresa to Zaragoza, which is where I live. Here I completed the provisional term. We were married in prison. I lived free while Manolo completed his sentence. But his misfortunes didn't end with the end of his sentence. I was seven months pregnant when he was incarcerated again. He was still in prison when the baby was born. When my husband finally was released from prison, our little boy was three years old. After his release he had many difficulties finding work; businesses would be advised not to hire him because of his prison record and political convictions.

As for me and other women in the party, discrimination still exists. A man's responsibilities in the party are considered more important than a woman's. If my husband and I both have political meetings on the same evening, I'm the one expected to stay home with the children. Women are excluded from positions of higher responsibility in the party because they say we're less well prepared than men. I hoped my husband would help educate me in the ideals and programs of the party, but he didn't. And he hasn't shared the work at home as I think men in the party should. We say that the party is for the masses, but in reality the few people who run it are interested in theories and lofty ideas rather than the everyday problems we women face.

# CHAPTER 22

# *The Burden and Strength of Clandestinity 1946–1948*

A boarder at Carmen's house on Mallorca street was waiting for me in a taxi at the prison door when I was released that February of 1946. When I saw Miguel again I told him how I'd given a false address.

"Does that mean you're going to continue working for the party?"

"We aren't done yet with the Francoist regime, are we?"

I stayed a couple of days in Carmen's house. Then a man who was active in our party and personally like a brother to us arranged a room for me in San José de la Montaña. My room had a terrace and looked out on a garden. He paid all my expenses for a month so I could consult with two or three doctors about my head and spinal column.

After seeing the radiograph, the doctors determined that the blow to my neck had knocked my spinal column out of alignment. None of the doctors agreed with the diagnosis from prison that I would have to have an operation. These doctors thought the blood clot would dissolve by itself, though not without causing me some difficulties. They insisted that I get complete bed rest and lie on a board. I spent a month in that house. Afterward I stayed with Miguel's parents in Madrid for two months. Then I returned to Barcelona where Miguel welcomed me with open arms. We had almost joined our lives together, but it was difficult even to consider marriage in our clandestine circumstances.

"Get along with you, my fine friend," I finally said to Miguel. "If we have to wait for the end of Francoism, we'll be old and gray."

Miguel laughed. He is and always has been an optimist. "This situation will end. We're in debt to our party and ought to continue fighting. If we get married, it's going to be all the harder for us to keep up the struggle."

I disagreed. I told him the two of us could continue together since we belonged to the same party and shared the struggle to end the dictatorship. I assured him I would never stand in his way and I couldn't imagine that he would ever stand in mine.

On that condition I was ready at any time to join our lives together for however long we could enjoy them. I was prepared to endure any separation. I would always think about him and I knew that when we were together, we could rejoice in our love. It took him a while to understand that I really wouldn't be an obstacle in his political life. We were married on June 29, 1946.

Our first home was a house on Sarria street near Avenida Infanta Carlota. There three married couples lived in a very pretty flat. One of the couples had a darling little girl, about two and one-half years old. The other couple was Moises and Agustina, some of the closest comrades with whom we had worked before the arrests of 1945. Also living there was our comrade, Celestino Carrete, nicknamed "the old man." The seven adults and little girl lived there for several months until we had to split up for reasons of security. Only María and her husband, the parents of the little girl, remained. As for the others, each went to a place with friends of the party. We went to live at 72 Urgel street in the first apartment on the third floor. We had two small rooms with kitchen privileges. On our same floor lived a marvelous family. The mother, Luisa, was like a mother to me. All of us called her Mama Luisa.

In our state of semiclandestinity we went on working for the party and the guerrillas. But when I found out I was pregnant I didn't make trips as frequently as before my arrest in 1945. I worked with the contact person between the party and the guerrillas. I had a lot of dealings with Pedro Valverde.

In April of 1947 there was another general arrest like the one in 1945, but this one was much more serious because of the consequences. In 1945 we had managed to get the death penalty lifted from a group of guerrillas that had been tried under exceptional circumstances, but in this new round of arrests our luck ran out. Our comrades were hideously tortured. Pedro's optic nerve was broken and he was left half blind. In spite of the beatings and torture, the police couldn't drag out of them the name of even one comrade or the location of one drop-off point or a single support house.

On February 17 Gómez Ponchón, who had been our lawyer in 1945, called Miguel at his office, told him his comrades had been arrested, that the police were looking for him and that he should leave town immediately. Without saying a word to anyone, Miguel left. His pen was on the desk in his office just as he left it and his coat still hung on the coat hook. He took the key to the strong box with him and came home to collect some things and see what we would do. Before we left, Miguel gave the key to the strong box to Luisa and told her to take it to the office after a couple of days and give it to Mr. Rivero, the man in charge.

I don't remember where we came to rest that day but I do know that the police were searching everywhere for Miguel. The word was they were looking for him but not me. Nonetheless, it was decided that Miguel shouldn't leave Barcelona but stay on for a while hidden in a house. I was to be taken to France where I could give birth. They put me on a train bound for some town where a car then took me to a textile factory where I stayed with friends. There I awaited the party's decision. If I went to France I might be separated from the party for a long time. In those days you couldn't know for how long.

But I flatly refused to cross the border. I was determined to stay in Catalonia come what may. Our friend, who was an engineer, communicated my decision to Barcelona and I returned to the city. When I reached Barcelona, I was taken to the same hiding place where Miguel was. There was a rather large shop on the ground floor and upstairs Miguel had make-shift living quarters, but no kitchen. Our friend "Coa" brought us food and papers every day; for furniture we had only a sofa and some big boxes. During the day the boxes were our table and we used the sofa for sitting. At night Miguel slept on the inside part of the sofa while I slept on the edge with my stomach, growing bigger every day, resting on a large box. We had no light except from the street. On the roof of the house was a terrace where we went at night for fresh air. We'd go on tiptoe in case a nearby neighbor out on the balcony or terrace might see us. That terrace was our refuge; no one could see us seated there, leaning back against the wall and breathing free air. During the day I would walk around barefoot through those empty rooms because I couldn't stand to sit all day with my big stomach. At dinner time when the workers left and we heard the machines stop, the two of us would walk around as we pleased and eat. Miguel would read newspapers and write. We stayed there for two months, all the time our companions were detained at police headquarters. It wasn't until 1962 that our hard work with international lawyers on behalf of prisoners paid off: prisoners couldn't be held in police stations longer than seventy-two hours. But that action came too late for the four companions in jail.

When we learned that the authorities weren't going to let up on their search for Miguel, we decided that I would go to Luisa's house for the birth of our child. When I left Miguel said to me: "If the birth is at night, let 'Coa' know and I'll come."

In a matter of a few days everything was ready for the baby's arrival. At night they would take me out for walks. The doctor had said I should walk a great deal. The house didn't have an elevator so we went down five floors and then along the avenue as far as the Plaza España. At that time there were gardens and a waterfall in the city center as well as benches. We would cross the square, sit down, and then return home along the same route.

I had a marvelous doctor. We called him Dr. Marcos, but that probably wasn't his real name. He was a young man, a refugee from Madrid, living clandestinely with his wife in Barcelona. Most of us didn't pay him anything when he examined us because we simply didn't have the money. On occasion some midwife—there were still midwives in those days—would come to help in case she was needed. But there wasn't much call for midwives because most women at that time had their babies in hospitals or clinics.

Labor started around noon, July 5. Luisa called Dr. Marcos. He came immediately. After examining me, he said: "Looks as if this will take a long time, so I'm going to leave. Call me if something happens. At any rate, I'll be back around eight or nine o'clock." When he returned that night he examined me again. There was reason for concern: I was older than most women having their first baby and it looked as if this would be a dry delivery. Dr. Marcos and his wife had supper and spent the entire night in Luisa's house. Since it was clear the baby would be born at night, Luisa let "Coa" know so he could get word to Miguel.

The July heat was suffocating. Luisa had bought ice which she kept in a dish pan along with beer for the doctor. I spent the night walking from my flat to Angelita's; hers faced the street. There I would peer out from the balcony for a glimpse of Miguel. Every time a car or taxi drove by, I thought it was Miguel. I knew that it might take a long time for Miguel to get the message. That's what happened. Miguel didn't know for several days that he had a baby daughter.

Estrella was born at four o'clock in the morning. That very day, July 6, 1947, the first referendum under Franco was held. As an exprisoner, I couldn't vote. Before Luisa went to vote, she made a good breakfast for us with chocolate, churros, and cream. Thanks to Luisa's incredible way with money, we had a real feast that day. After breakfast Dr. Marcos examined me and then left with the promise that he would return in the afternoon to see how mother and daughter were doing. Luisa left to vote. In fact Luisa was voting because she was afraid sanctions might be leveled against people who didn't vote and if so, she might lose her boarding house.

On Friday I learned that Miguel was coming the next day. Naturally I counted the hours until I would see him. When Miguel finally got there, I hardly recognized him; with his hair dyed blond even the mother who bore him wouldn't have known him.

That night Miguel explained our plan of action: we would leave Catalonia. Our departure had to be prepared carefully since Miguel couldn't just walk around the streets with the police still after him. I had to take charge of everything. We began by dying his hair dark again. I contacted comrades to get false documentation. The only document needed at that time was the rationing card, which didn't have a photo-graph stamped on it. Miguel took care of the baby and house while I went out to take care of these matters. He always watched to make sure no one was following me.

I would make lots of false turns before going in the house. Miguel would sigh with relief whenever I got back. By now we also had a false military service card, which was indispensable for Miguel who at his age certainly would have served in the military. Any policeman or Civil Guard or any other authority would have asked for this document. Finally the only documents we lacked were the safe conducts that were still required for train travel. The day I went for them was the most frightening time for Miguel, not that he was afraid for himself but rather that something had happened to me. I went out promptly in the morn-ing, right after nursing the baby at nine o'clock. I expected to be back by noon. But there was a long, long line of people waiting for safe conducts. I waited from quarter past ten until one o'clock. What must Miguel be thinking when I was supposed to be back by noon to nurse the baby? In short, Miguel had a bad time. He told me later that when the baby began to fuss at noon, he gave her a little bit of sugar water to quiet her.

Now all that was left was the actual departure, but that was risky business because the train stations were swarming with police. The baby was a month old when we left Barcelona. I caught the train at the Fran-cia station, carrying the baby in a little basket. Miguel got the train from another station. We changed trains in Calatayud and went on to my sis-ter's home in Soria. My mother was there, too. We had a marvelous month together. Then we went to Guadalajara where Miguel stayed while I traveled to Madrid to find out if our contacts were still in place. We were in Madrid only a short time before Miguel informed me that the party was sending him elsewhere to work. And me? I was left with a baby and two pesetas in my pocket. I didn't even know where my hus-band was going.

I was able to stay with a friend for three months and got work doing cross-stitch on trim for children's clothing. At the end of December I was told to leave the shop because I would be going with Miguel in January. I was to spend the Christmas holidays with the grandparents so they could enjoy their granddaughter for a little while. I had a wonderful Christmas and New Year's holiday helping prepare and take packages to the prisons. I often went to Miguel's parents' house and many friends came over curious to see the baby. Miguel's mother wasn't very happy about our marriage. She would have preferred her only son not to have a Communist for a wife and to give up the risk of clandestine life, which constantly jeopardized our freedom and perhaps our lives. What his mother couldn't understand was how difficult it was for her son to give up the political struggle. It's not easy to be separated almost constantly, to see each other only once in a while, and not to know where the other person is, to spend years and years in these circumstances. Our best years were spent in separations, either by prison or clandestine living.

When the holidays were over I went to see the man who had set a day for me to leave Madrid. The only plan I had to follow was to catch the train to Seville and meet someone who would identify himself with the countersign. So with Estrella in a little basket I took the train for Andalusia. The train left at half past eight at night. The car I happened to get in was occupied by a priest and a seminarian. When they saw the little girl in their car, the priest said in a voice I could hear: "So, we have a canary in the room. What a fine night we're going to have."

I looked at him but didn't answer. At that time I was rabidly anticlerical. To me the priests' cassocks smelled of the coup de grace shots they had administered when prisoners were executed. At nine o'clock I took the baby out of the basket and nursed her. After being fed and cleaned, she went fast to sleep. About ten or so the priest and the seminarian began to eat supper; then they took out their cigarettes. Up to that time they'd done their smoking outside on the car's platform but now, after dinner, they intended to smoke inside.

"Please, gentlemen, the canary isn't bothering you; she's sound asleep. But your tobacco smoke is going to harm her. So go outside to smoke."

The little priest turned red as a tomato but he nodded to the seminarian and they went outside. What must those men have thought! It was quiet in the compartment all night along. At nine o'clock in the morning we reached Seville. Those men behaved very well and said to me: "Madam, you get down with your suitcase and we'll lower the little basket."

So they did. They bid me good-bye and I remained standing on the platform with my suitcase in one hand and the basket in the other. I walked toward the station exit. Someone on the platform approached: "Communist and Catholic, right?"

I stood looking at him, thinking, "Tomasa, you're caught." But the comrade saw the expression of doubt on my face and immediately gave me the countersign. He looked at the little basket and seeing the baby girl, said: "This girl is yours?" But in Spanish his use of the plural form of "yours" meant that he knew Miguel.

"Yes, whose would she be? She's mine. And her father's, of course."

"But could such an ugly father have such a fine looking little girl?"

"Now, young man, you haven't looked at me," I said jokingly.

"Hey, you're not bad, but this little girl is something else. She's one of the prettiest babies I've ever seen. What's her name?"

"Estrella."

"I'm not surprised. With that name she must be prettier than the stars shining above. That child is sure to do honor to her name."

He took my suitcase and the little basket we carried between the two of us. We left the station and walked a short way.

"Good, now we're going toward a truck that's coming for food and supplies for the dam. That's where Fernando is working as a book-keeper, at least that's the name we give him. It's a big wooden barracks where the company has the commissary. You'll live with him there. Remember, when we're in the truck picking up people, we don't know each other. Understand? You told me you were the bookkeeper's wife, nothing more."

I got in the truck and we left. In Seville we picked up several people who had gone shopping. They were surprised to see me and asked where I was going.

"To the dam. My husband is the bookkeeper at the commissary."

Miguel was at the dam on party orders. By the beginning of 1948 the party had decided to dissolve the guerrillas and organize the party on a firmer basis. The main work in the area at that time was organizing workers for the party. My job was to visit the caves when the workers were eating their lunch or in the evenings after work and pass along messages or set up times when Miguel could meet with the party men working on the dam.

Eighty percent or more of the workers had fled their towns to avoid arrest or they had been exiled when they got out of prison. Without any other source of work they had been stuck in that hole where on the one hand they were safer than in their home towns but on the other more tied to the job than if they'd been prisoners. Their wages were so miserable that the money ran out before the week was up and they had to get credit from the commissary; their credit was on a weekly basis so the men couldn't leave the dam even if the conditions at home had been less dangerous.

Miguel was very happy to have us together again. And he was so proud of little Estrella, darling that she was. We established a relationship with the man in charge of the commissary that went beyond business. The Civil Guard were constantly in the store; they must have been afraid the guerrillas would sneak in and take away their food. What they didn't know was that Miguel was there by a plan established between the party and the guerrillas.

As for me, I would speak with the wives of the comrades. It hurt me so much to hear about the miseries and calamities they suffered. By the time the children reached the age of two, three, or four, they had rickets and were anemic. The death rate among children was very high. And it was impossible to guess the age of the women. They might tell me they were twenty-six or twenty-seven, but they easily looked ten or twelve years older.

One day, without being seen, I took a handful of caramels from the store. They never sold because the families didn't have money for candy. I went into the first hovel where they were two little kids and gave them caramels. They didn't want to take the candy. Their mother told them to go on and take the caramels. But even with the candy in their hands they didn't know what to do. They switched the candy from one hand to another and finally gave it back to me. "Don't worry," their mother said to me, "the children just haven't ever had a caramel." My eyes began to water. I took a caramel, removed the paper, and put it in the little boy's mouth. Of course he loved it. The kids were so happy and smiling eating their caramels. Their mother began to cry. I tried to make her feel better; I told her that this misery was going to end soon because we were working to overthrow the fascist regime that was choking people to death.

We didn't know if it was the weather or what, but Miguel became very ill, his fever so high he was delirious. Everyone was concerned about him; even the guards wanted to visit him. I played the part of the Civil Guard, prohibiting anyone from coming in. I couldn't leave him for a minute because everything he said in his delirium pertained to the work at the dam. I spent several days not knowing where we would end up if some guard walking through the commissary happened to hear what Miguel was saying. Sometimes I even had to put my hand over his mouth to stifle his words. When he was better, he realized that he couldn't continue there. We knew the guards were becoming suspicious. The precautions I had taken as well as refusing to let them see Miguel struck them as odd. After Miguel was well, he made a bus trip to Seville on the pretext of doing company business. During the trip he managed to send a message to our contact in Barcelona. By then he had accomplished what he'd set out to do.

After we reached Madrid, we were separated again. And again, I didn't know where he was going. But after a few days I got a cryptic note, letting me know I should go to Vitoria, which I did. I didn't see Miguel at the station, but when I got off the train a lady said to me: "You're Peque, right?"

"Yes."

"Oh my dear girl, how much I've wanted to meet you," she said, embracing me.

With the two of us carrying the little basket and me with my suitcase, we went to the house where I was to live. Meanwhile Miguel had been watching to see if we were being followed. When he was sure that no one had followed me, he came in the house. He explained that his work wasn't in Vitoria but in Vergara. He would come to see us some Sunday. In those days he combined his professional work with his work for the party. We received no salary from the party. Wherever we went we had to work to be able to eat; food didn't fall from heaven.

We didn't stay long in Vitoria. Not many days after our arrival, I went out shopping with Paquita, the woman whose house we shared. We bought some little sandals for Estrella. After we finished shopping, we went to a cafe for a refreshment. I had some black coffee and Paquita had coffee with milk. She was holding the girl and soon I saw that she was giving her a little spoonful of coffee with milk, which Estrella loved.

"Paquita, don't give the baby anything that doesn't come from home."

"Oh, don't be foolish. This can't hurt her."

She only gave her that one little spoonful. A fatal spoonful. That night Paquita got sick with terrible pains in her stomach and intestines. She tried to throw up but couldn't. I had her drink glasses of water with bicarbonate. She finally vomited. She had to get up several times during the night to throw up again. Meanwhile Estrella spent a very restless night. She usually slept soundly but that night she was restless and whimpered from time to time as if something were hurting her. By morning she was worse. She hadn't had a bowel movement and she threw up what I fed her. By then I was giving her orange juice and tomato juice besides nursing her. Everything came up.

That afternoon we went to see a pediatrician who had taken care of Paquita's children. He diagnosed some little infection and prescribed sul-fanilamides. The baby was sick all that afternoon and that night she got worse. The following day I told Paquita we should see the doctor again.

As pretty as the baby usually was, I could tell she was getting sicker by the hour. I phoned Miguel to tell him how our little girl was. After eating we went to the doctor, hoping to be among the first people he would see. The time for seeing patients came but the doctor didn't appear. We waited an hour. I could see Estrella getting worse all the time. I asked Paquita if she knew another doctor in Vitoria and not to think of the cost. She took me to an expensive but excellent specialist. When we reached his office the waiting room was filled with women and their babies. I thought my baby needed immediate attention or we might lose her at any moment. Paquita spoke to the nurse who took one look at the girl and said: "We've got one other case like yours. The doctor will see them first."

So it was. The other woman was the first to go in with a boy a lit-tle older than Estrella. When she came out she looked more desperate than when she'd gone in. When we went in, the doctor spoke to us so quietly we had to strain to hear him. I thought he must have a problem with his hearing, but that wasn't the case. His custom was to speak with children in a low voice. When I went in his office, he spoke in a normal voice. The first thing he said when I entered was: "Madam, you've brought me a dead little girl."

I got a knot in my throat. I could hardly breathe. But I managed to control my nerves and listen intently to the doctor's words. He examined her carefully, asking me how she had gotten to this extreme situation. I thought we should explain what happened in the cafe.

Paquita described her symptoms too. Without a doubt, the doctor said, the milk must have been bad.

"But I only gave her one little spoonful," Paquita said. "Her mother wouldn't let me give her more."

"Madam, poison comes in little doses. Remember that you knew what to do to make yourself vomit. But the baby couldn't tell you what was wrong with her."

Since she hadn't had a bowel movement and had vomited the nourishment I'd given her, her little body was filled with toxins. The situation was grave. At that age only one in a hundred children survived such a poisoning. Quick action was needed. First he prescribed a treatment at a nearby clinic. There they would give the baby a liter of antitoxin serum, half of a liter in each little thigh muscle. If the baby tolerated the first half of a liter, he explained, trying to encourage me, she would tolerate the second more easily. But nothing was certain.

The doctor also prescribed an infusion of some kind of liquid with a medication to be given every hour in a soup spoon. I was told that if the baby tolerated the liquid, she might throw up and have a bowel movement too. If this didn't work by nine in the morning, they'd have to try something else.

While Paquita dressed the baby, the doctor called me to one side to say that if she was still alive in the morning and hadn't vomited or had a bowel movement, he would have to operate. I had to give my approval right then because he needed to advise the surgeon. I asked him how much the operation would cost. I was taken back to hear 25,000 pesetas, but I reacted quickly: "Yes, yes, of course. You understand that everything must be done for the child. Advise the doctor. If we have to operate, then we'll operate."

When we left the doctor's office, I told Paquita about the operation. She stared at me. "Where are we going to get that kind of money?"

"Don't worry, be calm. The important thing is to save the baby."

We reached the clinic and I gave the clerk and nurse the sealed envelope from the doctor. They looked at each other, then at us. Then they quickly set about to give the injections. The whole time they put the liquid in the little leg the nurse took the baby's pulse. The first half of a liter was in. They went to the other leg. Then the nurse looked at the baby and said to me: "Relax, madam. The baby tolerated the first injection and she'll stand the other one, you'll see."

So it went. She tolerated both injections, that is, a liter of antitoxin serum divided in two parts. When we were ready to leave, they put the doctor's note in the envelope, saying: "There, madam, take it with you."

We were a long way from home. Paquita couldn't find a taxi so we had to walk home with the sick baby.

Miguel opened the door. "You're crazy to come and go at these hours with a sick baby."

Choking with fear that the baby was going to die, I burst into tears.

"What's the matter?" Miguel asked. "Why are you crying? What's going on?"

I explained what was happening. He stood there asking forgiveness for greeting me like that. He asked me to please calm down.

He explained that when he came in from Vergara and didn't find anyone at home, he'd gone to the station where Paquita's husband worked and gotten the doctor's address. But when he hadn't found us in the doctor's office, he'd come home.

Everything was cleared up and we set about to prepare the baby and give her the treatment. Miguel took a sheet of paper where he kept track hour by hour of the baby's symptoms each time she took her spoonful of medication. At the beginning she didn't take all of it, spitting some out, but after one or two in the morning she began taking the whole spoonful, even eagerly. When I put it in her little mouth she gave us the feeling she would have taken more, but we followed the doctor's directions carefully. We spent an anxious night: the baby wasn't passing anything, either above or below. But she was keeping the liquid down, which the doctor had told us was important. After seven o'clock in the morning the baby finally had a bowel movement. Her stools showed how badly poisoned her little body was.

Paquita made us a hot breakfast. We were worn out. I'd been able to lie down and sleep a little but Miguel had spent the night sitting next to the baby. I cleaned up the baby after breakfast and we went to the doctor with a stool sample. On the way Miguel said: "Last night with all this business about the baby I didn't ask how you could say yes to the operation. How did you plan to come up with 25,000 pesetas?"

"Look, Miguel, the main thing is to save the baby. I went to prison for political reasons. I would go again to save my baby."

Miguel stopped suddenly, took me in his arms, kissed me and uttered beautiful words that anybody would love to hear.

When the doctor saw us come in, the first thing he said was: "I can see already from your faces that everything turned out all right."

And so it did. When he saw the stools he was astounded. He told us that the little boy who had exactly the same thing had died that morning.

"One out of a hundred survives," he repeated. "You're lucky. That one is your baby."

Miguel gave him the record we had kept during the night. The doctor was impressed by how carefully Miguel had charted the baby's condition.

"All fathers should do this when their children are sick," he said. "Unfortunately, they don't."

How different the situation was now from the previous day when the baby had cried as the doctor put his hands on her stomach and sides. This morning all she did was sleep. She would open her little eyes from time to time and then close them again. He gave her a pat on the fanny: "There, there, little girl, the danger has passed."

Yes, that danger was over, but not the dangers of our clandestine living. By June Miguel and I were separated again. Shortly after we left Vitoria the police came to the house where we had stayed. They took Tomás to jail and interrogated Paquita. She only said that she had had some boarders by the names of Fernando and Juanita. They interrogated Tomás much more strongly, but he stood up well under it.

When we left Paquita and Tomás we told them we were going to Madrid. Tomás had even bought the tickets. But we got off before Madrid and bought two more tickets, one for Barcelona, where Miguel was going, and another for Soria, where my sister lived. I spent a quiet three months with my sister and her family in Soria until the morning my brother-in-law came in the house white as a sheet.

# CHAPTER 23

# *The Long Years 1948–1976*

My brother-in-law turned pale because the Civil Guard had turned up asking for a certain Juanita. He thought it was just their way of getting at him. He didn't know Juanita was my cover name. At that time he was the manager of a large farm with fruit trees, vegetable gardens, and a large herd of dairy cows. He barely made enough money to support his six children, wife, our mother, and now me. So he made an agreement with the man in charge of the cows to exchange goods: fruit and vegetables for a well-hidden pail of milk. There was also an understanding with the guards; he was under orders to fill their knapsacks with fruit and vegetables every fifteen days or so. The guards had been there just a few days before and left well supplied. It seems that the previous night my brother-in-law had brought home a sack of dried beans to have something hot to feed the children during the coming winter. These beans the older children were shelling by walking on them when the guards unexpectedly showed up asking about this Juanita. After the guards left, my brother-in-law came up to the room and began swearing: "This had to happen to me, this had to happen to me. They'll be back. Everything they asked was just a cover. They'll come back to check everything and then they'll find the beans."

"What did they ask you?" we all wanted to know.

"They were looking for some woman named Juanita."

Hearing that, I caught my brother-in-law, gave him a kiss and said: "Look, Manolo, calm down, this business about the beans isn't anything to worry about. We'll burn the shells and they won't find a trace of them if they come back. And for sure they won't find that Juanita on any farm around here. You see, that Juanita—it's me."

They all stared at me. They didn't know I went by the name of Juanita, but it didn't surprise them because they did know the kind of life Miguel and I lived. We put the beans in a sack and hid it under a dresser and then took the shells down to the kitchen and burned them in the hearth. Since the house was old, the hearth was always lit for cooking whether it was summer or winter. I told Manolo that if the guards returned I would do everything possible to make sure they didn't see him. He probably would have such a frightened expression on his face it would be better if he didn't come out. Besides, since he'd already told them that this Juanita didn't live there, there was no reason for him to face them again.

I went to the door and sat down outside on one of the stone benches to cross-stitch. My mother was in the kitchen and didn't know what was going on, and my sister wasn't at home. The entrance to the house was very pleasant with its little patio, fruit trees, stone benches, even a cute pine tree and large vegetable garden.

The guards weren't long in coming. They asked for my brother-in-law. I told them he probably was working out in the gardens.

"Would you like me to look for him?"

"You're not from these parts, are you?"

"No, I'm Manolo's sister-in-law. I've come to spend a few months with my mother and family."

"And where are you from? Where do you live?"

"In Barcelona."

"And your husband, where's he?"

"Bilbao."

"What's his name?"

"Fernando."

"Hmm, what a coincidence. We're looking for a woman named Juanita whose husband is Fernando, and she has a little girl named Estrella."

I looked at them in surprise. "Hey, that is a coincidence. I have a baby named Estrella and my husband is Fernando. But my name isn't Juanita. But tell me, why are you looking for them?"

"Oh, we're just acting on orders."

"Well, look, you're worrying me because we live in Barcelona. My husband works in a business and he has to go to Bilbao now and then to work for a few months in their branch office. Why would I want to stay alone in Barcelona when I've been so anxious to see my mother and family? My husband suggested I come to Soria until his work in Bilbao is done. But now you've got me worried. I wonder if something's happened to my husband. Maybe there's been a mix-up over names."

"Could you tell me the address where your husband works?"

A Basque name came to mind. "Yes, certainly, in such and such a street." And I gave a number.

The two guards looked at me, not knowing what to do. On the one hand they trusted my brother-in-law and were grateful for everything he gave them from the garden; on the other hand, they were suspicious.

"All right," one of them finally said, "all right, what can we do? If her name were the same there wouldn't be an issue, but it's not."

"Look," the other answered, "the best thing is to go to the station, call Barcelona, and get more details."

"If you think it would help, I could go with you to the station. The matter will be cleared up if I'm there with you. It won't take long to get the baby ready and we can be off."

My reply calmed them down a little but also made them reluctant to take me, Manolo's sister-in-law, to the station.

"Oh, no, madam, no. Look, we're going and if there's any news, we'll come back. But don't worry. Don't move from here."

And very respectfully they left for the station. In those days the same Civil Guard station served three or four villages, so they had to go to another village. No sooner had the guards left than my oldest nephew got the horse, left for Carbonera, the closest village, and hired a taxi to come for me. While my nephew was off getting the taxi, I got the baby ready, packed my belongings and as soon as the taxi arrived left for Soria. My plan was to leave the baby with her grandparents and go on to Barcelona: first, so I wouldn't be with Miguel's parents in case the police came looking for me there and second, to see what was going on in Catalonia. I was calm about Miguel because I knew I would have been advised immediately if something had happened to him.

I left for Soria in the taxi and from there went on to Madrid where I went straight to Mama Anita's house; she was a marvelous woman whose son was in prison. The grandparents came to her house and took the baby home with them. I spent the night at Anita's house. The next morning when she saw what pain I was in from my breasts, she went for the baby so I could nurse her. I wasn't comfortable with what Anita had done, though of course I realized she'd acted with the best of intentions. But it had been difficult enough to leave the baby the day before; now to say good-bye once again was more than I could bear. How many times since then have I thought: "Why did I leave her? Why didn't I stay with her or take her with me?" I know it was fear, fear that I might be arrested and have to take her to prison with me. But then again, why not? So many children had endured prison. What was one more child? It's possible, I don't know, but it's possible that in those moments I could only consider what I ought to do and I believed that I was doing the right thing. Perhaps I should have stayed in Madrid and done what I could clandestinely with a little girl at my side. Would this have been wiser? I don't know.

I reached Barcelona and according to procedure I didn't go to any comrade's house. Instead I looked for domestic work, which I found immediately. I told the family I had an aunt in Barcelona, Luisa, who might be calling me. Luisa, of course, was my connection with the party.

It wasn't long before I received instructions to go to Reus. Once in Reus, I walked toward the place where a comrade was supposed to meet me. I'd only gone a short way when I spotted a young fellow with a magazine in his hand, similar to the one I was carrying. He approached and gave the countersign. He took me to a house where I was to stay until night when he himself would come back for me and put me in touch with the person I was to work with. There was food in the kitchen and a radio and books to help pass the time. More than five months had elapsed since Miguel and I had separated and I hadn't had one bit of news from him. In spite of the fact that he had seen these men, I didn't ask them about Miguel. I didn't know what name to use or whether to reveal my own identity.

Just after nightfall the man came for me. He took me to a place called Sweethearts Walk. That's where engaged couples and sweethearts who weren't engaged yet would meet. He and I were to walk as if we were a couple also. He'd let me know when we met the contact man, but we were to keep on walking until we reached the end of the walk and then he was to leave and I would go back to meet the other man. So we acted like sweethearts, walking close to each other and chatting intimately. Suddenly I noticed a man coming toward us. There was something familiar in his silhouette. Was I dreaming? Were my desires to see him overcoming me? No, I wasn't dreaming. It was Miguel coming toward me.

"Look," my companion said, "that man coming our way is the one you're supposed to join. Look at him carefully so you don't make a mistake with all these couples around here and the path so poorly lit."

I didn't dare look at the man for fear of giving myself away. My companion realized I was scarcely looking.

"Look at him," he said, giving me the elbow, "look at him."

"Don't worry, I saw him. I won't make a mistake. Don't worry."

The guy wasn't convinced, which meant he didn't know the connection between the other man and me. We reached the end of the walk, stopped a few minutes, then said good-bye. He left the park. I walked around a little while and then returned on the same path. I walked in the shadow of the trees to avoid the light playing on the center of the path. Miguel was doing the same. Finally we met next to a tree.

"Wait," he said, not embracing me, "wait." And opening a large portfolio he was carrying he took out a big jacket and put it on me. "Now, girl, this fits as if it had been made just for you."

Then he took me in his arms, happy, of course, but also worried— he knew about my leaving Soria and how the baby was with her grandparents. He knew everything about me, but I didn't know one thing about him. Speaking with Miguel about our little girl was so painful. But how could we avoid talking about her. Miguel wanted to know if she remembered him.

"Remember you? Poor man. She doesn't even remember me. At her age children only remember people who take care of them, feed and bathe, dress and undress them and fuss over them. Others don't even exist for them."

"That's nonsense. Her grandparents talk to her about us."

"No matter how much they say, it's nothing. In her mind neither of us exists."

I couldn't stand it any longer. I burst into tears.

"Don't be like that, woman," Miguel said, putting his arms around me again. "Be strong. You've always been strong. You'll see, we'll have her with us before long. We'll be together soon. This business will end. Do you understand?"

Those words, "this business will end," had been on our lips since the end of the war, ten long years ago. Thanks to this optimism we had been able to keep up the struggle. Had we known then that the struggle would last for thirty-seven years, would we have acted differently? Would we have settled into a regular family life? But we never seriously considered that possibility. We continued fighting, up to the very end.

And what about the other couples that night in the park? Some sat on benches, huddled together for warmth. Others walked beneath the shadows of the trees or leaned against the trees. Perhaps there was no happiness for them either. Perhaps love was all mixed in with disgust and jealousy. Who knows? Each person has his world.

We, too, were leaning against a tree. And something was missing in our lives, our little daughter. I wept for her. I had the feeling that my conscience cried out to me that night—that I should not have left her. My grief was especially acute when I milked my breasts each morning and evening. Each day a little less milk came. But there was still some milk, milk my little girl should have had. And each day I wept when the milk came. But that grief I could stand. This was different, this night being with Miguel on the Sweethearts Walk. My grief made him suffer. He wanted to appear strong, but tears filled his eyes. We ended up not talking, not saying a word, in silent, painful embrace. Our grief gradually eased and we calmed down.

"Well let's leave," Miguel suggested when he saw me calmer. "I want to introduce you to a friend so you'll know the house where we are to meet tomorrow when you start a job with us. I'm not going to tell you anything tonight but tomorrow I'll explain what you're to do." The house belonged to a single woman, Teresa, a professor who had worked for the party for many years. She was the owner of the jacket Miguel had brought me.

So it was that Miguel and I both did party work in Reus, though I also worked for three small shops mending nylon stockings. During the mornings and part of the afternoons I worked at home mending; then at half past four I walked to Teresa's house in time to listen to Radio Independent Spain at five o'clock. The news stories, which they read slowly, we copied down. We also got news of Spain which we used for a bulletin we put out called *The Guerrilla*. This work Teresa did after she left school, along with another comrade. Teresa taught me a lot; with her help I came to understand politics much better and I also improved my reading and writing.

During this time in Reus, Miguel and I behaved in front of the others as if we were just friends. From time to time we made love secretly. By December 24, Miguel knew that he was being sent elsewhere. He asked the leadership in Catalonia—at that time it was Gregorio López Raimundo—if we could spend the Christmas holidays with other friends in the party. Gregorio agreed. So on the twenty-fourth four of us women spent the entire day cooking and preparing packages for the prisoners in Tarragona and Reus. Naturally we talked about everything while we were working. Among other things we talked about our families and how they would spend Christmas. They hadn't ever asked me any questions about my personal life. Such questions would be dangerous in clandestine life. To them I was just one more comrade who happened to be called "Luisa." That day I told them I was married with a little girl. They asked to see a photo of her. Miguel had always said he was married and had showed off Estrella's photo. He was very proud of her. Even today, when he has grown grandchildren, he carries that little photo in his billfold. When I showed them Estrella's picture, two of them looked at each other, then said: "But this is Fernando's daughter."

"And mine. She's one and the same."

The girls couldn't get over their surprise. "Look, girl," one of them said, "if I had to spend months living the way you do, I couldn't stand it. Everyone would know in days who my husband was."

"But if the party told you beforehand to keep that a secret, wouldn't you do it?"

"I'm not sure. No, I don't think so."

At dinner time we ate together. There was no dearth of jokes about how we were going on our honeymoon and so forth. Later, when we finished preparing the packages and the men's political meeting broke up, Miguel and I were left alone in the house for the first time. Miguel was set to leave the next morning between eight and nine o'clock. That would be January 17. He didn't know where he was being sent. Naturally we wanted to spend this last night together. We couldn't go to Miguel's boarding house; besides, he'd already left the dirty place. So we decided to meet later at Teresa's.

When Miguel got to Teresa's, I met him at the door. He had a little square package in his hand, like a pastry box, and some other packages, including one that appeared to hold a bottle. We walked to a park and sat down on a bench under a tree. I was trembling with cold. We opened the little box of pastries and drank from the bottle of liqueur. Then we went back to Teresa's house. It was freezing cold. I was especially cold, in spite of the swallows of liqueur. But the political meeting at Teresa's was still going on. Then Miguel remembered another house; he went to see if we could stay the night there.

"Yes, we can go there," he said when he returned, "but there's no bed or bedroom, just a place under the stairs. But it's completely separate with enough room for a mattress."

That's where we spent our last night in Reus. With the little bit of liqueur I had drunk, the cold, and hugging Miguel tightly between the blankets, I went to sleep quickly, something he still teases me about. The very night before we had to say good-bye for how long we didn't know I went to sleep while he lay awake looking at me and thinking about having to leave me. I like to tease him that if I went to sleep it was because I felt at peace in his strong, safe, and loving arms.

Very early in the morning we went to Teresa's house to get his few things. There we said good-bye. I remember his saying: "Look, you're still young and if you think you can't wait for me, I'll never hold it against you. Just let me know somehow. You'd tell me the same thing if I were the one who had to wait."

We agreed not to deceive each other and always, always, good or bad, we would tell each other the truth. That promise we have kept, right up to the present time. There is no one better to solve our difficulties than we. We have always stood together, in good times and in bad.

On the seventeenth of January in 1949 I was alone once more, without the baby and with little news of her. What news I did get came through Mama Luisa. I don't remember exactly if it was the end of January or the first week of February when there was an attack on a train. A bomb had been placed on the track. One of the comrades who came by the house was very upset because at the time we weren't involved in guerrilla activities. He thought it might be a police ruse or the work of guerrilla groups who didn't agree with the party's policy to disband them. The fear was that there would be reprisals against the comrades who had been condemned to death more than a year before. There was a neighbor on the floor above who listened to the radio. This man was very reserved; he would greet me but nothing more. In those days it was a crime to listen to Radio Independent Spain. This neighbor would put the radio on the floor, right where his dining room was, so it wouldn't be heard through the walls. In order to listen to his radio I would put a chair on top of the table and climb up to listen. Two mornings had gone by without listening to his radio because I had a bad cold. On February

17, 1949, I heard the radio go on. No sooner had the broadcast started than I heard a heavy stomp on the floor. I jumped out of bed and got up on the table, thinking something had happened already. And something had.

That very morning our four comrades had been executed: Numen Mestres, Angel Carrero, Puig Pidemunt, and Pedro Valverde.

I remember how difficult it was for me to get down from the chair to the table and from the table to the floor. I wept bitterly for the loss of our comrades. The Francoist assassination was one more among the many that had been perpetrated. That morning I cried even more than other times when friends had been snatched away to be shot. Maybe it was being alone that sharpened my grief. It used to be that my reaction had been one of fury and renewed courage to keep fighting. This time, February 17, my tears were bitter—that the struggle would have to be continued.

I looked up at the ceiling and remembered the knock the upstairs neighbor had given listening to the news. Was he a comrade or simply a citizen opposed to Franco? What must he be thinking? Revenge, like me? In those years many of us wanted more from the party's struggle than a national political reconciliation; for myself and many others it was very difficult to accept a change in the party's political philosophy that would settle for compromise.

Still today there is etched in my memory one day and two months: the seventeenth of January and the seventeenth of February. The first seventeenth was the day I said good-bye to Miguel. I was not to see him for another four years and eight months, during which time I would not receive a single bit of news about him. The second seventeenth was the day in February they shot our comrades.

A couple of months later, on the way back from delivering the mended stockings to the shops and just as I turned into the street where I lived, I saw a man at the other end hide when he saw me approach. At least I thought he hid when he saw me. It might just have been a coincidence. But the following day when I returned a little later, there was a man in the same spot as the day before. Was he waiting for someone? Watching me? I made a third test. The time was different, but the guy was there again.

There wasn't a doubt in my mind. Something strange was going on. I went up to the flat and without turning on the light I very carefully opened the door to the balcony. I stretched out on the floor and watched the man in the street. He began to walk. When he reached the entrance to my building, he looked up at the balconies and windows. Clearly he was trying to ascertain if a light had gone on with my arrival home. If he recognized me, he could have me arrested. Why didn't he do it? Or was he watching the house? Had someone tipped off the police about the meetings held there? If they've recognized me, I thought, they're probably waiting to catch someone in this house because they know there's a reason why I live here. It's not my arrest alone that interests them. It could be they're just watching the house. At any rate, it was clear I had to leave Reus.

I left Catalonia for Madrid and went directly to Luisa's house. She told me the baby was fine. I made arrangements to stay with the parents of Miguel's previous sweetheart, Alfredo and Maximina. Luisa let the grandparents know I was at her home. That afternoon they came with the little girl. Estrella was twenty-two months old at the time, a precious child with long, curly hair and a cute way of talking. I could hardly believe I was seeing her so near to me. But there was one huge blow: she didn't know me and didn't want to have anything to do with me. When I asked her to come to me, she answered: "You aren't my mommy. You're stupid and ugly and I don't like you."

I spoke with the grandparents about my staying with them. But I saw they were very confused about this, perhaps because they feared the police or perhaps because they had made the baby their own.

I sublet a room with kitchen privileges, found work giving permanents and made contact with the party. Although I saw my little girl frequently, she refused to accept me as her mother. Perhaps she couldn't understand the situation.

In the month of July I went to Los Molinos in the mountains for a summer job in a hotel. I still hadn't succeeded in having my daughter give me a kiss or hug. And I had no news at all of her father. It was a bad time. I was also suffering from pains in my spinal column and neck.

The hotel in Los Molinos was very pleasant, with three floors and a big garden. The owners were a married couple with a daughter who was a professor and did the bookkeeping during summer months. I was the oldest person among the personnel they had chosen for summer work. They gave me lots of responsibilities in the hotel. As usual in clandestine life I had to tell stories about myself: my husband was working in Germany, my daughter was with her grandparents in Madrid, my name was Eugenia. They didn't try to confirm who I was or who I had ceased to be. From extra jobs I took on I was able to save some money and rent a room so the grandparents could visit with Estrella.

The first Saturday they came the owners realized right away that the little girl didn't like me. I was usually the only person to eat with the owners in the kitchen, but that first day the grandparents and little girl also ate there. She went to play in the garden with the owner's daughter, preferring Elisita to me. On Sunday when they left, I still hadn't had a single kiss or hug. Estrella continued with her usual talk of how I was stupid and ugly and not her mommy. I wondered how she could keep up this same song after all these months when I had seen her often enough, though not every day. I went with them to the train station to say good-bye and when I returned to the hotel, my eyes were red from crying all the way back. Mr. Torquemada, the owner, was a pleasant and compassionate man.

"Eugenia," he said when he saw me return, "look at me."

"Why? What's wrong?"

"Nothing, go on with your work."

The following week the grandparents and Estrella returned. The same thing happened. There was nothing to be done. The girl didn't want anything to do with me. On Sunday I was preparing the table in the kitchen for our meal and Estrella was playing in the garden with Lucky, the owners' big German shepherd. The grandparents were seated at the table in the garden where Mr. Torquemada had invited them for a cold drink.

"Eugenia," he said, "if you agree, I'm going to speak with your in-laws. It's not right that your little girl doesn't like you. They don't realize what they're doing to you."

Fed up with the situation, I answered that he had my permission to speak with the grandfather and tell him whatever he liked. After dinner they went out to the garden for a coffee and later I found out they had spoken. When the grandparents left, I went as usual to the station with them. The walk was very tense and we scarcely spoke. I didn't know if the two had spoken with Mr. Torquemada or if it had only been the grandfather. The strain on me was terrible. When I returned from the station, Mr. Torquemada told me he had spoken with the grandparents and their answer was I couldn't care for the child because I worked all day. They did take good care of her and were always attentive to her. Mr. Torquemada had told the grandfather: "If the girl is here with Eugenia she can take care of her in the most essential ways. When she's working in the dining room, Estrella can be with my daughter. What you cannot do is make that child dislike her own mother. You don't realize how much Eugenia is suffering."

"Do you think they'll give in?"

"Possibly. Let's wait until next week. They promised to think it over. We'll see."

The following Saturday they returned as usual. This time they brought a little suitcase. Mr. and Mrs. Torquemada looked at me satisfied as if to say, "We've won."

"Here, take the girl's things," the grandparents said. "We need to talk when you have time."

"Well, right now."

The grandfather told me they were leaving the child with me to see if she got along, but I should be very careful because she didn't know me. Besides, I should watch what I gave her to eat because she didn't eat everything yet and the hotel wouldn't be able to give her the food she was used to eating. I answered that however much they loved Estrella—and I understood how deeply they cared for her—I was still her mother and knew how to take care of her. They said I could let the room go because the girl was going to stay with me. But I replied they could continue coming every Saturday because just as I wanted to see my daughter I knew they wanted to see their granddaughter.

I also had the idea that the money I earned in tips would pay for the room so they could spend the month of August in Los Molinos when grandfather had his vacation. On Sunday they didn't want me to accompany them to the station for fear the little girl would throw a fit when they left. They couldn't stand to see her cry.

Mr. and Mrs. Torquemada set up the crib they had used for their daughter in the room where I slept. That night my daughter cried herself to sleep.

"Don't worry, Eugenia," Mr. Torquemada said. "Don't suffer. You'll see that the girl will have changed in a few days."

The next day she didn't want a thing to do with me. She called and called for her little grandpa and grandma. Elisita was the only one who could do anything with her: she got her ready, took her out to the garden and played with her and Lucky. I took her to the upstairs rooms to be with me, but everything seemed so strange to her that she didn't pay any attention to me. She watched how I dusted and then took the handkerchief out of her pocket to dust.

"No, Estrellita, not with your handkerchief. You'll use it on your nose and it will be all dirty. Look, mommy will give you a dust cloth."

She grabbed it from me and threw it on the floor angrily. So it went for three days. On the fourth I didn't put the handkerchief in her pocket. When I took her to the upstairs rooms, she tried to dust but when she realized she didn't have a handkerchief, she stood looking at me.

"Well, give your mommy a little kiss and I'll give you a dust cloth so you can clean. Okay? Will you help me?"

It was the first time after months that she took hold of me and gave me a kiss. Everything changed after that.

Her grandfather was surprised the next Sunday when we all ate together and had paella. I put some rice from the paella on the girl's plate, only the rice, with a bit of chicken cut up in little pieces, mixing it with the rice. Seeing this, the grandfather said to me: "Are you going to give that food to her? She's not used to such food."

"Don't worry. She'll get used to it. She's getting used to eating everything and as of today no harm's been done. Look, grandpa, remember that I'm her mother and I don't want to hurt her in any way. Do you think you love her more than I do? Well, you don't. You may love her as much as I do, but not more."

That Sunday when the grandparents left, we didn't hide the girl. She said good-bye to them without crying. Apparently she realized that it was better to play in the big garden of Los Molinos than in the grandparents' small house. The following week the grandparents stayed in Los Molinos for their vacation, and when it was over they left happy to see that Estrella was running the hotel. She was everybody's favorite.

I stayed at the hotel until the beginning of October. The owners had told me they hadn't taken vacations for years. Now they had found a person to run the hotel during September. They spent fifteen days in Santander while I stayed with my daughter to help the other person manage the hotel. I returned after the summer season to Madrid, happy to have recovered my little girl but physically a wreck. The hotel work had aggravated my spinal column and the pain was driving me crazy. Many times when I was out on the street I would lean as straight as possible against a wall to ease the pain. At home, since I didn't have the hundred pesetas it cost to buy a board for the bed as the doctor had advised, I slept on a mattress on the floor. I went to several clinics; they all agreed I must enter a bone sanatorium to improve. The method of getting better was to spend several months in a body cast. But to get admitted to a sanatorium I had to present a birth certificate. Every time I had gone to a clinic I had used a different name. I would tell the doctors that yes, I would return to ask for admission, but they'd never see me again. A lot of clinics in Madrid have my file under different names.

The provincial prison in Guadalajara had been converted into a penitentiary for prisoners with long sentences. Since I'm from that province and know the city and its people, I was given the job of setting up contact between the prison and the party. I used the excuse of visiting my married brother for going to Guadalajara. Of course, I had some fears about being caught since I was known in the area. And it was a huge risk to set up contact with a prison where I myself had been detained.

One morning I took Estrellita and went to the prison to ask for visiting rights. I recognized a girl who was also asking for visiting rights; we had been in the JSU and later in prison together. Her brother had been transferred to this prison with a thirty-year sentence. When he saw us at the window, he stared at me and then broke into a smile. But I shook my head as if to say "Don't say anything to me." He understood perfectly. When it was my turn to go in for a visit, I walked with my head down talking to Estrella so the officials I knew wouldn't recognize me.

When I entered the visiting area, the man I'd come to see wasn't there yet. When he finally came in I saw why it had taken him so long: his lungs were in very bad shape and his doctor had forbidden him to walk or talk. Two other prisoners held him up on either side. When the officials made the two men leave, he held himself up the best he could by clutching the bars. I explained the reasons for my visit as they had been presented to me. On that visit and the following one we were able to set up a system for communication between him and the outside: the person who came in for his dirty clothes and brought them back clean would be his contact.

About this time I renewed friendship with María Valés who had been released from prison and was doing housework. Through her I found work in a sewing shop embroidering fancy sweaters. María also made Christmas possible for us—once again she cut off her beautiful braids for money, this time to buy a gift for her little boy and one for Estrella. About this time I also found out that Amalia Morales had been released and was living in a shanty by the Manzanares river. Thanks to her social security card I still have my sight.

By now I had been told that I had anemia of the retina; later I was diagnosed with an embolism. With treatment my left eye could be saved; but I barely saw out of the right one. I couldn't finish the eye treatment because my spinal column deteriorated so badly I had go into a sanatorium. In November of 1950 I was admitted to the sanatorium in Pedrosa, Santander, under the name of Emilia Roldán. In one respect, my stay there was worse than prison. There were twenty-one beds in the room and everyone received daily communion and prayed continuously all day long; they even took turns praying throughout the night. I wouldn't take part, which displeased the other patients. Interestingly, neither Sor Primi nor the priest badgered me.

In April of 1951 the political scene in Spain changed as strikes and arrests broke out everywhere. One of our friends gave information to the police when she was arrested. As a result, my little girl and her grandparents were confined to their home and the authorities took me— immobile in a body cast—for three days of interrogation. They threatened to haul me to Madrid: if the Barcelona police had dislocated my spinal column, they said, the Madrid police would stomp on it until it broke. But the doctor at the hospital refused to discharge me.

The authorities forbade any contact with the outside world. The priest came to my rescue. He mailed my letters from Santander and picked up ones for me that were sent to a certain address in that city. He knew my true identity, but he never asked any questions. The other patients in the room now respected me. And the doctor, who also knew my real name, said that my file would always bear the name of Emilia Roldán.

The months passed. I wanted to move my body, but the doctor refused to take off the cast. In October of 1952 he admitted that he could have discharged me six months earlier, but he didn't want to risk my safety. But now they needed my bed very badly. He felt terrible to tell me I must leave. I asked him not to discharge me. I would try to get up.

"What are you going to do?"

"It's better you don't know. That way you'll have no responsibility to the police."

When he left my bedside, tears of emotion filled my eyes. What a good man! No wonder the people of Santander called him "God on Earth."

By the end of November everything was set for my escape. By now I was able to get around. Shortly before supper one day I told my companions I was going down to the first floor to see the children. I met Sor Primi in the hallway. She had suspected a possible escape, but she hadn't said a word to anyone. Now she embraced me and wished me good luck.

I left the sanatorium and walked with a man to his boat, for the sanatorium was on an island. When we reached the mainland, I followed him to the train station and boarded. He put the little package with my belongings on the seat and left. Not a word had passed between us. I stayed the night with friends in Santander and the next morning took the bus for Burgos. Ultimately I made my way back to Barcelona where Luisita, as usual, helped me. I needed help: after all those months in the body cast, I was very thin, my feet were deformed, and I was all bent over. Luisa found out the police were looking for me. I hadn't wanted to leave Spain but now it seemed the best thing to do. My friends and Sor Primi at the hospital had advised me to go to France. But first I wanted to see my daughter and the grandparents; maybe they had news of Miguel. I'd heard nothing from him since January 17, 1949.

Estrella was five and one-half years old and a darling. She preferred to stay inside the house with me than go out to play with her friends. "Mommy," she'd say, "if the bad men come looking for you, I won't tell them I saw you." The grandparents promised to send Estrella to me as soon as my health improved. Promises aren't always kept.

From Madrid I went to Santander and then to a contact house in San Sebastian. At the beginning of January, 1953 I crossed into France, though not without some problems. A member of a Spanish refugee family met me in Paris. This person was a boy who had been released from prison only recently and also had crossed the border. His family chose to live in a wood shack so they could save money for their return to Spain. They believed each year would be their last one in exile. They wondered how the Franco regime could last. They had to wait thirty-nine years. I contacted a comrade to ask that he let the party know I was in France and ready to make a verbal or written report.

I stayed with the family of this contact person a few days in a small village nearby. From there I was taken to Nemours to stay with a family that had previously offered refuge to a certain "Manuel," known to me as Miguel. Other refugees lived there, too. I was known as Auntie Amalia. But I wanted to hear from the party so I returned to Paris.

On April 14 there was a big celebration in a large movie house. Maybe I'd meet someone I knew. I didn't recognize a soul. But suddenly I heard my name called. It was a woman from my days in Les Corts. She said not to worry, the party would reach me, but first I'd have to legalize my status as a political refugee. For that I needed a job. I found work as a housekeeper for a family of White Russians. My document said I was a widow with a daughter in Spain. My employer offered to have my daughter come and attend school with their six-year-old son. By now I was well recuperated. I thought the grandparents would let Estrella come. But they didn't. I would not see my little Estrella again until she was ten years old. By then her father would not have seen her since she was eleven months old. Some hurts are too painful to talk about.

In July the party asked for my report. I did it between July and August. One evening at the end of September a friend came to the house where I worked. He asked me to come to the door because his mother was with him. I was serving supper, so I gave him the key to my room and asked him to wait for me there. After supper I went upstairs. Someone opened the door. Not a woman. It was Miguel. I could only stammer, "you, you, you." It had been four years, eight months, and fifteen days since I'd had word of him.

Miguel had found out in April at a meeting in Paris that I'd escaped from the sanatorium and gone to France. He'd asked to see me, but the party had refused, saying they didn't have my report. "How can she do it if you don't ask her?" was his reply. He had returned to Madrid and then in September come back to Paris for another meeting. That's when we met.

Miguel went back to Barcelona but returned to Paris for Christmas and New Year's of 1953–1954. I left the house where I'd been working and Miguel and I spent some time together in a little house in Saviny that belonged to a comrade. After Miguel left again, I stayed with close associates of his in Paris and resumed clandestine activities. I was with them until 1959. A lot happened during those five years. In August of 1957 Estrella and her grandparents finally joined us. In March of 1958 Miguel was arrested in Barcelona. I immediately asked for a passport, with the party's authorization, of course, and in January, 1961 I made my way back to Spain. Miguel was still imprisoned in Burgos. He finally was released on September 20, 1967.

But life still wasn't peaceful. Franco remained in power. When a state of exception was declared in January of 1969 we had to live clandestinely in Barcelona once again, this time until the beginning of 1976. By then Franco had died and we obtained legal documentation. We were home at last.

# AFTERWORD

## Mary E. Giles

Tomasa's final words in the third volume of the trilogy of testimonies speak to her undying commitment to the ideals of peace, freedom, and democracy. And, as she wrote me early in 1997, she continues to search out the stories of men and women from among the hundreds of thousands who suffered execution, imprisonment, exile, and clandestine living, that they, too, may be a part of Spanish history. Miguel is no less dedicated: though retired, he travels to Central and Latin America to help organize political groups on behalf of the poor and unrepresented.

The peace and freedom for which Tomasa and Miguel have fought and suffered may not be realized yet on the scale they envision, but their love for each other and for their family and friends is a glimpse into the truth of their ideals. Estrella, once carried as a baby in a basket, is now a beautiful, mature woman who lives in Paris with her husband, an architect, and spends a great deal of time in Spain. Estrella's four children, Tomasa writes, "me adoran y les adoro"—"adore me and I adore them." Some people past eighty years of age are content to resolve their lives in the seclusion of family. Not Tomasa. Adore her family she does, but not at the expense of the larger arena in which she has forged her identity for decades. The spark of the fighter still lights her eye, straightens her back, steels her resolve. Wife, mother, rebel, fighter, friend, all these you are, Tomasa, yes, all these, and how much more!

# GLOSSARY

*AJA Alianza Juvenil Antifascista* (Antifascist Youth Alliance)

In November, 1937 the Communists succeeded in establishing an alliance of leaders of youth groups on both national and local levels. The main contingents of the alliance were the Libertarian Youth and the JSU. The Communists estimated that 70 percent of all Spanish youth adhered to AJA.

*Calvo Sotelo, José* (1893–1936)

He was a radical counterrevolutionary who rejected democratic procedures and looked for an authoritarian Spain to be established by the army. He was shot on July 13, 1936, at 3:00 A.M., as he sat in the front seat of a government car, after having been taken from his house by a captain of the Civil Guard. The political right saw his murder as the complete collapse of order.

*Carrillo, Santiago*

Early in his political career, in the 1930s, he was secretary to the JSU. As Secretary General of the Communist Party in the 1950s he advocated a policy of strikes; in the following decade he worked to reconstruct the Popular Front of 1936.

*Casado, Colonel Segismundo* (b. 1893)

As Republican commander of the Army of the Center, he opposed Juan Negrín's policy of continuing the war in the face of inevitable defeat. Forming an opposition government and taking for himself the portfolio of defense, at midnight of March 4, 1939, he broadcast the revolt to the people of antifascist Spain. After days of unsuccessful negotiations with the Nationalists, he ordered the surrender of Madrid to the Nationalist commander in University City, after which he flew to Valencia and ultimately to Marseilles.

*casas de pueblo*

Established by the UGT, these Socialist club houses held commmittee rooms for the local trade unions, free lending libraries, and cafes.

237

*CEDA, Confederación Española de Derechas Autónomas*
(Spanish Confederation of Right Wing Groups)

Formed in 1933 as a general national Catholic party, it backed revolt against the Republic even though it had supported socialist positions in principle.

*CNT, Confederación Nacional de Trabajo*
(Anarcho-Syndicalist Trades Union)

Formed in 1910–11, the union rejected political action and electoral participation in favor of direct action against employers. In November of 1936 it changed policy and joined the Popular Front government, though some purists remained absolute anarchists. Its strength was in Barcelona, the Levante, Aragon, and among the landless laborers of Andalusia.

*Falange*

The nearest thing to a fascist party in Spain, the organization was made up of authoritarian nationalist parties under the leadership of José Antonio Primo de Rivera (1903–36), who was executed on November 20, 1936, by the Popular Front in Alicante. The party grew rapidly in the early years of the Civil War and in April, 1937 Franco fused it with the Carlists, long-time traditionalists and monarchists, to form *FET de las JONS (Falange Española Tradicionalista y de las Juntas de Ofensiva Nacional-Sindicalistas)*.

*Guardia Civil* (Civil Guard)

A militarized police force created in 1844, it served under the Ministry of the Interior and was commanded by a regular soldier. Especially notorious for rigorous methods of keeping order in rural Spain, the guard fought on Franco's side because when war erupted villagers throughout Spain reacted by slaughtering the hated Civil Guards.

*Ibarruri, Dolores* (b. 1895)

Known as La Pasionaria, she was the most recognizable figure in the Communist Party, especially effective as an orator.

*JSU, Juventudes Socialistas Unificadas* (Unified Socialist Youth)

In April of 1936 the Communist Youth and the Socialist Youth were joined. Although the initial membership of Communist Youth was far less than that of the Socialist Youth, the Communist Party gained control of the *JSU* and used it as a successful example of uniting efforts of both Communists and Socialists. The Communist Party also used the *JSU* to promote cooperation with the Anarchists, against whom they had been working. The *JSU* worked vigorously for the Republic and was praised for its role in defending Madrid in 1936 and 1937.

### Largo Caballero, Francisco (1869–1946)

A leading figure in the *UGT (Unión General de Trabajadores)*, a Socialist trade union with power in Madrid, the mining regions of Asturias and the Basque industrial zones, he was prime minister from September 4, 1936, to May 17, 1937.

### militias

In February, 1936 the unions formed paramilitary forces in Catalonia, and after July 18, 1936, they were expanded elsewhere in Spain. There was an effort to centralize them into a disciplined and regular Popular Army that would be dependent on the central government rather than on unions and political parties. The militarization of the militias was a controversial issue because on the one hand the image of men and women fighting in their uniform of workers' overalls was appealing but on the other the irregularity of training and equipment and inefficiency of a system left to random were not promising of victory. By December, 1936 the government refused to pay nonregular units and the process of militarization of the militias was complete by the summer of 1937.

### Mujeres Antifascistas (Antifascist Women)

This was one of many organizations set up by the Communist Party to attract members who otherwise might have been reluctant to become Communists.

### National Front

This "umbrella" group was made up of all the organizations and parties that supported Franco.

### Negrín, Juan (1889–1956)

Prime minister from May, 1937 until the end of the war, he found himself in sharp disagreement with Colonel Casado about continuing the war against the Nationalists.

*PCE, Partido Comunista Española* (Spanish Communist Party)

The orthodox, that is, Stalinist, Communist Party was founded in 1921 when a younger radical youth group joined with members who had left PSOE, a Marxist-Leninist party founded in 1879 by Pablo Iglesias that advocated a workers' state and government. The party became very popular during the war and afterward maintained the only consistent opposition to the dictatorship. It gradually lost power, however, and in the elections of 1996 its influence was negligible.

*Popular Front*

During the October Revolution of 1934 leftist groups unified and in the elections of February 16, 1936, united under this rubric to emerge as a major force in the political scene. Socialists, Republican Left, Republican Union, Esquerra (Left Republican Catalan nationalist party) and Communists collaborated as the Popular Front, a clear opponent of the rightist National Front.

*POUM, Partido Obrero de Unificación Marxista*
(Workers' Party of Marxist Unification)

This revolutionary Marxist party was founded in September, 1935 from the former Trotskyist Left Communist Party of Andrés Nin (1892–1937) and Joaquin Maurin's block of workers and peasants. The party advocated workers' seizing political power.

*PSOE, Partido Socialista Obrero Español*
(Spanish Socialist Workers Party)

A Marxist-Leninist party founded in 1879 by Pablo Iglesias, it advocated a workers' state and government. Although the party did not oppose the dictatorship as vigorously as did the PCE, after Franco's death it emerged as an effective rival to the PCE, and after winning the 1982 elections managed to hold political power until its defeat in the 1996 elections.

*PSUC, Partido Socialista Unificado de Cataluña*
(Unified Socialist Party of Catalonia)

Established in July, 1936 with the uniting of the Catalan Communist Party, the Catalan branch of PSOE and two other organizations, it is, in effect, the Communist Party of Catalonia.

*Requetes*

They were the political descendants of the Carlists, who fought in two wars for the right of Don Carlos (1788–1855) to ascend the throne in opposition to Isabella II (1830–1904), who was seen by them to be too yielding to liberalism. This protest movement was centered in the Basque provinces and the mountains of Aragón and Catalonia. Defenders of the Catholic Church by tradition, the latter day Carlists, known as requetes, put their paramilitary militia at the service of the Nationalists. They were identifiable by the red berets they wore.

### SIM, *Servicio de Investigación Militar* (Bureau of Military Investigation)

A secret police organized by Soviet specialists in August, 1937, it maintained "law and order" through the harshest of means, spreading terror and employing torture in the manner of the Soviet secret police.

### *sindicato* (syndicate or trade union)

To a large extent the trade unions were dominated by the Anarchists, the more militant of whom wanted formal government abolished and replaced with agreements and pressures of trade groups. In the 1930s some syndicalists favored a degree of cooperation with society. Syndicalism spread to Madrid in July of 1936 as a result of an anti-popular uprising.

### SRI, *Socorro Rojo Internacional* (International Red Aid)

The international Communists established a number of relief agencies headed by Willi Muenzenberg in Paris, of which SRI was the most important. Helping revolutionaries of the Left in Spain since 1934, it counted 992 local committees and 353,000 members in February of 1937. Because it distributed relief and aid, it had real power and gained prestige for the Communist Party and the Soviet Union among Spaniards.

### UGT, *Unión General de Trabajadores* (General Union of Workers)

A socialist-led trade union founded in 1888, it was strongest in Madrid, the Asturian mining region, and the industrial parts of the Basque provinces.

### UHP, *Unión de Hermanos Proletarios* (Union of Proletarian Brothers)

In Asturias the Anarchists, Socialists, Communists, and semi-Trotskyists of the Workers and Peasants' Alliance cooperated under this rubric and rallying cry.

# NOTES

## INTRODUCTION

1. Information about the Civil War and the Franco regime is drawn primarily from Raymond Carr, *The Spanish Tragedy: The Civil War in Perspective* (London: Weidenfeld and Nicolson, 1977); David T. Cattell, *Communism and the Spanish Civil War* (Berkeley: University of California Press, 1955); Helen Graham and Jo Labanyi, eds., *Spanish Cultural Studies: An Introduction* (New York: Oxford University Press, 1995); Hugh Thomas, *The Spanish Civil War* (New York: Harper & Brothers, 1961); Sergio Vilar, *Historia del Anti-Franquismo 1939–1975* (Barcelona: Plaza & Janes Editores, S.A., 1984).

2. The military unit was named after Ernst Thaelmann (1886–1944), a harbor worker in Hamburg, Germany, whom Stalin regarded as the leader of the German Communists in the late twenties.

3. See especially "Women and Social Change" by Helen Graham in *Spanish Cultural Studies*, 99–116.

4. See especially "The Urban and Rural Guerrilla of the 1940s" by Paul Preston in *Spanish Cultural Studies*, 229–37.

## CHAPTER 1. GROWING UP IN PREWAR SPAIN

1. Before February, 1936 the Communist Youth claimed membership of about 14,000. When the organization joined with the Socialist youth group in March of that year, membership increased.

2. For his activities Carlos Prestes later was incarcerated; efforts from supporters outside of Spain and within the country to effect his release finally were successful. Ernst Thaelmann (1886–1944) was a harbor worker in Hamburg, Germany, whom Stalin regarded as the leader of the German Communists in the late twenties. In Spain his name appeared with the "centuria," or group of 100 men, German emigrés who had come to the "Workers Olympiad" at Barcelona and worked under Hans Beimler, a Communist ex-deputy of the German Reichstag.

## CHAPTER 2. COMING OF AGE IN POLITICS AND WAR

1. Tomasa says in the original text that it was the second or third day of March when they went to Madrid, but more than likely the day she describes

was the fourth because it was at midnight on the fourth that Casado's revolt was broadcast to the people.

## CHAPTER 6. MY PRISON ODYSSEY

1. On April 12, 1931, the monarchist candidates were defeated in municipal elections. The following day King Alfonso issued a statement that he was stepping down; driving from Madrid to the coast, he left Spain for exile. The next day the Second Republic was established.

## CHAPTER 7. THE DYNAMITER

1. José Ortega y Gasset (1883–1956) was the most influential thinker in Spain from 1914 to 1931. Educated in Germany, he later occupied a professorship at the University of Madrid. A prolific writer, he developed his ideas in journals, newspapers, and books. Like many other intellectuals, he left Spain shortly after the Civil War began.

2. Miguel Hernández (1910–1942), a member of the Generation of '39, expressed themes of the poor and working class in his poetry. He died in prison.

3. Vicente Aleixandre (b. 1898) is considered to be one of the finest poets of the Generation of '27.

4. The battle of Brunete took place from July 6–25, 1937. The Republic intended to move toward the village of Brunete from the north of the road running from El Escorial to Madrid in order to cut off the Nationalists who were besieging the capital from the west. The battle was not a victory for either side, and the losses in terms of men and equipment were heavy.

5. The Littorio Division was an Italian division on the Nationalist side. After the defeat in the Battle of the Ebro, Mussolini decided to concentrate the Littorio and the March 23 Divisions into one large division and to withdraw the rest of the Italians.

## CHAPTER 9. A MINOR IN PRISON

1. Colonel Gabaldo was an inspector in the military police of Region I who was responsible for the archives and documents that made possible the arrest of many people on charges of Communism and Masonry. He was a major force in political repression and his death on July 27, 1939, produced a flurry of arrests in the next two months.

2. Another reason for the increase in arrests of Communists in July and August of 1939 was that Roberto Conesa, who had been a member of the JSU, began to work for the Francoist police. On August 4, 1939, sixty-five death penalties were handed down to sixty-seven militants. On August 5, 1939, in the East Cemetery, sixty-three people were shot, including the thirteen roses (*las trece rosas*), young women between eighteen and twenty-one years old.

## CHAPTER 10. THE CEMETERY OF THE LIVING

1. The Ebro campaign from July 24 to November 18, 1938, was one of the most important of the Civil War. The Republican War Council in Barcelona devised a plan for reestablishing communications between Catalonia and the rest of Republican Spain that involved crossing the Ebro river in several places, about sixty miles from the sea. Infantry battles were fierce and Nationalist air attacks relentless. Hugh Thomas states that "during the first five weeks of the counter-offensive the Nationalist aircraft dropped an average of 10,000 bombs every day" (549). What began as a successful offensive by the Republican forces eventually turned into defeat. During this period the International Brigades were withdrawn from Spain.

## CHAPTER 12. SOLIDARITY AND COMPASSION

1. By 1941 there was an effort to consolidate Communist organizations within Spain. Heriberto Quiñones took the lead in this effort. His position was that party leaders should stay in Spain. During the war he had been part of the Provincial Committee in Valencia and had worked in military information. While in the concentration camp in Albatera he had met the Polish Communist, Josef Wajsblum, who had been sent by the Communist International during the war to help Republicans. He escaped from the camp and with Wajsblum's help came to be in charge of the party committee in Madrid, which became the main leadership of the PCE within Spain. He never forgot that such leaders as Santiago Carrillo and Dolores Ibarruri had abandoned the party within Spain. He was bound to suffer for his criticism of their leadership. Quiñones worked on a national union that was to include Republicans and even Monarchists, but not Falangists. His image of the PCE challenged Communists outside of Spain. His efforts were restricted by both the Franco police and Communist leadership in exile. Quiñones was arrested on December 30, 1941, as he was going along Alcalá street in Madrid with a Communist militant, Angel Fermín Cardín. He was tortured until his spinal column broke. He was condemned to death and on October 1, 1947, shot along with his closest comrades, Luis Sendín and Fermín Cardín.

## CHAPTER 13. REFLECTIONS ON PRISON LIFE FOR WOMEN

1. Tomás de Torquemada (1420–1498) is infamous for his role as the Inquisitor General of the newly established (1482) Inquisition in Castile.

2. Benito Pérez Galdós (1843–1920) is regarded as the finest Spanish novelist of the nineteenth century. Unlike his contemporaries whose novels were regional, Galdós cultivated a national voice.

3. The Free Institution of Education was founded in 1876 by Francisco Giner de los Ríos (b. 1839), who was a professor of law at the University of Madrid. In the 1870s the Spanish minister of education had decided to call for a loyalty oath from all professors at the University of Madrid in support of the

crown, the dynasty, and the Catholic religion. Refusing to sign the loyalty oath, many professors decided to organize a union of their own dedicated to educating young people in an atmosphere of freedom. The aim was to graduate liberal men who would lead Spain into the modern world.

4. The main character in Miguel de Cervantes's classic novel, *Don Quixote of La Mancha* (*Don Quijote de la Mancha*), Don Quixote is for many people the quintessential symbol of unflagging idealism.

## CHAPTER 14. THE COSTS OF SACRIFICE

1. Catholic Action was a large Catholic social movement started in the early 1920s.

## CHAPTER 15. A STRANGER IN A STRANGE CITY

1. Antonio Creix was head of the Political-Social Brigade, which was directly responsible for the torture and mistreatment of prisoners at police headquarters in Barcelona. His brother, Vicente Juan, was also a member of the secret police. Eduardo Quintela was chief of the Brigade in Barcelona. On March 2, 1949, there was an assassination attempt on him near the cathedral of the Sagrada Familia in Barcelona. Three anarchists machine-gunned the car they mistakenly thought he was riding in. Poloco, or Pedro Polo Borrequero, was a commissar of the secret police in Barcelona. The methods of the Political-Social Brigade were so bad that on May 11, 1966, thirty priests marched in protest from the cathedral to police headquarters. When the police found out about the intended march, agents Olmedo and Vicente Juan Creix went to dissuade them, but the priests went ahead with the march. When the police took action, the demonstrators were forced to disperse and with the help of the common people managed to escape.

## CHAPTER 18. ESCAPE

1. Cristino García had been an outstanding guerrilla during the war and later was a member of the "maquis" who resisted the Nazis in France. In April, 1945 he entered Spain with a double mission: to create guerrilla groups and to liquidate Gabriel León Trilla. Trilla had been an original organizer of the PCE in the twenties, but had been ousted in 1932, then readmitted in 1936. From 1944 on he was in Madrid editing the clandestine paper, *Mundo Obrero* (*Workers' World*). In the spring of 1945 the external leadership of the party decided to take control away from Trilla and Jesús Monzón. Trilla was assassinated September 6, 1945, in an old cemetery. On September 22, 1946, García was arrested in Alcalá de Henares and on February 21, 1947, he was shot along with nine other guerrillas. He was decorated posthumously by the French government in recognition of his resistance work in France.

2. Fighting Youth was the youth branch of the *Unión Nacional Española* (*National Spanish Union*). During August and September of 1941 the Communists had called for a national union of Spaniards against Franco. The keystone in their program was a guerrilla invasion of Spain to overthrow Franco.

3. Jesús Monzón was the son of a comfortable family in Pamplona. He studied law and was a lawyer in one of the popular tribunals during the Civil War in Bilbao. He later functioned in Valencia and Madrid and was named civil governor of Alicante. In March of 1939 he left Spain for exile in France where he organized efforts for exiles to go to Iberoamerican countries and the Soviet Union. He made several clandestine trips to Madrid.

## CHAPTER 19. THROUGH THE GATE TO FREEDOM

1. See the Glossary for information on S.I.M., the *Servicio de Investigación Militar*.

## CHAPTER 20. CROSSING THE BORDER

1. Joan Comorera was a leader of the PSUC in Catalonia who was opposed by Santiago Carrillo and his followers in a fratricidal struggle that was at its worst from 1948 to 1956. On November 10, 1949, the Central Committee of the PCE expelled him for betraying the party, the working class, and the people. Although Carrillo took the lead in plans to liquidate him, Comorera managed to enlist support and on December 31, 1950, secretly made his way from France back to Barcelona. He worked four years clandestinely until his arrest on June 9, 1954. He was interrogated for fourteen days and on August 23 sentenced to thirty years in prison. He was taken to the penitentiary at Burgos where he died on May 7, 1958. With Comorera out of the picture, Carrillo managed to put the PSUC under PCE control. Wenceslao Colomer was one of the leaders of the PSUC. He convinced his wife, Nuri, to write an open letter repudiating her father, Joan Comorera. The letter of March 21, 1950, was addressed to the comrades in the Communist Party at Paris.

2. Dr. Bonifaci wrote the epiloque to Tomasa's first volume of oral testimonies, *Cárcel de mujeres. Ventas y Segovia*.

## CHAPTER 21. THE GUERRILLA

1. Although Esperanza refers to this man by the name of José María de Oriol y Urquijo, he is probably one Antonio Oriol Urquijo identified by Sergio Vilar in his *Historia del anti-Franquismo. 1939–1975* (416) as being supportive of the regime even though, as a lawyer, he had presided at an important conference that had passed two liberal measures.